DESIGNING DREAMS

Modern Architecture in the Movies

DONALD ALBRECHT

Published by Harper & Row in collaboration
with The Museum of Modern Art

For my parents

DESIGNING DREAMS. Copyright © 1986 by Donald Albrecht. All rights reserved. Printed in the United States of America. No part of this book may be used or reproduced in any manner whatsoever without written permission except in the case of brief quotations embodied in critical articles and reviews. For information address Harper & Row, Publishers, Inc., 10 East 53rd Street, New York, N.Y. 10022. Published simultaneously in Canada by Fitzhenry & Whiteside Limited, Toronto.

FIRST EDITION

Copy editor: Marge Horvitz

Index by Brian Hotchkiss

Library of Congress Cataloging-in-Publication Data

Albrecht, Donald.
  Designing dreams.
  "Published . . . in collaboration with
the Museum of Modern Art."
  Filmography: p.
  Includes index.
  1. Moving-pictures—United States—Setting and scenery. 2. Architecture, Modern—20th century—United States. I. Museum of Modern Art (New York, N.Y.) II. Title.
PN1995.9.S4A4 1986   791.43′025′0973   86-45077
ISBN 0-06-055020-1   86 87 88 89 HAL 7 6 5 4 3 2 1
ISBN 0-06-096106-6 (pbk.)
                      86 87 88 89 HAL 7 6 5 4 3 2 1

Contents

Preface

The idea for a book exploring modern architectural film sets of the 1920s and 1930s had its origins in the late 1960s with Ludwig Glaeser, a curator in the Department of Architecture and Design at New York's Museum of Modern Art. Glaeser proposed a study that would begin as a comparison of the Museum's vast files of architectural photographs with its enormous collection of movie stills. The result, he hoped, would suggest a new interpretation of modern architecture, one that took into consideration the perceptions of the general public, who made cinema *the* popular art form of the Depression era, and not only the "official" account of this period offered by architects and professional historians. Glaeser's supposition remained untested, however, until late 1978, shortly after I had volunteered to work for him and the Museum's Mies van der Rohe Archive. His provocative idea fascinated me, as did the prospects for casting my architect's eye on the designs of my passion since childhood: the movies.

Over the next few months, as we narrowed this wide subject down to a focused project statement, we developed a number of questions that would guide my subsequent explorations. Which visual features of modern architecture did moviemakers adopt for film sets? What factors guided their choices: the aesthetics of movie designing, the economics or technology of moviemaking, fashion? Was there a relationship between modern architectural sets and certain movie genres, plot lines, and character types? Were modern architectural film sets exclusively the efforts of modern architects who occasionally designed for the cinema, or was there a group of in-house movie designers who created modern film sets without firsthand knowledge of the buildings and ideology of the modern movement? The result of my efforts to answer these questions, and the many more questions my research raised, is *Designing Dreams: Modern Architecture in the Movies*.

In organizing the book, I have selected a format that in successive chapters presents a progressively "deeper" reading of the material. The introduction lays out the book's thesis in general terms, then examines it as displayed in a typical film of the period, *What a Widow!* (1930). Chapter 1 follows, with a brief history of modern architecture from 1925 through 1939. Chapter 2 gives an overview of film decor before its designers adopted modernism in the mid-1920s. Chapters 3 and 4 run chronologically through four periods between 1916 and 1939 and chart the first steps, breakthrough, dissemination, and decline of modern architecture in the movies. These chapters are objective and descriptive, and concern the designers themselves, when and where they worked, why they adopted modernism to the screen, what the decor looked like.

Chapter 5 examines nine specific types of modern film decor, and explores subjectively the connotations moviemakers gave to modern architecture and how these meanings reflected facets of popular culture of the time. The epilogue is a case study of a film released ten years after the heyday of modern architecture in the movies. *The Fountainhead* (1949) is the best-known example of cinematic modernism, yet is ironically one of its least successful manifestations. Its particular failure sheds light on why its predecessors worked so well.

Throughout the book I have analyzed a set design by three criteria. While the primary one has been the architectural qualities a set possesses—whether its designer has created memorable spaces and forms, dramatic lighting, striking surfaces and textures —I have also looked at the various ways in which a set embodies the movie's themes, defines its characters, and underlines psychological nuance. Finally, I have tried to determine how successfully a set has combined high-quality design and expressiveness, engaging its public to become a cultural icon in their lives, a collective dream.

This book took much longer to fund, research, write, edit, and publish than I ever expected—an eight-year period that did, nonetheless, bring me luckily into contact with enough savvy, scholarly, and generous people to last a lifetime of bookwriting. First and foremost is Ludwig Glaeser, mentor and friend. I am grateful to the outstanding staff of the Department of Film at The Museum of Modern Art, especially Mary Lea Bandy, its director, and Ron Magliozzi. My thanks also go to the Museum's Department of Publications and the Department of Architecture and Design, especially Arthur Drexler, its curator and director, and Mary Jane Lightbown. The late Margareta Akermark made most of the all-important contacts to film archives that I needed; I deeply regret that she did not see finished a project she was so instrumental in launching.

The following people offered continuous assistance and time: In New York, Lee Chiaramonte, William Everson, Joanne Greenspun, Brian Hotchkiss, Deirdre Houchins, Richard Koszarski, Jay Leyda, William Luckey, Holly McNeely, Thomas Navin, Judith Richman, Janice Russell, Elliott Stein, and the staffs of the Performing Arts Research Center at Lincoln Center, and the Avery and Butler Libraries at Columbia University. In Los Angeles, the late Paula Armel, Henry Bumstead, Edward Carfagno, Ursula and Jan de Swaart, Erica Edwards, Thomas S. Hines, Harry Horner, William Hubbard, Eugène Lourié, John Mansbridge, Al Nozaki, Herbert Nusbaum, Bonnie Rothbart, David Shepard, Marc Wanamaker, Michael Webb, Lyle Wheeler, Eric Wright, Maurice Zuberano, the staffs of the Film Archive, the Theater Arts Collection, and the Department of Special Collections at the University of California at Los Angeles, the staff of the Margaret Herrick Library at the Academy of Motion Picture Arts and Sciences, and the Department of Special Collections at the University of Southern California. In Madison, Wisconsin, the staff of the State Historical Society of Wisconsin, Film and Manuscript Archive, at the University of Wisconsin. In Santa Barbara, the staff of the University of California. In Washington, D.C., the staff of the Library of Congress, Motion Picture Division. In Paris, Diane O'Callaghan Aktan, the late Lotte Eisner, Mary Meerson, and the staffs of the Cinémathèque Française and the Bibliothèque Nationale. In Bois d'Arcy, the Centre National de la Cinématographie, Service des Archives du Film. In London, Stephen Bayley, Kevin Brownlow, Patrick Downing, and the staff of the British Film Institute. In southern France, Anne and Marc Kandelmann. In Berlin, Alfred Krautz, Jan Schlübach, and the staffs of the Deutsche Kinemathek, the Bauhaus-Archiv, and the Staatliches Archives der DDS. In Koblenz, the staff of the Bundes-Archiv. In Weisbaden, the staff of the Deutsches Institut für Filmkunde. In Rome, Joyce Johnson, Mario Verdone, and the staff of the Cineteca Nazionale. In Brussels, the staff of the Cinémathèque de Belgique.

Designing Dreams could never have been researched and written without generous funding. The Graham Foundation for Advanced Studies in the Fine Arts, under the directorship of Carter Manny, funded the writing phase. The National Endowment for the Arts, under the Design Arts Division, and the New York State Council on the Arts, through the Academy of Educational Development, supported the research. And, finally, the Pinewood Foundation of Mr. and Mrs. Armand Bartos came to the rescue of the project twice: once to support a research trip throughout Europe, and again during publication, with funds to ensure the high level of quality achieved in producing the book.

My thanks to my agent, Eric Ashworth of Candida Donadio & Associates, and to Rick Kot, my editor at Harper & Row, who helped make a reality a book that would convey my enthusiasm for the modern movie designs and my respect for the outstanding film architects who created them.

Introduction

In the early decades of the twentieth century, modern architects developed a new architectural style, one that had little historical precedent. Their buildings were distinguished by flowing, unencumbered spaces and bold, abstract forms, their use of industrial materials in daring and unusual ways, and their establishment of artificial illumination as an exciting element in design. Partisans of an international avant-garde, the modernists defined a new role for architecture in industrial society; ideologically, theirs was an architecture of vigorous optimism and utopian thrust. "The new environment, which we thus create," declared the writer Paul Scheerbart in a statement that would become for many a fundamental assumption of the modern movement, "must bring us a new culture."[1]

Many factors contributed to the popularization of modernism throughout the 1920s and 1930s. Not only did architects themselves promulgate their work with unprecedented fervor in books, manifestos, and exhibitions, but artists in other media soon began to adopt the characteristic features of the new style. Novelists and playwrights set high-toned comedies and dramas in ultra-modern penthouses. Fashion photographers shot layouts aboard sleek ocean liners. Comic-book illustrators drew their super-human heroes flying through the air above futurist cities. The simple surfaces, lines, and planes of modernism made ideal decorative backdrops, setting off with their elegance everything from a Chrysler automobile to a *Vogue* model dressed by Chanel.

But appreciation for the modern style went deeper than for just its graphic value. Many members of the generation born at the end of the nineteenth century welcomed it as an antidote to the Victorian clutter and fussiness of their parents' interiors. Modernism for them became a rallying point, a battle cry, and an emblem, not only of taste in design, but also of the liberated lives one could lead by living, working, and playing within the new buildings. Modernism was alluring, too, precisely because it was "new," a not inconsiderable attribute in a period when so many were infatuated with the new in every sphere of life, from the

"New Frontier" of American business proclaimed in 1920 by the banker Guy Emerson, to the "New Objectivity" (Neue Sachlichkeit) movement of German art in the '20s, to *l'esprit nouveau* promoted by the architect Le Corbusier, to Franklin Roosevelt's "New Deal."

The adoption of architectural modernism by the popular arts had two notable effects. First, it successfully promoted the modern style to the general public, making it both more accessible and more palatable. Even more significantly, it helped create a potent new iconography for architecture: Through frequent exposure in the media in a similar range of contexts, the "modern look" became associated with affluence and with progressivism in taste, if not necessarily in political beliefs.

No vehicle provided as effective and widespread an exposure of architectural imagery as the medium of the movies. Statistics of cinema attendance during the first half of the century suggest the ability of the movies to rival, if not actually surpass, exhibitions as a major means of promoting new design concepts. Consider that the New York World's Fair of 1939–40 attracted 45 million visitors in eighteen months, while a scant 33,000 saw the 1932 New York mounting of The Museum of Modern Art's *Modern Architecture: International Exhibition,* which was instrumental in defining the new architecture for the United States. Then consider that shortly after World War I a *single* picture palace like Chicago's Central Park entertained 750,000 moviegoers in its first year of business alone. By 1939, *weekly* attendance at America's 17,000 movie houses was an astonishing 85,000,000, while seven years later, Hollywood's best year in domestic attendance figures, the number had reached 98,000,000 moviegoers.[2]

The allure of the new twentieth-century style of architecture proved as irresistible for the creators of the newest art of the twentieth century as it had for other visual artists, and for many of the same reasons. In addition to its novelty and connotations of affluence and progressiveness, modernism was attractive to moviemakers on aesthetic grounds: Like modern architecture, film design was fundamentally a manipulation of the elements of space, light, and movement. A number of key film producers, directors, stars, and art directors who were aware of the influence that the cinema had come to wield on its vast audience were, in fact, able to develop a film aesthetic that fostered architectural experimentation. Building film sets indoors on soundstages encouraged explorations of out-of-the-ordinary designs by liberating film designers from the structural, economic, and climatic constraints within which architects are forced to work.

The cinematic adaptations of modern architecture created by moviemakers of the 1920s and 1930s not only provided a glamorous visual mise-en-scène, but also supplied moviegoers with an optimistic view of the workings of society. By shooting stylized architecture on soundstages, which dominated popular film production between the wars, filmmakers sought to exceed audiences' expectations of what the future would hold for them by suggesting undreamed-of possibilities and ways of life. These upwardly mobile aspirations, shared by the majority of filmgoers at the time, had been reinforced by the deep financial crisis of the Depression. Ominous financial warnings ignored by shortsighted American investors during the booming 1920s had culminated in the collapse of the New York Stock Exchange on October 29, 1929, and within six months, four million Americans were unemployed. Within two years the number doubled, with many forced to depend on soup kitchens for their sustenance and on "Hoovervilles" for their shelter. After the United States began to withdraw its investments from overseas, Europe, too, felt the crippling effects of the Depression.

Compared with this bleak reality, the allure of the glamorous, heightened version of reality on view inside many moviehouses becomes clear indeed. The social order that populates the films discussed in this book was by no means fixed: Its ranks were open to any ambitious salesman or secretary who had the pluck or luck to ascend the ladder of success. Cinderella scenarios held the promise that everyone could conceivably become a fashion model or ingenue, playboy or tycoon, rising from rags to riches. In this context, modern architecture formed the standard backdrop for newly attained affluence. Penthouses, nightclubs, executive suites, and ocean liners were the perquisites of prosperity – dream dwellings, pleasure palaces far removed from the harshness of many a moviegoer's life.

A major endeavor of *Designing Dreams* is to explore the contrasts between the popular dreams realized in set designs of film architects of the 1920s and 1930s and the utopian visions expressed in the drawings and writings of modern architects working during the same period. The modernist utopia was an egalitarian one where good design would be available to all, not just to the upper classes, who had traditionally been its main beneficiaries. The average man would live in hygienic housing, work in sunlit factories, and exercise in spotless health clubs. Moviemakers, by contrast, created a utopia of wealthy nonconformists. Instead of workers' housing, many popular films depicted deluxe villas and rooftop apartments; instead of factories, they featured executive offices for capitalist captains of industry; instead of sports clubs, sparkling nightclubs. It is one of the ironies of the modernist movement that the cinema, the twentieth century's greatest egalitarian visual art form, took modern architecture's collectivist agenda and transformed it into a fantasy of

privilege to be enjoyed only by the celluloid wealthy—meanwhile broadcasting that message to an audience composed of the widest segments of society that the architects sought to reach. More than any other visual medium, film, by virtue of the size of its audience and its growing influence over culture as a whole, helped shape popular perceptions of architectural modernism.

The cinema of the 1920s and '30s thus offers a challenging new perspective on modern architecture, as well as an unusual case study of how mass culture assimilates radical visions in the arts. Unlike contemporary histories of modern architecture written by partisans of the movement, this book aims to present a picture of modernism drawn by art directors who were not professionals directly associated with the movement and whose sources were therefore secondhand, via the magazines, books, and exhibitions through which modern architects promoted their style. Finally, this view also gauges the influence modernism had on the public, who had been exposed to the movement through movies that had wholeheartedly adopted its most vanguard imagery, while usually ascribing connotations to that imagery that modern architects never intended, nor perhaps even perceived.

A typical feature produced during the Depression, the 1930 Hollywood film *What a Widow!*, directed by Allan Dwan, offers a paradigm for the story of modern architecture in the movies, and as such introduces some of the major themes of this book.

What a Widow! opens with wealthy American Tamarind Brooks, whose natural vivacity and zest are only temporarily shadowed by the untimely death of her husband, enjoying life again by sailing for France on the magnificent liner *Île de France*. Accompanying Tam on the transatlantic journey is a host of international bons vivants, among whom are Gerry Morgan, a successful lawyer, and Victor, a nightclub dancer. In the course of the trip Tam attracts the amorous attentions of many of the male passengers, yet when Gerry Morgan proposes marriage, she declines: Her freedom is still too new. When the group finally arrives in Paris, Tam holds court at the ultramodern town house she rents from the Marquise de la Fousbouget. A brief fling with José, a Spanish baritone, followed by a squabble with and separation from Gerry, leads to a short tryst with Victor. After passing out during an evening with Victor, Tam wakes with the mistaken belief that they have been intimate. She agrees to marry him out of her firm sense of propriety, but when the misunderstanding is cleared, she realizes that it has been Gerry she has loved all along. Returning to New York via a Dornier DO-X airship, the couple are married, while outside the window pass the Statue of Liberty and the Manhattan skyline.

Few stars dominated this era as did the charismatic Gloria Swanson, the heroine of *What a Widow!* During the 1920s Swanson reigned at the peak of the American cinematic aristocracy along with Fairbanks, Pickford, Valentino, and, of course, Chaplin. Their adoring public, when not thronging the grand cinema palaces to see Hollywood's latest pictures, followed every detail of the stars' personal lives via the enormous amount of publicity hype generated by the studios. Of the female members of the film pantheon, Mary Pickford was America's down-home sweetheart, more often than not cast as a simple, innocent lass, playing children half her age in traditional settings free of modernism and its connotations of chic sophistication. Swanson, in contrast, was America's "New Woman," a daring, sexually liberated cosmopolite and Hollywood's mannequin for the most glamorous contemporary fashions.

Like the modern woman she portrayed in *What a Widow!* Swanson herself was no stranger to modern design. Her screen image had been shaped largely by director Cecil B. De Mille. In *The Affairs of Anatol,* De Mille's 1921 fancy-dress Viennese froth, he surrounded his young star with intoxicating decor by European designer Paul Iribe. Although the sinuous, nature-inspired Art Nouveau style of Iribe had long passed its prime by 1921, the picture nonetheless served to introduce Swanson to modernist art trends. In 1924 she was the subject of a celebrated photograph by Edward Steichen. During extensive travel in Europe in the same year, she came in contact with avant-garde art movements and, even before the wives of Europe's leading modern architects, commissioned cubist-inspired fashions from Parisian artist Sonia Delaunay. Five years later, the chance meeting between Swanson and the modern architect Paul Nelson (Illus. 1), who was visiting the Pathé studios in Los Angeles with relatives, gave her the impetus to take a decisive step in the production of the forthcoming *What a Widow!* Nelson's zeal for the new architecture sparked Swanson's own enthusiasm for modern design, which she may have hoped would also help boost box office receipts. Yet the task of convincing the film's conservative producer, Joseph Kennedy, could not have been easy, and without the efforts of the remarkable Swanson, Nelson's designs might never have reached the American screen.[3]

Billed in the publicity for *What a Widow!* as "Paul Nelson, Paris," for added cachet, the thirty-four-year-old, Chicago-born alumnus of Princeton University had lived in Paris since his graduation from the prestigious architectural program at the École des Beaux-Arts. Proficiency in the grandiose, neo-classical style of the École would have virtually guaranteed him a successful architectural career in America, where leading architects and their clients were infatuated with French culture. Yet Nelson rejected his conservative training and advocated instead the architectural modernism of Le Corbusier, a leader of the vanguard, whose talent flowered in the 1920s. Throughout a fifty-year career committed to rational design, Nelson boldly experimented with twentieth-century technologies in several hospital designs and in such innovative unbuilt projects as the Maison Suspendue (1936–38),[4] a multistory residence of floating stairs, mezzanines, and sculptures suspended within a shell of perforated metal.

Nelson's film architecture for *What A Widow!*, which stands as one of the earliest examples of the new architecture to be executed in America, echoes in its stylistic features Richard Neutra's Lovell House (1927–29). Located only a few miles northeast of the Pathé studios, the Lovell "Health" House, built for Los Angeles doctor and health columnist Philip Lovell, hovers dramatically over steep slopes in the Hollywood Hills, its advancing and receding volumes wrapped in a taut industrial skin of glass and concrete. The cool, austere style opted for by vanguard patrons like Lovell was still largely a European phenomenon. In contrast, many Americans were building with a flamboyance influenced by the exposition of decorative arts that had been held in Paris in 1925. For these novelty-seeking Americans excluded from the latest European art trends by the First World War, the decorative appeal of the cubist, machine-inspired imagery (which has come to be known as Art Deco) was considerable, and by the late 1920s it had become *the* chic, commercial style in urban America.

Nelson's stylistic experiments during his nine months of work on *What a Widow!* were largely guided by Le Corbusier's "five points of architecture." Le Corbusier had published these formulations in 1926 as the

1. Gloria Swanson and Paul Nelson on the set of *What a Widow!* in the Pathé studios, Los Angeles, circa 1929.

syntax for a new architectural language and, with his cousin Pierre Jeanneret, employed them to brilliant effect in the Villa Stein (1926–28) and the Villa Savoye (1929–31), both outside Paris. In Nelson's own design, Le Corbusier's influence is especially noticeable in the open living space of Tam's Parisian villa, which is shaped by freestanding curvilinear walls and further defined by groupings of metal tubular furniture (Illus. 2). The living space opens without walls onto an equally expansive terrace, which is raised to afford a view of a bucolic landscape. In the multilevel music room (Illus. 3), Nelson exploits the advantages of freestanding columns, which here allow the ribbon windows to run uninterrupted across the facade.

2. *What a Widow!* (1930, Allan Dwan). Art Director: Paul Nelson.

The use of open, flowing space in the sets for *What a Widow!* illustrates one of modern architecture's most significant contributions to film—namely, the vivid rendering of three-dimensional space on the flat, two-dimensional movie screen. Representing spatial depth is a primary challenge of film architecture, a burden laid on it largely by the limited recording abilities of the movie camera itself. Human beings are able to perceive depth and space by means of stereoscopic vision, which relies on visual data received from two eyes. The camera, however, has only a single lens, which seems to flatten the images it records. Set designers compensate for this phenomenon by employing a series of optical tricks to achieve the illusion of depth. The simplest of these is the placement of walls, screens, or other large objects in the foreground of the picture. Functioning as frames, these elements heighten the perception of distance between foreground and background. Equally effective is the use of false perspective, in which objects in the distance are built in a smaller

virtually pull the viewer's eye to the rear of the scene along an axis perpendicular to the screen. The existence of further space extending outside the frame is also implied: through a doorway behind the S-shaped wall to the right; onto the terrace through broad openings to the left; and around as

3. *What a Widow!* (1930).

scale than those in the foreground, again creating the semblance of depth.

In addition to such optical ploys, space could be suggested by the skillful manipulation of set design, and modern architecture proved to be especially suitable for that purpose. Look again at Nelson's designs for Tam's villa. Freestanding walls in the living room (Illus. 2) not only demarcate space but

well as above the semicircular stairway to the rear. In the music room (Illus. 3), expanses of glass open to an almost infinite depth beyond.

Nelson's innovative use of space was matched by his experiments with artificial lighting. Film sets require a tremendous amount of illumination, which in studio shooting is usually provided by light fixtures of various wattages (sometimes as high as ten thousand watts) attached to pipes running across the top of the set. Nelson ingeniously incorporated much of this illumination into features he designed for the set itself, which suffused the decor (Illus. 4) with a brilliant light. More than almost all the modern architecture of its day, Nelson's schemes for *What a Widow!* realized the dream of a world transformed by light that had been foreseen by early modern theorists. Consider, for example, the originality of the translucent panels, recessed cove lights, and metallic finishes in Tam's living room, and especially Nelson's design for a freestanding neon light fixture (Illus. 5). A cinema original—and a remarkable architec-

tural innovation as well—is the use of the fixture's lighting tubes to replicate the cubist profiles of the painting in the background. Nelson even commissioned a Hollywood sculptor to create a relief (Illus. 6) of an enlarged version of Picasso's painting *Three Musicians,* whose overlapping cubist planes are given further definition by artificial illumination.

Nelson also studied in great detail the problem of suggesting color on black-and-white film stock. Although modern architects themselves relied primarily on black-and-white photographic images to publicize their work, a rich color palette was nevertheless available to them for the materials of the actual buildings. For example, Mies van

der Rohe's Barcelona Pavilion (1929), a temporary exhibition structure, has earned its reputation largely on the basis of the black-and-white photographs taken of it.[5] Yet the building itself was equally notable for Mies's use of green marble, blue-green glass, and red curtaining. For film designers during the 1920s and 1930s, however, the predominance of black-and-white cinematography limited their use of lush color to achieve surface richness in cinema decor. To compensate for this deficiency, film architects used striking black-and-white motifs, all-white decor, and dramatic lighting effects to impart the luster of luxury. Nelson built the sets for *What a Widow!* in a wide range of grays and black, with a celestial blue used in place of pure white, impossible to film at that time because it produced a glaring effect. Brilliant materials placed next to matte ones, and textures next to solids, helped achieve a rich and lively palette.

What a Widow! was Paul Nelson's only film set, and he seems to have had no further interest in pursuing a film career in Hollywood or in France, to which he subsequently returned. His departure was far from spelling the end of modern film decor in Hollywood; *What a Widow!* marked the onset of a great decade of outstanding set design. To some degree, the successful introduction of the new architecture into the United States fueled this period of creativity. But the late 1920s also witnessed a shift

4. (OPPOSITE) *What a Widow!* (1930).
5. (LEFT) *What a Widow!* (1930).
6. (ABOVE) *What a Widow!* (1930).

in movie studio policy from luring architects with avant-garde credentials like Nelson to relying on staff design specialists to create the modern "look." These designers, nurtured from birth, as it were, within the walls of the studios themselves, performed the functions of artist, craftsman, technician, and businessman. Most could claim only a tangential relation to the architectural profession; few, in fact, actually practiced architecture; and none were avowed partisans of the modern movement. All, however, showed as strong a modernist sensibility as many of their architectural counterparts.

Without subscribing to its program, film design specialists absorbed the new style's repertoire from secondary sources ranging from printed material to exhibitions. Among the latter, as the next chapter will show, certain key exhibitions provide a convenient framework to trace a brief history of modern architecture during the 1920s and '30s. These were exciting forums not only for publicizing architectural experimentations but also for offering provocative suggestions on progressive ways to live in the twentieth century. New inventions, new technologies, and new media had heralded the modern age, which would now be given shape by a new architecture.

DESIGNING DREAMS

CHAPTER 1

Projecting the New Architecture

A view down the most fashionable streets of the West at the turn of the century would reveal a medley of styles of urban architecture inspired by the achievements of the past. One of the most prominent styles, neo-classicism, replicated the columns, pediments, and moldings of ancient Greece and Rome, and both imparted a civic grandeur to museums and railway stations and lent prestige to the villas of the affluent. Other buildings were reproductions ranging from the neo-Gothic to the neo-Tudor, recreated with archaeological accuracy or eclectic whimsy. Solidity and permanence were suggested by the use of traditional building materials, sculpted, chiseled, and honed into decorative details that manipulated light and shadow to produce lively chiaroscuro effects.

But not all architects were satisfied with carefully constructed evocations of the past. Many strove instead to reconcile their art with the changes wrought by the Industrial Revolution, an inescapable reality of the modern world. These builders sought inspiration for a new architectural language and often found it in the great works of engineering of the nineteenth century. They looked to structures like Joseph Paxton's Crystal Palace for London's 1851 Great Exhibition, for example, which rejected facile imitations of historical styles in favor of simple expressions of structure and function and the bold use of modern materials like steel and glass. These new architectural ideas began to achieve wider currency around the turn of the century throughout Europe and America. In Vienna, the banking hall of Otto Wagner's Post Office Savings Bank (1904–6) combined riveted steel columns, shining ceramic walls, a glass ceiling, and aluminum furniture for an architectural evocation of machine-like precision and sleekness. At the same time, in Chicago, the

3

leading center of architectural innovation in the U.S., Louis Sullivan spearheaded the development of a forthright commercial style for the city's pragmatic business community. The facades of Sullivan's Carson, Pirie & Scott (originally Meyer and Slessinger) department store (1899–1904) openly acknowledged its industrial metal skeleton by sheathing it in only lightweight panels of terra-cotta and filling in the frame with large sheets of glass.

Such buildings introduced features that would be the foundation for the modern architectural style of the late 1920s and early 1930s. Le Corbusier's 1931 Maison de Refuge, a hostel for the poor, represents modernism at its peak (Illus. 7). A shocking departure from its traditional neighbors, the building meets the street with an asymmetrical composite of freestanding elements, including a white-tile-and-glass-block cylinder, a dramatically cantilevered canopy, and a cubic pavilion clad in primary-colored panels. These provide the foreground for the main, multistoried body of the building, a structure clad in a skin of metal and glass. To many contemporary eyes, the building must have seemed fragile, naked, and frankly "functional."

Le Corbusier expressed his architectural theories not only through buildings like the Maison de Refuge but also through the printed word, where he could elaborate their philosophical underpinnings. His 1923 book, *Vers une Architecture,* urged architects to redefine their art so that it kept pace with modern life, whose ideal embodiments he considered to be automobiles, ocean liners, and airplanes. *Vers une Architecture*'s section on mass-produced housing, illustrated with many of Le Corbusier's designs, proposed that architecture must be an egalitarian art serving a broad segment of the population. Le Corbusier's definition of modernism as a non-elitist art became a major tenet for many modernists, who willingly accepted

the task of proselytizing for the new style. As architects sought to reach clients beyond the traditional avenues of religious and aristocratic patronage, they began to publicize their work with ingenuity and perseverance. Manifestos, one of modernism's preferred forums, satisfied the movement's penchant for polemics and gave architects an opportunity to criticize the errors of the past and promote visions of the future. For example, in 1909 a group of architects, artists, and writers launched Italian Futurism, a precursor of modernism, with a manifesto extolling the Machine Age, which appeared on the front page of the Paris newspaper *Le Figaro.* Although few modernist tracts would ever again make so widely heralded a debut, architects continued to use manifestos to disseminate their beliefs, even if their readership tended to consist mainly of their avant-garde colleagues.

Books, however, both reached a wider audience and gave architects an opportunity for a more elaborate presentation of their ideas. One particularly effective format consisted of a short, spirited introduction followed by a wealth of illustrations drawn from modern architecture throughout the world. Modernism was broadcast through periodicals as well. Vanguard scholarly journals were an important outlet to the mid-1920s. But from the middle of the decade onward, most modernist journals withered and disappeared as more modernist buildings were constructed and general-circulation magazines began covering this design.

However effective the advocacy of the printed word, these publicity outlets relied heavily on architectural photography. The photographic image often achieved the purity and machined precision that architects sought but could rarely accomplish in actual construction. Red filters, for example, made the preferred white stucco cladding appear whiter, and if necessary, photos could be

7. Maison de Refuge, Paris (1931,
Le Corbusier).

retouched to remove all blemishes. Of
course, the visual image itself was, to the
public, an easily accessible means to and
vivid expression of modernist aesthetics.

But the most effective medium modern
architects had at their disposal was the exhibition, where full-scale examples of modern
architecture often went on display before the
public. The exhibition pavilion and its
express function as a publicity event also
fostered a spirit of experimentation not
normally possible under the more restrictive
conditions of professional practice. In this
respect, exhibitions were comparable to

movie sets, which were likewise temporary
constructions having useful publicity value
for studios. Although exhibitions never attracted spectators to the same extent as did
the movies, they did allow architects to
reach an unprecedentedly large audience,
consisting not only of those in attendance
but also of inestimable numbers through
magazine and newspaper coverage, souvenir
programs, and promotional brochures.

As modernism's most eloquent method of
self-promotion, exhibitions provide a convenient means of tracing the development of
modern architecture as viewed by the public
—and, of course, by the movie designers
who adopted what they saw for the movies.
Between 1925 and 1939, the years of mod-

ernism's flowering and the period in which the movies adapted it most successfully for set decor, five major exhibitions in particular defined the progress of modernism.

In 1925, Paris hosted the first of these shows, the *Exposition Internationale des Arts Décoratifs et Industriels Modernes*. At approximately this time, the distinctive design features of the modern movement had coalesced in a group of key buildings, many of them making their debut before the public at the exposition. The earliest film to employ modern architectural decor had appeared the previous year, and was, in fact, a project of the French avant-garde undertaken in anticipation of the exposition. The Paris exposition also introduced the general public to Art Deco, a cluster of decorative motifs that would later be applied to both buildings and film design.

Two years after the Paris exposition, modernism's greatest period was inaugurated by the 1927 Exhibition of the Deutscher Werkbund at Stuttgart, which presented an entire housing development featuring contributions by virtually every major modern architect working in Europe at the time. In 1932, the *Modern Architecture: International Exhibition* at New York's Museum of Modern Art celebrated the modernist style and signaled its emergence in America. Modern film decor, meanwhile, had followed a similar pattern, with a dramatic rise in the number of modern film sets built beginning in 1927 and peaking in 1932, when more films with such decor were produced than in any other year. While Europe dominated modern film work of the late 1920s, it was eclipsed in the early 1930s by American designers.

Two other American expositions of the 1930s traced the evolution of modern architecture in the United States during these years and spread the influence of Art Deco. An angular, cubist-inspired style of Art Deco, introduced in America through the Paris exposition of 1925, reached its apogee at the 1933 Chicago Century of Progress. A streamlined version of Art Deco was also promoted there; it reached its peak of popularity six years later at the 1939 New York World's Fair.

Exposition Internationale des Arts Décoratifs et Industriels Modernes, Paris, 1925

Although shortly before World War I, many French artisans would likely have considered France preeminent in the decorative arts, the new modernist trends emanating from Germany and Austria had already begun to assert themselves and challenge French self-confidence. The enormous popular success of the designs from Germany exhibited at the annual Paris *Salon d'Automne* in 1910 posed a sufficient threat to spur French industry to plan an exposition that would reaffirm France's own talent for innovation. The outbreak of war, however, forced the project to be shelved until 1922, when France seized the opportunity to react against German influence before the war and to reassert its own artistic culture after the war's devastation.

When, after three years of preparation, the *Exposition Internationale des Arts Décoratifs et Industriels Modernes* finally opened in April 1925, it was a triumph for its organizers, a lavish showcase for a diverse assembly of buildings and decorative objects. Covering both banks of the Seine at the Alexander III and Invalides bridges, the exposition consisted of a collection of pavilions, each sponsored by an attending nation, manufacturer, store, or individual designer. While the Soviet Union, Japan, and most of Western Europe were officially represented, a United States contingent was conspicuously absent: Herbert Hoover, then secretary of commerce, had declined the organizers' invitation, indicating that his country could not fulfill one of their stipulations, that all items displayed be modern. Nevertheless, he sent a visiting delegation of more than one hundred American manufacturers and artists, and thousands of American tourists visited during the exposition's six-month run.

The dominant style at the exhibition was a pastiche of design trends that have since been grouped under the heading Art Deco. This decorative style has emerged in France as early as 1909, reached its culmination at the exposition, and was popularized and diluted afterward. Despite its extravagant ingredients—elements that made the designs seem "modern" to many observers—Art Deco was essentially a conservative style. Many Art Deco designers transformed late-eighteenth-century neo-classical models into generously proportioned furniture in rare and exotic materials such as ivory, heavily veined wood, tortoiseshell, and lizard skins. Stylized flowers, plants, and fountains set in octagons were recurring motifs. The outstanding design in this repertoire was that by the furniture designer Émile-Jacques Ruhlmann, whose salon in the Pavillon d'un Collectionneur was accorded lavish praise by critics and was the most popular exhibit with the general public. A suitably dignified setting for some of Ruhlmann's most luxurious furniture, the room featured violet and gray wall covering applied to surfaces decorated with a simplified cornice and base moldings (Illus. 8).

More exotic themes influenced Art Deco designs in the form of African and Egyptian motifs (Tutankhamen's tomb had been opened in 1922) and the theater designs of the Ballets Russes, which had its premier performance in Paris in 1909. The company offered Parisians intoxicating evocations of the East in *Schéhérazade* and primitive barbarity in Stravinsky's *Le Sacre du Printemps*.

8. Salon of Pavillon d'un Collectionneur, Paris (1925, Jacques Ruhlmann).

Through stage decor by artists such as Léon Bakst, Art Deco designers became infatuated with vivid colors, as opposed to the subtle nuances that had been characteristic of Art Nouveau. Russian ballet also heightened the already popular fad for the Orient. No chic Parisian salon was complete without a set of low divans piled with pillows and a decor that featured sharply contrasting patterns. Orientalism reached its peak in the fashions and interior decorations of Paul Poiret, France's leading couturier from before the First World War until the late 1920s. Poiret held a series of parties on Arabian themes and published luxurious volumes devoted to his clothing designs, which set the period's standard of extravagance. With typical flamboyance, Poiret was

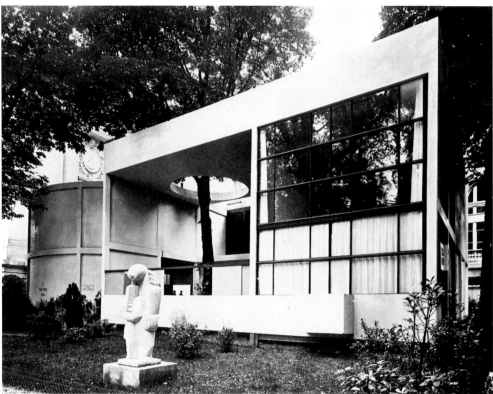

represented at the Exposition by three barges—*Amours, Délices,* and *Orgies*—floating along the Seine.

Cubism, a major prewar movement in painting and sculpture, was another influence on Art Deco designers, who had adopted the angular forms of cubist paintings as decorative motifs. At the exposition, cubist-inspired appliqué covered books and cigarette cases and was even used as ornamentation for automobiles (Illus. 9). While these motifs were only a minor current at the exposition, they would provide an important source of later design, especially in the United States.

In contrast to the richly decorative contri-

9. (OPPOSITE TOP) 1925 Citroën B12 and fashions, Paris (1925, Sonia Delaunay), with Pavillon du Tourisme beyond (Robert Mallet-Stevens).
10. (OPPOSITE BOTTOM) Pavillon de l'Esprit Nouveau, Paris (1925, Le Corbusier).
11. (ABOVE) Pavillon de l'Esprit Nouveau (1925).

butions of the Art Deco designers, the designs of the modern architects, a small but provocative contingent at the exposition, were of a startling simplicity—so startling, in fact, that Le Corbusier's Pavillon de l'Esprit Nouveau (Illus. 10) was assigned only a peripheral site and was initially hidden from general view by a six-foot wall. The wall was removed before the exhibition opened, however, and the public was allowed to view a most extraordinary structure by one of the most innovative designers of the twentieth century.

Born Charles Édouard Jeanneret in Switzerland in 1887, Le Corbusier adopted his professional name shortly after he moved to Paris in 1916. The 1920s would be for him an incredibly fertile decade, during which he would emerge as a major creative force in the modern movement. By the end of the decade, he had established himself as one of the century's great architects, mainly as a result of the villas he had designed in and around Paris for fellow artists and wealthy patrons of the arts. These buildings displayed Le Corbusier's talent not only as an architect but also as a painter, a sculptor, and a theoretician. His achievement in the villas was to take everyday materials of the modern industrial world—items like pipe railings, metal-framed windows, ship's ramps —and, by placing them in an unusual or unexpected context, elevate them into expressions of the progressive spirit of the age: *l'esprit nouveau,* which was the name chosen for the avant-garde magazine that Le Corbusier and the painter Amedée Ozenfant had begun in 1920.

Le Corbusier's exhibition pavilion is an asymmetrical composition of open and closed volumes wrapped in undecorated surfaces of stucco and large glass windows. Its floating roof, pierced by a circular cutout, suggests the structure's airiness and an illusion of weightlessness. This geometric vocabulary is carried to the interior as well (Illus. 11), where, in contrast to the fussy neo-classic decoration of Ruhlmann's exhibit, monochromatic walls, built-in furniture, and abstract paintings impart a spirit of order and clarity.

Another important modernist exhibitor was the French architect Robert Mallet-Stevens. His five projects, some of which were collaborations with France's leading modern artists, included a garden of abstract trees executed in cement by the Martel brothers and the Pavillon du Tourisme, an asymmetrical grouping of floating horizontal planes and soaring vertical fins.

An equally notable contribution of Mallet-Stevens to the exposition was a studio on the Champ de Mars for the Société des Auteurs de Film, a building that reflected his own involvement in French cinema. The previous year, he had designed sets for the first important film to adapt modern architecture to the screen, *L'Inhumaine* (see page 45). Participating in this effort had been a coterie of vanguard architects, artists, and filmmakers. The exposition loosened the vanguard's dominance over modern film decor, however, for more than any other single event, it focused the attention of popular filmmakers on the merits of Art Deco and modern architecture. Both were fully drawn into the mainstream of film design; the former immediately, the latter within a few years. The eventual success of modernism in this cinematic context could only have been guessed at by the editors of *Art et Décoration,* the lush magazine that previewed the exposition's fashions, architecture, and film decor, when they asked their readers if modern, "cubic" design was not in fact the *grand moyen* of cinema decor.[1] The answer, given by filmmakers who carried modern architecture home to studios from Hollywood to Berlin, was a resounding affirmation.

Exhibition of the Deutscher Werkbund, Stuttgart, 1927

While modern architects played only a minor role at Paris in 1925, they were the sole exhibitors at the 1927 exhibition sponsored by the Deutscher Werkbund at Stuttgart. The Werkbund was a design organization that had been founded in Germany in 1907 to foster collaboration between art and industry and to raise the aesthetic quality of machine-made products. But as the designs of many of its members demonstrate, this goal often led them beyond commercial considerations toward a philosophical quest to capture the very spirit of the machine age.

The Werkbund pavilion that Walter Gropius and Adolf Meyer designed for the group's first exhibition in 1914 at Cologne elevated industry to an almost religious pursuit. In their pavilion, a model factory, the architects attempted to negate the connotations of filth and foulness that had become attached to industrial production by bringing a gas turbine engine into the light and treating it as a monumental outdoor sculpture. The building itself conveyed a mystique of technological efficiency and order through sleek details such as the rhythmic banding of the brick walls and the taut glass cages surrounding the helical stairways that flank the entrance.

This design vocabulary, brought to an even more polished and simplified state, was used for the buildings at the Werkbund's second exhibition, thirteen years later. The 1927 Stuttgart show can be considered the first large-scale, cohesive presentation of modern architecture to the general public. Focusing now on the modern dwelling for an industrial society, the Werkbund commissioned sixteen prominent modern architects or teams to design a housing complex for a section of the city called the Weissen-hof. Germany was represented by, among others, Walter Gropius and Ludwig Mies van der Rohe, who had been appointed first vice-president of the organization in 1926 and directed the exhibition the following year. As his contribution, Mies designed an apartment house (Illus. 12), an impeccably proportioned block with large windows set in thin metal frames pushed flush with the smooth white stucco of facades of pronounced horizontal emphasis.

The French contingent at Stuttgart included Le Corbusier, who designed two dwellings (Illus. 13) that strikingly realized the five points for a new architecture that he had proposed the previous year. The first of these was the use of a thin structural column, or *piloti,* to replace the heavy, load-bearing walls of the traditional building. The result of technological advances in reinforced concrete construction, the piloti permitted radical freedom in the manipulation of space both within and without the structure. By lifting the house off the earth, it returned the ground to nature, as it were, and freed it to be planted with gardens.

The *flat roof,* Le Corbusier's second point, replaced the standard pitched roof with a functional space that would also contain a garden for exercising, sunbathing, and relaxing. The same piloti that made possible the banishment of load-bearing walls around the ground floor would make them obsolete in the interior as well. Instead of relying on the conventional arrangement of discrete, self-contained rooms enclosed by thick walls, the modern interior would be open: just a floor, a ceiling, and a grid of pilotis for support. Spaces such as living and dining rooms now flowed freely into one another, defined only by low walls and groupings of furniture. The result: the *free plan,* Le Corbusier's third point. Finally, interior and exterior spaces were essentially merged by Le Corbusier's fourth and fifth

points: *thin facades,* which served as the merest of taut skins wrapping around the open interior space, and *long horizontal windows,* which flooded the interior with light.

The effect of Le Corbusier's five points on architecture was to produce an illusion of

12. Apartment house, Stuttgart (1927, Ludwig Mies van der Rohe).

weightlessness, to make his buildings seem as if they hovered above the ground. The modern house therefore presented itself as an analogue to the airplane or the dirigible, which ranked among the outstanding and dynamic results of scientific achievement in the century. With its roof garden that suggested the deck of an ocean liner, and an interior that echoed the clean, well-lit environment of a scientist, the contemporary dwelling firmly asserted its position in the forefront of the new age of progressive technology.

The architect's desire to align his work with forward-looking, healthy life-styles was unequivocally expressed by Sheldon

13. Residence, Stuttgart (1927, Le Corbusier).

Cheney when in 1930 he wrote in *The New World Architecture:*

Many times I have mentioned "openness" as an ideal of the new home building. I use the word with more than a spatial connotation. It seems to me clear that there is going on a freeing process in regard to both our physical and our mental lives. While the old walled-in house, the essentially castle-refuge sort of structure, is giving way before less-confined living space, women are discarding most of their clothes, and human minds are freeing themselves slowly of old superstitions, old limiting religions, old narrowly selfish motives. This is a general coming-forth—which seems to me calculated for the better health and the greater happiness of mankind.[2]

The period following the Deutscher Werkbund exhibition of 1927 saw the modern movement reach its peak in Europe, and during the next half-dozen years some of the century's most extraordinary buildings were erected. These designs shared a common architectural language whose vocabulary included asymmetrical compositions of simple geometric shapes; taut, skin-like enclosures of glass, stucco, and metal, free of ornament; and open interior spaces. These features, distilled from the diverse precursors of modernism that had arisen during the first quarter of the century, came to represent the ideal of modern architecture at a rare moment of stylistic unity.

Yet by the early 1930s, European modernism was already on the wane. Due in large measure to the deepening world depression, which forced cutbacks in building construction, and to the rise of authoritarian regimes in Germany, Italy, and the Soviet Union, which for ideological reasons rejected the modern style and, in Germany, at least, drove out its best modern architects, the focus of architectural development shifted to the United States.

Modern Architecture: International Exhibition, The Museum of Modern Art, New York, 1932

In the late 1920s, American familiarity with the achievements of the European modern movement was limited to only a small coterie of intellectuals, many of whom relied on the initiative of small, specialized publications for the latest word of artistic developments overseas. In 1927, for example, the journal *The Little Review* sponsored an eye-opening "Machine Age Exposition" devoted to the works of the avant-garde abroad, including pieces by Soviet constructivists like architect Constantin Melnikov, the French architect André Lurçat, and the Russian-born sculptor Alexander Archipenko. Perhaps the most important forum for new architectural ideas was *Architectural Record*. Although for most of the decade it had paid only slight attention to European modernism, *Record* underwent a dramatic change in editorial policy in 1928. Bold, abstract graphics replaced the picturesque covers of the past, and architectural historian Henry-Russell Hitchcock began contributing articles on the European modern architects, bringing their designs to the attention of many American architects for the first time.

It was Hitchcock, as well, who played a major role in exposing the American public to modernism when, in 1932, he directed with Philip Johnson the *Modern Architecture: International Exhibition* at New York's newly founded Museum of Modern Art. With models, photographs, drawings, and plans in five rooms of a mid-Manhattan office building (the Museum's own quarters would not be constructed until 1939), Hitchcock and Johnson sought to demonstrate that the prominent design features of the best modern architecture formed the basis for a worldwide consensus, a unity of vision that often allied itself with progressive social concerns. One room of the exhibition stressed this international character of modernism by displaying the work of almost fifty architects and designers from sixteen different countries. The movement's commitment to improving society through architecture was the subject of a second room, devoted to mass-housing projects in Germany and the United States.

Nine outstanding architects and partnerships, whose designs represented a high percentage of the most successful modern buildings to date, were featured throughout the show. The Europeans in this select group were remarkable for the individuality of their invention within the context of a common modern architectural language. The work of Mies van der Rohe had during the late 1920s evolved into a style poised between classical calm repose and the dynamic sense of movement the twentieth-century architect had raised to the level of a symbol for his time. The German Pavilion for the 1929 International Exhibition at Barcelona (known as the Barcelona Pavilion) was Mies's masterwork (Illus. 14), a structure Hitchcock would later praise as "one of the few buildings by which the twentieth century might wish to be measured against the great ages of the past."[3] Freestanding walls of sumptuously colored marble, onyx, and glass manipulated an apparently uninterrupted flow of space punctuated by cruciform-shaped, chrome-plated columns. The main roofed areas provided distinguished settings for official ceremonies; the open, unroofed areas formed courtyards of pools and statuary.

While Mies's buildings at this time led the

14. Barcelona Pavilion, Barcelona (1929, Ludwig Mies van der Rohe).

occupant along spaces that flowed into one another horizontally, those by Le Corbusier moved one along vertically as well. His Villa Savoye and Villa Stein, both outside Paris, stand as flawless demonstrations of the range of architectural expression possible within the five points of architecture. Their severe yet elegant facades barely hint at the spatial grandeur inside, where gently sloping ramps, curving walls, and spiral stairways draw the occupant along dramatic passages Le Corbusier called *les promenades architecturales*. At the Villa Savoye, one travels through the house along a scissor ramp of constantly shifting views, beginning at the glass-enclosed ground floor; continuing up through the main level, open on one side

with a terrace; and ending, finally, at the roof terrace (Illus. 15), partially enclosed by curving walls and affording spectacular views of the countryside.

Both the Villa Stein and the Villa Savoye played prominent roles in *L'Architecture d'Aujourd'hui,* an avant-garde documentary written by Le Corbusier and directed by Pierre Chenal. The film's opening sequence declares movement as a major theme of the new architecture by establishing an implicit connection between it and two of the century's foremost achievements in the field of transportation. A shot of an auto, followed by an intertitle that explains it is "a machine for driving," leads to one of an airplane, "a machine for flying," and finally, to a shot of

15. Villa Savoye, Poissy (1929–30, Le Corbusier).

the Villa Savoye: "a machine for living." Throughout the film the buildings of Le Corbusier are not merely presented as successfully executed art objects for the viewer's contemplation, but seen in the context of action: People wind around their spiral stairs, ascend their ramps, and play and exercise on their roof terraces. Similarly, the Villa Stein is introduced with a shot of a car sweeping toward it; when the vehicle stops, a man (Le Corbusier himself) alights and jauntily enters the building.

The third member of the European triumvirate that dominated The Museum of Modern Art show was Walter Gropius, who had been chosen as the first head of the Bauhaus (Illus. 16), the most prominent design

school of the century. Located originally in Weimar, where it was founded in 1919, the school moved to Dessau in 1926 into its new teaching and living facilities designed by Gropius. The glass-walled workshop wing housed facilities that were devoted to virtually every branch of the visual arts, from graphics and painting to metalwork and textiles. The Bauhaus conceived the design process as the conjunction of a variety of disciplines that together created a total architectural environment. The school's auditorium, for example, formed within its modern shell the perfect setting for the innovative metal tubular chairs by Marcel Breuer, the industrial light fixtures by László Moholy-Nagy, and the performances of avant-garde ballets with dancers costumed as abstract shapes, designed and choreographed by Oscar Schlemmer. Under Gropius's direction, members of the Bauhaus staff carried out the school's goal of merging design with modern industrial production methods—or at least a suggestion that such methods had been employed—and brought their creations to the public through books, exhibitions, patents, and license agreements. So successful were they at publicizing their work that by the late 1920s, the "Bauhaus style" of simple lines and functional elegance became synonymous with modern design in Germany, an influence that spread worldwide through the emigration of its most famous members after the school was closed by Nazi order in 1933.

Gropius shared the prestigious first room of The Museum of Modern Art show with Irving and Monroe Bowman, two young brothers from Chicago, whose exhibited work, which consisted almost entirely of designs for unbuilt projects, testified to the general scarcity of modern buildings in the United States. A significant exception was the work of Austrian-born Richard Neutra, whose Los Angeles designs were the most accomplished American representatives of the new style. Neutra benefited from publicity generated by the exhibition, especially when it traveled to Los Angeles. Although his Lovell House there (Illus. 17) had been the occasion of a local sensation upon its completion in 1929, when fifteen thousand astonished Angelenos poured through the house on four successive open-house Sundays, the Museum's exhibition solidified his position among the vanguard as the leading modernist of the West Coast.

The Museum of Modern Art exhibition also was distinguished by a number of designs for skyscrapers. This very American building type had evolved in the late nineteenth century as the product of a combination of forces. Two technological factors

that encouraged vertical expansion were the development of lightweight steel construction and the invention of the elevator, while the possibility of concentrating ever greater amounts of business activity on relatively small parcels of urban land prompted speculators to build even higher. Early skyscrapers were often modeled on an elaborate historical precedent, fashioned, for example, to resemble a church bell tower, a stack of Greek temples, or a Gothic cathedral. After the First World War, however, architects began to develop a non-revivalist skyscraper vocabulary, a hybrid drawn from many sources, including, by the mid-'20s, the fashionable motifs of the Paris exposition. The Chrysler Building (Illus. 18), designed by William Van Alen and completed in 1930, at the end of a decade of fevered construction in New York City, was a masterpiece of this popular style. Built for the automobile manufacturer Walter Chrysler, the building rises in a series of receding setbacks and ends in a silver crown of semicircles pierced by triangular windows. Van Alen set the black, white, and gray walls of the structure in elaborate geometric patterns, often simulating hubcaps and mudguards. This program of automobile motifs culminated in the giant silver hood ornaments decorating some of the skyscraper's corners.

Neither Van Alen nor the Chrysler Building was included in The Museum of Modern Art show, which featured instead a skyscraper style that was less decorative, tending toward simpler, less chiseled shapes. The skyscraper career of Raymond Hood, which was charted in the exhibition, exemplified this shift toward greater simplification. Hood's 1924 American Radiator Building in New York was an extravagant, neo-Gothic tower in black and gold, but by the time he created New York's Daily News Building in 1930, a stripping down had obviously taken place. Confining ornament to

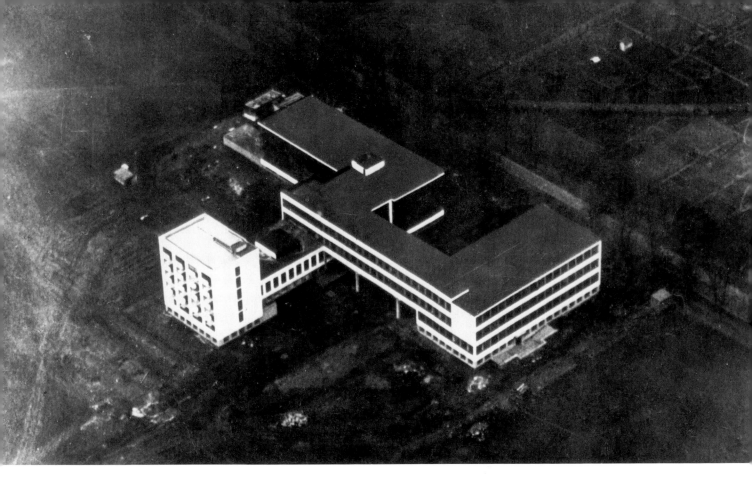

16. (ABOVE) Bauhaus, Dessau (1926, Walter Gropius).
17. (BELOW) Lovell House, Los Angeles (1927–29, Richard Neutra).

18. Chrysler Building, New York City
(1928–30, William Van Alen).

the ground floor, Hood designed the building as a series of austere, flat-topped slabs clad in uninterrupted vertical stripes of two colors of brick and glass. A year later, Hood collaborated with J. André Fouilhoux on the McGraw-Hill Building, which marks a moment of transition in American skyscraper design, reflecting the declining popularity of Art Deco and the rising acceptance of modernism. Although Hood retains his Art Deco heritage in the multicolor banding applied to the ground floor and the setback top, he looks ahead to modernism with the tower's wrapping of industrial glazing placed flush to the building's blue-green terra-cotta panels.

The most progressive skyscraper included in the exhibition was not located in New York and, in 1932, was in fact still under construction. The Philadelphia Saving Fund Society (Illus. 19) brought into the mainstream of American skyscraper style virtually all the design precepts of European modernism. Its architects were the American George Howe, whose solid Philadelphia reputation was instrumental in securing the commission, and the Swiss-born William Lescaze, to whose European training can be attributed many of the building's bold, modern features. These elements, expressed more cogently in PSFS than in any other skyscraper built in the 1930s, would evolve after World War II into the dominant forms of modern high-rise design.

While The Museum of Modern Art exhibition furthered the cause of modernism in the United States, it did not bear sole responsibility for introducing the style to the American architect or, for that matter, to the general public. As already mentioned, American moviemakers had exposed their audience to modern designs as early as 1930 in *What a Widow!*, whose designer, Paul Nelson, was represented at the Museum's show by a Parisian pharmacy. And, as will be seen in a later chapter, the use of modern decor was not confined to avant-garde designers like Nelson, but had by the time of the exhibition already spread to the studio-employed film design specialists. The general conviction among some architects and historians that the Museum's exhibition marked the initial appearance of modern architecture before the general public thus grants too much credit to the power of American high cultural institutions while overlooking the swift and far-reaching influence of the nation's popular cultural sources. The Museum's show was, nonetheless, a most significant event in the early years of the adoption of modernism in the United States, in that it clarified a canon of design principles that, in an even more simplified form, would influence a large consensus of American architects after the war.

Century of Progress Exposition, Chicago, 1933–34

While modern architecture was still in its infancy in the United States, a zigzag, cubist-inspired version of Art Deco had concurrently reached the peak of its popularity. This new style had been introduced at the Paris exposition of 1925, and Americans had returned eager to use it in their work. The Art Deco look was launched with enormous press coverage and publicity bonanzas at such major department stores as Macy's, Lord & Taylor, and John Wanamaker. The American Association of Museums even circulated an exhibition of decorative objects from the Paris exposition to nine cities in 1926. Within a few years, Art Deco established itself as the most up-to-date style for fashion, shops, nightclubs, movie houses, and skyscrapers.

Despite its popularity (or perhaps because of it), the fashion for cubist Art Deco was to be short-lived, and the style enjoyed its last hurrah at the 1933 Century of Progress Exposition in Chicago.

19. Philadelphia Saving Fund Society Building, Philadelphia (1929–32, George Howe and William Lescaze).

Visitors to the Century of Progress, which stretched along Lake Michigan, were able to view technological wonders on display—the photoelectric cell, for example, and the latest concepts in cars and trains—and perhaps saw in these progressive inventions the means by which they might escape from the hardships of the Depression. No less startling was the architecture of the pavilions themselves, executed in a variety of styles. A few modern examples were featured, including John C. B. Moore's residential design for the Home and Industrial

Arts Group. Moore's pavilion, which adopted orthodox modern aesthetics—monochromatic walls, rectangular geometry—and ideology (it was constructed by prefabricated building methods), was heralded in the architectural press as "a house designed for occupancy by an average family."[4] Promoting itself as pragmatic, functional, and efficient, Moore's design was, in the end, bland.

A more theatrical display of modernism could be seen at the exposition in two buildings designed by the local architect George Fred Keck. In his "House of Tomorrow," Keck took the setback massing that was a typical design feature at the top of an Art Deco skyscraper and gave it a modernist wrapping of floor-to-ceiling glass and pipe railings. Keck outdid himself the following year, though, when he unveiled his Crystal House (Illus. 20), a constructivist fabrication of exposed metal structure and glass, and, in its anticipation of developments after the war, one of the most remarkable American designs of the 1930s.

However outstanding Keck's designs were in quality, they were far outweighed in quantity by pavilions (many of which were devoted to American industry) that echoed the Art Deco skyscraper, with its receding setback shapes chiseled into vertical fins, jagged against the sky (Illus. 21). This effect of restlessness was heightened by the vivid blue, gold, orange, and violet hues used to paint the buildings, a scheme that colored lighting enabled to be carried into the night.

While the aesthetic of these pavilions looked backward to the exuberance of the jazzy '20s, the emergence of a smoother, less angular version of Art Deco could be detected in the designs for the many transportation vehicles the exposition displayed. Streamlining, as this style was called, was originally conceived as an aerodynamic design principle: By incorporating teardrop contours and rounded corners, a vehicle would offer the least possible resistance to a current of air or water through which it traveled. At the exposition, the teardrop contour and a radical three-wheel design distinguished the Dymaxion Cars, invented by the American R. Buckminster Fuller. In the airspace above the pavilions, the sleek, ovoid shape of the Goodyear blimp seemed to appear everywhere. But the designs that most galvanized the public's infatuation with streamlining were those of two trains: in Union Pacific's M-10,000, later named the City of Salina, and Burlington's Zephyr (Illus. 22), on which the Chicago architects Holabird and Root acted as consultants for the exterior and Philadelphia architect Paul Cret consulted on the interior. The Zephyr's 197-foot length was sheathed almost entirely in stainless steel—from its helmet-like engine car through its body, ribbed in long, linear corrugations, to its teardrop-shaped passenger lounge. Taking its name from the Greek god of the west wind, a romantic evocation of the notion of speed, the Zephyr made a spectacular arrival at the opening day of the exposition's second year. It had left Denver's Union Station early on the morning of May 26, 1934, raced eastward at an average speed of 77.6 miles an hour, and reached Chicago in the record-breaking time of thirteen hours and five minutes. Thousands cheered as it crossed the finish line at the Century of Progress, and over 700,000 additional visitors would tour the train over the following summer.

Streamlining had actually begun to make inroads into architecture and design prior to the Chicago exposition. In his widely publicized 1932 book, *Horizons,* Norman Bel Geddes, who had during the 1920s designed for the theater and for store displays, created a magnificent ocean liner (Illus. 23), which, with its smooth metal shell, swept-back stacks, and long, tapering stern, was a study of design in motion. *Horizons* also included

20. (TOP LEFT) Crystal House, Chicago (1934, George Fred Keck).
21. (BOTTOM) General Motors Building, Chicago (1933, Albert Kahn).
22. (TOP RIGHT) Logo for the Burlington Zephyr (1930s, originally designed by Raymond Loewy).

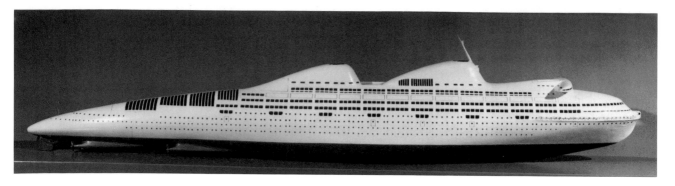

23. Proposal for an ocean liner (1932, Norman Bel Geddes).

a model for a revolving restaurant, one of nine architectural projects intended (none was built) for the Century of Progress. Here Bel Geddes precariously cantilevered off a pylon three segmented circles holding restaurants and terraces, a theatrical and fanciful design of the type usually frowned upon by avant-garde critics for its superficial and decorative application of modernistic motifs.

It was largely as a result of the popularity of the Century of Progress, though, and the wide media attention it attracted, that streamlining became a considerable commercial force. Throughout the 1930s, Bel Geddes—along with other leading industrial designers, such as Raymond Loewy, Walter Dorwin Teague, and Henry Dreyfus—not only helped American businessmen redesign their products in the search for higher profits but also provided moviemakers and their public with visions of a modern future. Common household items like telephones, radio cabinets, and irons were soon transformed by streamlining, their stylish contours far removed from their aerodynamic origins. The success of streamlined goods in the American home attested not only to the allure of the modern "look" but also to the appeal of its promise that the following century would be as progressive as the last—once the Depression had been overcome.

New York World's Fair, New York, 1939–40

The apotheosis of American streamlining occurred at the end of the decade in the form of the 1939 New York World's Fair, an event that dealt only in superlatives. Initiated in 1935 as a financial stimulant to arouse the still stagnant economy of the Depression, the fair was the first exposition to take place in New York in almost a century (the last had occurred in 1853), was the largest reclamation project ever attempted in the eastern United States, and covered more land (1,216.5 acres) than any other fair since the one held in St. Louis in 1904.

Responding spiritedly to the fair's theme of "Building the World of Tomorrow," designers gave free play to their imagination of things to come. Some of the architecture, such as the dominating seven-hundred-foot-tall Trylon and the two-hundred-foot-diameter Perisphere, strove for a sublime quality through abstract geometry. Other structures, such as the National Cash Register Building, which was surmounted by a giant cash register ringing up attendance figures, were pure kitsch. Automobile manufacturers, ready to supply Americans with the means to escape the city for suburbia after World War II, ranked among the most eager and adventurous exhibitions. The Chrysler Corporation commissioned Raymond Loewy to design an oval-shaped hall and a rectangular showroom with two soaring towers. Albert Kahn and Walter Dorwin Teague were responsible for the Ford Motor Company Building, where the Road of Tomorrow gave fairgoers the opportunity to drive the company's latest model.

The triumph of the fair was Norman Bel Geddes's General Motors Building (Illus. 24). Approaching on undulating ramps, visitors (about 27,500 daily) entered a dark, vertical cut in the building's monolithic, curving facade and proceeded to its auditorium. There the audience was escorted by uniformed ushers to their seats, which carried them by train on a sixteen-minute ride which simulated an aerial view of *Futurama,* Bel Geddes's model of America in 1960, which included superhighways, streamlined cars moving at speeds of one hundred miles an hour, and enormous power dams. The train began its descent over a futuristic city

of skyscrapers. After a close-up view of a split-level urban intersection, the viewer left the darkened auditorium and saw an actual re-creation of that intersection: The future had become a reality.

Although streamlining was the dominant design of the American entries at the fair, modern architecture did make a number of striking appearances. The building of Glass, Incorporated (Illus. 25), designed by Shreve, Lamb & Harmon, the architects of the Empire State Building, struck a decidedly modern note in its use of glass to virtually dematerialize the building's volume, especially when illuminated at night. An excellent example of a new tendency in European modernism, Finland's exhibit at the Hall of Nations was the effort of the architect Alvar Aalto and his wife, Aino Marsio-Aalto. Although Aalto's modern Turku Sanomat building of 1928–30 had been included in The Museum of Modern Art's

24. General Motors Building, New York City (1939, Norman Bel Geddes).

25. Glass, Incorporated, Building, New York
City (1939, Shreve, Lamb & Harmon).

1932 exhibition, Aalto's later works pointed
away from the regular geometry and machined materials of the late '20s and early
'30s. They now moved toward more sculptural, biomorphic forms and traditional
building materials like wood and stone. This
trend toward a less austere modernism
would be a theme of The Museum of Modern Art's 1944 exhibition, *Built in USA
1932–1944,* the catalogue for which advocated the development of a modern American architecture from "the mingling of
traditional American techniques and materials with the forms of Wright and the Europeans."[5]

Although Frank Lloyd Wright did not
himself participate in the New York
World's Fair, his work of the decade cannot

be overlooked in even a brief discussion of
the architecture of the 1930s. The Museum
of Modern Art's choice of Wright as a
model in 1944, while consistent with the
course modernism was taking, was nonetheless an ironic turnabout in the architect's
critical reception. Wright's career had always been that of a great individualist, an
architect who picked and chose from a number of different movements, never aligning
himself with any one of them. Although his
Prairie Houses had had enormous influence
on European architects earlier in the century,
his Mayan-inspired, lushly ornamental residences of the 1920s revealed that Wright did
not subscribe to contemporary European
modernism. Johnson and Hitchcock exhibited work by the sixty-three-year-old
master in the 1932 Museum show, but excluded it from their book, *The International
Style,* of the same year. Many believed
Wright's career had ended, his architecture
merely a branch off the mainstream of modern architecture. The eulogy was premature,
however, as two extraordinary buildings of
the mid-to-late 1930s proved Wright's genius was still fertile: the S. C. Johnson and
Son Administration Building in Racine,
Wisconsin, and one of his most brilliant creations, Fallingwater.

The Kaufmann family, owners of one of
Pittsburgh's biggest department stores, had
commissioned Wright to built a house on a
heavily wooded piece of land, a favorite spot
for picnics, some fifty miles east of the city.
The siting was the most dramatic in the
architect's career, and he responded by
designing Fallingwater (1935–37). Perched
as a series of concrete trays cantilevered directly over the falls of the Bear Run stream,
the house is a dazzling amalgam of Wrightian and European modernist themes
(Illus.26): the open planning that was
Wright's greatest influence on European architects, combined with features more char-

acteristic of their work, like the hovering horizontal spandrels and the ribbon windows set in metal frames.

Equally remarkable is the central hall of Wright's Administration Building for the S. C. Johnson and Son Wax Company (1936–39), which features concrete mushroom-shaped columns, and is protected by almost windowless curvilinear walls of terra-cotta red brick. Although such smooth, streamlined curves would play an increasingly important role in Wright's later work, the streamlined style itself—to which the Johnson building did owe some debt—would die with the New York World's Fair. The architectural historian David Gebhard attributes its quick demise to two factors: The movement's glorification of technology may have disenchanted the public, who during the war witnessed a much more destructive side of technology; after the war, during the stable and afffluent '50s, streamlining's futurist stance may have lost the seductive power it had had during the turbulent '30s.[6] Whatever the reasons, streamlining, even more quickly than it surfaced, would disappear during World War II and Bel Geddes's vision of an America streamlined twenty years into the future would never be realized.

By the middle of the 1930s, after a decade of heady invention, the high tide of modern architecture began to ebb and was followed by a period of greater conservatism, a phenomenon that occurred in many of the arts. Not only had the deepening Depression stymied building activity, but the rise of totalitarian governments in many European countries was accompanied by an active hostility to modernism and the sponsorship of a revival of neo-classicism as a state style. Signs of this trend could be read at the 1937 World Exhibition in Paris, where the German and Soviet pavilions forced a bombastic

26. Fallingwater, the Bear Run stream (1936, Frank Lloyd Wright).

juxtaposition as they faced each other across the fair's main axis.

This period also saw the splintering of the stylistic unity that had bound many of the best architects under modernism around 1930. Some, like Le Corbusier, came to reject the highly rationalist, machine-honed precision of the buildings of the late '20s. At the 1932 Museum of Modern Art show, for example, Le Corbusier exhibited two buildings that suggested that the consensus the Museum was celebrating was already disintegrating. Both the de Mandrot House of 1931 and the Maison Suisse at the Cité Universitaire in Paris, still under construction at the time of the exhibition but shown in drawings, diluted the pristine forms of Le

Corbusier's work of the 1920s with a more sculptural sense of form and the use of natural materials like stone and rough concrete. In the design of other modern architects, a neo-classical flavor reappeared. Although Mies, in his 1933 scheme for the Reichsbank in Berlin, stopped short of reviving the architraves, columns, and pediments of neo-classicism, he did, nonetheless, recall the style in the building's symmetrical massing, its grand double staircase in the lobby, and the tripartite division of the facade into base, *piano nobile,* and top.

In 1938, Mies emigrated to the United States, where, through his teachings at Chicago's Illinois Institute of Technology and his successful architectural practice, he emerged as the most influential architect of the postwar period. Although the style he developed became the basis for insipid imitations that were widely adopted as the orthodox style for corporations around the world, structures like Mies's Seagram Building (1954–58) in New York City, with its unerring sense of proportion, meticulous attention to detail, and sure handling of materials, testified to the still-fertile possibilities of modernism at midcentury.

CHAPTER 2

Building the Seventh Art

Midway through the six-month period during which the 1925 Paris exposition was introducing modernism to the general public, the movies celebrated their thirtieth birthday. Improvements in cameras, film stock, and lighting had transformed the grainy, variably focused, shuddery images of the turn of the century into an expressive medium capable of the most subtle and beautiful effects. Likewise, steady advances in decor had completely replaced the theatrical flats of the early 1900s with a cinema architecture brilliant in its manipulation of light and totally convincing in its suggestion of spatial depth. In a remarkably short time the cinema had evolved to an impressive enough degree of maturity that French films were being projected at the Paris exposition in Mallet-Stevens's studio for the Société des Auteurs de Film. So assured were the exposition's organizers that the cinema had become the seventh art, they rightfully elevated the moving image to the status of an artwork, as worthy of serious study and attention as any building, chair, painting, or vase displayed that year along the Seine.

Although the birth of the movies as popular entertainment occurred in the 1890s, the history of the medium itself had begun several years earlier. Initially, in the 1870s and '80s, scientists like the English-born Eadweard Muybridge had developed simple "motion pictures" as a tool to reveal the phases of human and animal movement that were imperceptible to the naked eye. The success of experiments like Muybridge's, and the sensation that they aroused wherever shown, sparked a race among inventors to create a machine that would make serial projections. In Paris, on December 28, 1895, Louis Lumière publicly unveiled his Cinématographe, a device whose fundamental concept is still current in movies today.

In the United States, the history of film

27

and of film decor had reached an important milestone in West Orange, New Jersey, in 1894, when Thomas Edison's film company had built the Black Maria. A small, tar-paper-covered shed that was able to rotate to capture the sun's rays, the Black Maria was the earliest known construction especially created for movie production. Inside the building, the company took filmmaking's first, tentative steps toward a movie decor with crude approximations of architecture painted on flats and filmed before a stationary camera. Although primarily a holdover of the notion of the fixed vantage point afforded the theatergoer, the use of the static camera may also have been determined by economics. Moving cameras required wider, more costly flats. For the exterior shooting of the earliest nonfiction movies, Edison and others used a mobile camera mounted on moving trains, subways, or even a gondola.

America's position in the field of set design was soon lost to France, where the full potential of film decor was realized by the man who built the first movie studio, Georges Méliès. Through the nearly five hundred movies Méliès made between 1896 and 1913, the youngest art of the century began to achieve a distinctive style and a sophistication that would make a pioneering contribution to the visual culture of the twentieth century. Méliès filmed the most important events of his day, and movie audiences far from France were able to visit the 1900 Paris exposition through his films, as well as witness the Czar's visit to Versailles. For his nondocumentary films Méliès established a style that combined elements of realism and stylization, two formal choices that movie designers would henceforth combine in varying proportions to form their own individual and characteristic synthesis. Méliès's own favorite subjects included industrialism's latest technological and scientific discoveries, such as the splen-

did machines set in glass-and-iron halls that he recreated in the The Impossible Voyage (1904; Illus. 27). His most innovative work, however, was in the area of fantasy and illusion, and he successfully portrayed on film the foreign and exotic worlds of Robinson Crusoe, Cleopatra, Faust, and Hamlet. Méliès's most popular success was a film that took his audience farthest from home, the 1902 A Trip to the Moon, thirty fabulous scenes that portrayed laboratories, launching pads, and, of course, the pockmarked landscape of the moon itself.

Creating illusions for the cinema came almost as second nature to Méliès, whose artistry as a conjuror had been exciting Parisians at his Théâtre Robert Houdin since 1888. His interest in using film as a medium for his magic had been sparked when he attended the premiere of Lumière's Cinématographe. Lumière focused his audience's attention on the ordinary, everyday objects that everyone looked at but never really stopped to see. Parisian audiences thrilled to the realism and immediacy of the typical Lumière offering, Arrival of a Train, a film that delivered exactly what its title promised. So taken was Méliès with Lumière's device that he abandoned his stage career and began to devote all his attention to making films of his own. He initiated his own production company, Star Films, within a year, and finally, in 1897, built his pathbreaking studio.

Méliès described this structure as "the combination of the photographic studio (with immense proportions) and the stage of the theatre."[1] Built on land he owned outside Paris in Montreuil-sous-Bois, the glass-roofed structure measured fifty by thirty feet, and had glazed walls to take full advantage of the sun for filming. (The advent of artificial illumination for movies was still about a dozen years in the future.) To achieve his fantastic effects, Méliès equipped the studio with all the paraphernalia of the illusionist theater, including the trapdoor,

27. *The Impossible Voyage* (1904, Georges Méliès). Art Director: Georges Méliès.

chutes, and revolving panels that would allow actors and props suddenly to appear and disappear. At one end of the shed, raised on a small stage, stood the first fully realized movie sets: theatrical flats or backdrops painted with trompe l'oeil architectural elements. Although a few props or pieces of furniture were added to lend some verisimilitude, both they and the actors in fact only pointed up the artificiality of the painted backdrop behind, and stamped the Méliès set with the charming primitiveness that is his unmistakable trademark.

Highly stylized studio re-creations also provided a means with which the new medium was able to take advantage of the flood of imagery that had recently been made available by inexpensive printing processes for consumption by the general public. Under Méliès's influence, movies became a kind of clearinghouse, animating the static images of picture postcards, chromolithographs, and family albums, which inspired the mise-en-scène of many early films. These decorative if mundane sources satisfied the scenic requirements of the period's moviemakers, who saw no reason to depart from a successful formula. But a few of the more advanced film producers believed that better-quality design would not only give the movies more artistic respectability but also make them more remunerative. Through their efforts, many a venerable painting began to turn up as the basis of film decor. In France, for example, where the cinema has always had a strongly pictorial emphasis, the sculptor-turned-filmmaker Victorin Jasset enriched Alice Guy's *La Vie du Christ* (1905) with copies of watercolors by the famous academician James Tissot.

As for Méliès himself, the international success that *A Trip to the Moon* earned him planted the seeds of his downfall. As his marvelous settings and novel techniques became more common in the cinema, the singularity of his achievement was soon forgotten. Always the consummate artist, Méliès was more often than not an amateur as a businessman, and, unable to stop the rampant piracy of his ideas, he watched helplessly as his fortunes dwindled and disappeared. Only at the end of his life did his genius, the spark that made the movies dream, once again become recognized.

A further factor in the decline of Méliès's popularity—and one more significant to the history of film—was his inability to keep pace with progressive film techniques. Though he did employ some devices to suggest movement, Méliès, like Edison, usually retained from the theater the fixed relation between spectator and stage. By keeping his camera stationary and structuring his films as series of tableaux, he gave the moviegoer a "privileged fifth-row seat." The system Méliès employed to define the range of what the static camera could actually photograph in a specific scene involved stretching from the camera two strings, one to the left edge of the flat and one to the right. The strings marked on the floor of the stage a triangle within which actors would be visible within the frame of the picture. A second set of strings, running parallel to the flat, marked the points at which an actor could be photographed full height, from the knees up, and from the waist. This method imposed definite restrictions on Méliès. Had he chosen to move the camera, the artificiality of

his flats would have been betrayed: If the camera approached the set too closely, its trompe l'oeil architectural details would become painfully obvious; sideways movement would have revealed its paper-thin edge, destroying any illusion of perspective painted on the canvas.

Other moviemakers had meanwhile been making great strides in set design and cinematography. Camera placement was being varied for dramatic effect, and the camera itself was gradually beginning to move, bringing into the studio some of the dynamism that had been familiar from exterior shots from speeding vehicles. The construction of more sizable studio space permitted moviemakers to build larger sets, ideal arenas for camera movement. The aesthetic possibilities inherent in more elaborate sets attracted the attention of architects and artists. Nowhere was the impact of this development more immediate than in Italy, where aristocratic patrons had already helped move the country's film industry to a vanguard position. Able to draw upon high-level talent from Italian literary and operatic circles, the aristocracy considered film as a spectacular means to extol Italy's rich historical tradition—in which they were the major participants.

While Italy began its first major set construction around 1910, its outstanding accomplishment occurred three years later, in Giovanni Pastrone's *Cabiria* (Illus. 28). Shortly before its public premiere in the United States, at New York's Knickerbocker Theater on June 1, 1914, the *New York Dramatic Mirror* praised *Cabiria* as "the greatest photographic spectacle ever shown in America."[2] The sheer sweep of its historical pageantry, which lasted for the virtually unheard of running time of three consecutive hours, astonished the reviewer. *Cabiria* told the story of the third century B.C. fall of Carthage to Rome, followed through the

28. *Cabiria* (1914, Giovanni Pastrone). Art Director: uncredited.

lives of Cabiria, a young Carthaginian woman, and her brave Roman lover, Auxilla Fluvius. Yet even more than the scenario, continued the *Mirror*'s ecstatic critic, it was *Cabiria*'s visual feast that would unquestionably "convince many doubtful people that high art and the motion picture are not incompatible."[3] For the first time, the term "film architecture" could be applied without reservation: With its sets of unprecedented scale and detail, *Cabiria* took full advantage of the potential of architectural effects. Great stairways and landings form staging platforms, and walls constructed of wood and surfaced with staff (a composition of plaster and fiber) give a splended impression of solidity, especially when lit from behind.

The influence of *Cabiria* was enormous. It established the longer feature film or pair of films as standard fare, and struck the final blow to the practice of showing a program of shorts. The success of the longer and more spectacular format convinced producers of the value of investing more time, effort, and money on design. And finally, *Cabiria* decisively ended the trompe l'oeil tradition of Méliès: The constructed set, with few exceptions, now stood as the standard means of representing reality in film design.

Almost immediately the potential for creative work available in the cinema attracted architects, a development that was encouraged by contemporary commentators. The poet Vachel Lindsay, who wrote *The Art of the Moving Picture* after the success of *Cabiria* urged American architects to be the advance guard in the production of films that would foster an appreciation of architecture throughout the United States. Architects should appropriate the movies as their means of propaganda, because with film's "intrinsic genius it can give [their] profession a start beyond all others in dominating this land."[4] With the cinema leading the way, America could soon become a glorious permanent fairground, modeled after the Philadelphia Centennial of 1876, or the San Francisco and San Diego exhibitions of 1915. Indeed, Lindsay, as well as a large segment of the architectural press, correctly foresaw that the movies would soon challenge the exposition as the leading force in shaping architectural taste.

During the first wave of architects' establishing themselves in the cinema, many moved with too great a vengeance to replace the theatrically artificial set. In Italy, set design degenerated into a dry, if historically accurate, academicism, while in America, Robert Haas, an architect turned film designer working for Famous Players–Lasky Studios in New York, lavished real materials and overwrought architectural details on the re-creation of Spanish convents and Victorian streets. Lindsay's vision of America as a fairground inspired by the movies seemed almost to come true with the Scottish town built under the direction of Cedric Gibbons for Goldwyn studio's *Bunty Pulls the Strings* (1921): The set was so realistic that the film's producers opened it to the public for a full year!

But a movement toward tempering this architectural excess had already begun during the teens, and would create a climate for modernism's appeal to film designers in the 1920s. Kenneth MacGowan, for example, writing in 1921 in *Photoplay* magazine,[5] singled out for special praise the efforts of Joseph Urban (see page 39) and Hugo Ballin, a painter and muralist with architectural training, who created handsome sets with only curtains and a few tall stone pillars. As well as eliminating many unnecessarily fussy elements of set decor, this new generation of designers discovered that illumination, properly placed, would allow settings to be reduced to powerful, abstract compositions of light and shadow.

A leader in the attempts to simplify film design was Wilfred Buckland. Although Buckland himself was trained in the theater, as were many of the cinema's first set designers, his great film work was undoubtedly architecturally inspired, dealing fundamentally with form, space, and the quality of light. Buckland had worked with the theatrical producer David Belasco in New York; in 1914 he began to commute between New York and the West Coast, until he finally settled in Hollywood in 1922, the year one of his greatest design achievements appeared in Allan Dwan's *Robin Hood* (Illus. 29). Buckland's arrival in Hollywood signaled a design revolution as decisive as the one Italy had launched a few years earlier by his bringing to the films of Cecil B. De Mille and producer Jesse Lasky the chiaroscuro effects of the New York stage. Buckland only fully realized his genius through constructed sets built in such a way that light could be carefully controlled. Thus he found unsuitable for his aesthetic goals such standard West Coast practices as filming on unroofed stages, shielded from the glare of the southern California sun by sails of gauzy cloth (Illus. 30), or in glass sheds, unless he could paint or drape the glass to regulate the

29. (LEFT) *Robin Hood* (1922, Allan Dwan). Art Director: Wilfred Buckland.
30. (BELOW) Outdoor stage of the Selig studio, Los Angeles (circa 1910).

amount of sunlight. His strong preference, of course, was for filming in indoor sound-stages, where he promoted the use of artificial illumination for total control. As a result, films with Buckland designs looked dark to viewers accustomed to the standard brightness of outdoor shooting, and film producers in New York worried whether audiences would pay a full admission to see half a movie. Thinking quickly, Lasky claims that he responded by hailing the new look as an artistic breakthrough—Rembrandt lighting, as he called it. The East Coast moguls accepted that explanation, sold the film as art, and raised the price of admission.[6] Eventually, Buckland's techniques prevailed and furthered the development of the totally opaque soundstage, a standard still in use today.

The aesthetic possibilities open to the film designer around 1920 were thus virtually unlimited. The theatrical flat had given way to the constructed set, the three-dimensional model with which the film designer became an architect and created space. The glass stu-dio had evolved into the opaque soundstage, where light could be manipulated to shape form and space out of darkness. And the static camera moved, enabling the film-maker to explore space with a freedom unthinkable in the theater.

The expression of space, light, and movement, a problem that now challenged film designers, had already been confronted by modern architects earlier in the century, and would continue to inspire their work into the following decades. It was during the 1920s that the paths of film and architecture would converge, as the cinema sought more sophisticated modes of visual expression. The new architecture of the twentieth century—bold in its spatial inventiveness, ingenious in its manipulation of light, dynamic in its suggestion of movement—provided an ideal answer to the same three imperatives of film design. That movie designers were often as talented and successful as their architectural counterparts in creating modern designs is the premise of *Designing Dreams*.

CHAPTER 3

Europe at the Forefront

The story of modern architecture in the movies properly begins in the middle years of this century's second decade. As a cataclysmic world war drew to its close, prewar experiments in the arts were taken up with renewed intensity. Paris reclaimed its aesthetic preeminence. Weimar Germany developed into a center of artistic activity. And in America, New York established its position on the world's stage as a great cultural power. The warfare that had inflicted so much devastation on Western Europe helped contribute to the destruction of the now outmoded notion that insisted on a separation between the "high" arts, like painting, architecture, and sculpture, and the "low" ones, like the cinema. A new purposeful realism emerged, one that sought to combine all aesthetic efforts—elite and popular—with modern technology into a coherent, egalitarian agenda for the arts.

It was against this background that cin-

ema and modern architecture took the first steps toward their fruitful confluence. Film designers, no longer bound to the painted flat as the basis of a mise-en-scène, were ready to assimilate modern design trends. This chapter will trace four phases in the rise and fall of modern architecture in the movies. Between 1916 and 1924, modernism made its first tentative appearance in the cinema via short-lived efforts launched by proponents of four pathbreaking aesthetic movements. Although Futurism, Expressionism, Vienna Secessionist style, and Art Nouveau had all seen their most fertile years by the end of the war, when the cinema began to adopt them, they each contained a number of stylistic features that would eventually coalesce into the distinctive look of modern architecture. Their cinematic adaptations stood in a similar relation to modern architectural film decor. The second phase began in 1924, when in anticipation of the Paris exposition, modern architecture made its film debut through the efforts of French pioneers, who hoped to promote the movement through the medium of the cinema. By 1928, the beginning of the third phase, these efforts had begun to dwindle, yet the next decade saw modern film decor attain its widest visibility and greatest triumphs. This was a period dominated by the film design specialist, who often had no direct experience of the modern movement itself. The first half of this phase, from the late 1920s to the early 1930s, saw the release of films from both Europe and the United States, and can be considered a kind of international "modern moment." After the early 1930s, however, the focus shifted to the United States. The decline of modern film decor, the result of the final phase, occurred first in Europe in the mid-1930s, but by the end of the decade it affected American film design as well.

Five countries—France, Germany, Italy, the United States, and, to a lesser extent, the Soviet Union—were the scene of most modern architectural activity in the cinema during this era. It should not be concluded from the following discussion, however, that the amount of modern architectural film decor produced in each of these countries stood in direct proportion to the degree of acceptance modern architecture itself had achieved there. If a preponderance of the film sets used as illustrations here are American, that bias reflects the numerical dominance of films produced in America rather than any particular success of modern architects in America. They were in fact much less visible than their counterparts in, say, Holland, where modern architects held prestigious positions in city government and designed housing complexes. The film industries of large countries had the distinct advantage of large national audiences to ensure that successful producers could recover the high costs of moviemaking, and, in the

case of the American studios, of aggressively successful international marketing and distribution networks. The lure of capturing a profitable segment of the national markets fostered risk taking on the part of producers, which led to a steady increase in the production of movies, and in turn the construction of studios, with opportunities for creative personnel seeking full-time film employment. A small country like Holland, therefore, while a leader in the development of modern architecture, seems to have produced little in the way of modern architectural film decor: Its tiny population simply could not support a sustained national film industry.

Beginnings

By the end of World War I, many national film industries already had well-developed cinematic traditions. The Italian cinema, which had with *Cabiria* established an innovative standard for constructed set design, witnessed a dramatic decline in the quality of its decor. Debilitated by the economic crisis of the war, Italy seemed content merely to follow its proven design formulas, and Italian set design succumbed over the next decade to what architect and film designer Virgilio Marchi termed "the decadent arabesques of D'Annunzianism,"[1] a reference to the literary style of Gabriele D'Annunzio.

Avant-garde opposition to this stagnation was attempted in the wartime period by the Futurists, members of the influential but short-lived movement, centered in Italy, that involved poets, painters, sculptors, architects, and filmmakers. The Futurists were the first artists to advocate an aesthetic that would reflect the speed, violence, and cacophony of the twentieth century. The movement's most fertile phase had occurred between 1909, the year of its first manifesto, and 1914, the year war broke out in Europe.

The bold and austere urban buildings depicted in the drawings of architect Antonio Sant'Elia, conceived circa 1913 and 1914, rank among modernism's first and certainly most evocative examples of an abstract architectural language drawn from the forms of industrialization. In the films they produced, the Futurists were adamantly opposed to the use of photographic realism, and instead promoted an abstract cinema based on concepts like simultaneity and the juxtaposition of jarring, irrational images against traditional narrative forms. Between 1910 and 1912, a group of Florentine Futurists created six short abstract films on subjects ranging from color and music to dance. *Una Vita Futurista* (1915) stirred audiences to near rioting when they saw one scene that consisted of a "discussion between a foot, a hammer, and an umbrella."[2] In 1916, the year of the *Manifesto of Futurist Cinema,* one leading Futurist partisan, Enrico Prampolini, collaborated as a film designer with Anton Giulio Bragaglia for *Il Perfido Incanto.* For this film, which featured what was probably the earliest examples of film decor to display the modernist style, Prampolini combined Art Deco settings reminiscent of Paul Poiret's interiors, with decor of striking abstraction that overlap layers of black-and-white patterns (Illus. 31).

These Futurist experiments went unheeded by the Italian film industry, and not until the early 1930s did it again produce a number of films that attempted to apply modernism's interest in abstract geometry to the constructed set. Such a development did occur, however, in Germany, where moviemaking was about to embark on a period of remarkable creativity. The German film industry had established itself early, through the efforts of brilliant producers, stars, and directors, some of whom had entered the field even before 1900. By 1914, Berlin boasted many film studios, and although a few of the country's best film de-

signers were already at work, their most successful period would come after the war, when the greatest influence on set design was Expressionism.

Expressionism had arisen early in the century as a movement that stressed the subjective and symbolic aspects of objects and events, which were often realized as abstract distortions of color and form. While plans for Expressionist architecture remained largely unexecuted, the Expressionist aesthetic had a great impact on painting, sculpture, and theater decor, most notably in Germany, where it flourished from the early years of the century until shortly after World War I. The movement was actually on the wane when it made its first and most striking appearance in film design. In 1919, three Expressionist painters—Hermann Warm, Walter Reimann, and Walter Röhrig—created a studio-bound, claustrophobic decor whose highly stylized, angular repertory was an uncanny reflection of the demented psyche of a madman, in the most famous of Expressionist films, Robert Wiene's *The Cabinet of Dr. Caligari (Das Kabinett des Dr. Caligari)* (1920; Illus. 32).

Although *Caligari*'s anti-realist mode of film design never formed the basis for a particularly cohesive school of set decor, it did initiate a short-lived series of films that copied its stylized aesthetic. Architect Hans Poelzig developed a sculptural Expressionism of organic shapes, spatial complexities, and mysterious lighting to illustrate the bizarre themes of *Der Golem* (1920). A decorative application of Expressionist motifs was used by designer César Klein in his decor for Wiene's *Genuine* (1920), while the Russian Andrei Andrejew mesmerized audiences with his work for Wiene's *Raskolnikow* (1923; Illus. 33), based on Dostoyevski's *Crime and Punishment.* The stairway for the latter film was one of the decade's great designs, fusing German Expressionist fantasy with the dynamic, spi-

31. *Il Perfido Incanto* (1916, Anton Giulio Bragaglia). Art Director: Enrico Prampolini.

raling suggestion of movement characteristic of Soviet Constructivism.

In America, *Caligari* had an unsuccessful popular premiere in 1921, followed five years later by a revival that initiated its "art film" status there. It was only in France, where the film's premiere was organized in 1921 by filmmaker and critic Louis Delluc, that it exploded as *"la bombe de l'expressionnisme allemand,"*[3] establishing a Berlin-Paris cinematic axis that would persist throughout the decade. Expressionism pervaded the films of Jean Epstein (Illus. 34), an avant-garde French filmmaker of the '20s, and, to a lesser extent, influenced the work of the prominent director Marcel L'Herbier. The noted jagged angles of his *Don Juan et Faust* (1923) may have owed a debt to Expressionism as well as to cubism, and in *L'Inhumaine* (see page 45), the obvious artifice in overlapping planes of plants in its heroine's winter garden were the most overt reference to the German classic. Even the French design world took note of the film.

While by 1924 the European film scene contained a number of isolated film designers struggling to break free of prewar styles and to breathe life into cinema decor through the introduction of modernism, the United States was taking its first steps toward the new style via the attempts of shrewd producers to lure European designers to the American cinema. A small but lively art cinema developed as a result of their efforts, whose most prominent and influential designer was Joseph Urban. Fifty years ago, Urban was a figure who was continually before the public. His was an eclectic career, spanning almost all the arts: He designed movie decor and a skyscraper for publishing magnate William Randolph Hearst; a Spanish revivalist villa for social lion Marjorie Merriweather Post; lavish revues, Broadway shows, and a theater for impresario Florenz Ziegfeld; operas in Vienna, Boston, Paris, and New York; and one of America's first modern buildings, New York's New School for Social Research (1929–30). Urban was born in Vienna in 1872, during one of the most intoxicating periods in the cultural life of the Austro-Hungarian capital. His diverse commissions, which included book illustration as well as decoration for the palace of the khedive of Egypt, promised a brilliant career even before his graduation from architectural studies. It was during the early 1900s that Urban came under the influence of the newly formed Secessionist school. Usually associated with the Wiener Werkstätte, the Viennese workshop of furniture and decorative objects established in 1903 by Josef Hoffmann and Koloman Moser, the Secessionist style is distinguished by its use of cubic shapes tempered with lush decoration set in geometric frames.

Urban's award-winning rooms that displayed Austrian art at the 1904 St. Louis World's Fair introduced him to the American public, which would soon provide his most ardent patrons. Eight years later, Urban's position as artistic adviser to the Imperial Opera of Vienna earned him a similar position with the Boston Opera Company. The company's bankruptcy in 1914 left him

32. (ABOVE) *The Cabinet of Dr. Caligari* (1920, Robert Wiene). Art Directors: Hermann Warm, Walter Reimann, and Walter Röhrig.

33. (RIGHT) *Raskolnikow* (1923, Robert Wiene). Art Director: Andrei Andrejew.

34. *Le Double Amour* (1925, Jean Epstein).
Art Director: Pierre Kefer.

momentarily unemployed yet determined to pursue his career in the United States, and soon he received the commission to design the stage sets for a fantastic New York production entitled *The Garden of Paradise*. The acclaim he received attracted the attention of impresario Florenz Ziegfeld, a patron as aristocratic as any Romanoff. Urban's work immediately brought new luster to the Ziegfeld Follies, and for the next two decades the colorful and portly Urban worked feverishly from his studio in midtown Manhattan and from his residence in Yonkers to design almost all the Ziegfeld productions.

The high point of the collaboration came in 1926 with the completion of Ziegfeld's new theater in Manhattan, financed by William Randolph Hearst. In addition to his theatrical and publishing ventures, Hearst had turned his eye toward the movies—modestly at first, but more actively after 1919, when he inherited his mother's fortune. His most significant step was to con-

vert an old amusement park on Manhattan's northeastern tip into Cosmopolitan Productions, to promote the film career of Marion Davies, a Ziegfeld showgirl who became his lifelong companion. Urban accepted the commission to head the studio's art department and retained the position for four years, during which he designed almost forty movies. Although most of Urban's work for Cosmopolitan was painstakingly researched historical decor (Hearst adored the sight of Davies in elaborate period costume), a number of his sets echoed the Secessionist style of the exhibit he had designed for the Art Institute of Chicago (Illus. 35) to promote the work of Viennese artists impoverished by the war.

Of the half-dozen modern films Urban designed, two stand out as especially remarkable. *Enchantment* (1921; Illus. 36) contains elegant decorative ensembles, advertised in a promotional brochure as "ultramodern in every sense of the word."[4] In the dining alcove of the tearoom, white flower boxes supported on miniature brackets separate the delicate wallpaper below from multipaned clerestory windows. Urban's most forward-looking design, and the culmination of his work at Cosmopolitan Productions, was the boudoir for a film putatively titled *Snow Blind* (Illus. 37). Here, the entire room of faceted walls and shelves is based on a square motif, repeated in the structure of a chair reminiscent of designs of Josef Hoffmann and Charles Rennie Mackintosh, a Scottish architect whose work paralleled that of the Viennese at the turn of the century. Urban's film set for *Snow Blind,* in rejecting historical precedent in favor of an elegant use of simple planes, was the immediate precursor of modern architecture in the American cinema.

Other members of the small vanguard designing for the American cinema of the 1920s included two protégés of couturier Paul Poiret—Paul Iribe, who designed Art

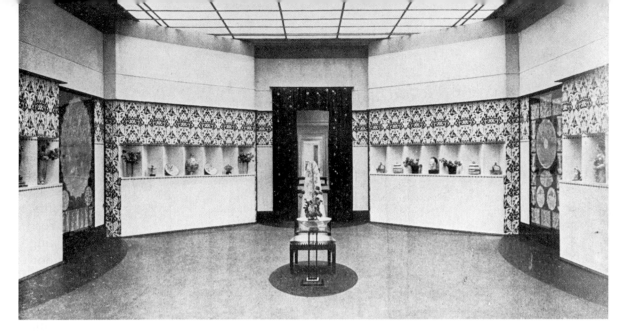

35. (TOP) Exhibit Room of the Wiener Werkstätte, Art Institute of Chicago (1922, Joseph Urban).

36. (BOTTOM) *Enchantment* (1921, Robert G. Vignola). Art Director: Joseph Urban.

37. *Snow Blind* (circa 1924). Art Director: Joseph Urban.

Nouveau sets for De Mille's *The Affairs of Anatol* (see page 116), and the flamboyant Erté (see page 88)—and Natacha Rambova. Although she lacked the design pedigree of Urban, Rambova nonetheless created effective "high-art" settings for two of early Hollywood's most unusual productions. Born Winifred Shaunessy in 1897 in Salt Lake City, young Rambova was educated in England and traveled extensively throughout Europe after her divorced mother married millionaire cosmetics magnate Richard Hudnut. Having decided to become a ballet dancer, she joined the entourage of Ted Kosloff, a member of the Imperial Russian Ballet, through whom she was introduced to modern design trends. After returning to the United States with Kosloff, Rambova went to Hollywood, where she created the settings for *Camille* (1921) and *Salome* (1922), both starring Alla Nazimova, the Russian-born theater and film actress, who shared Rambova's interest in artistic film productions.

Rambova's designs for *Salome* reproduced the flat, Art Nouveau illustrations of Aubrey Beardsley for Oscar Wilde's play from the same Biblical source; the decor of *Camille* recalled the work of the Spanish Art Nouveau architect Antonio Gaudí. The amorphous walls, floors, and stairs of *Camille*'s theater lobby (Illus. 38) seem to be freely sculpted from one organic material, its latent energy emphasized by exotically veined trompe l'oeil marble. Voluptuous giant moldings highlight the sensual shaping of arched openings. The pair of lampstands are overt references to the lobby lighting designed by German architect Hans Poelzig for Max Reinhardt's Grosses Schauspielhaus in Berlin, although in Rambova's hands these become even more plastic and serpentine than the originals.

The reign of the avant-garde in the American cinema was brief: Designers like Rambova and Urban became exceptions with the

38. Alla Nazimova (center) in *Camille* (1921, Ray C. Smallwood). Art Director: Natacha Rambova.

emergence of studio designers in the late 1920s. Although Urban did return to the cinema in the early 1930s after a half-decade hiatus, his settings for Fox studios were routine Art Deco exercises, copies of the decorative motifs popularized at the Paris exposition of 1925. However regrettable his decline, Urban had in his work for Hearst not only created the first American film sets to display modernist tendencies, but also established through his considerable visibility a place for the modern film designer in America, one that Hollywood art directors who followed him would exploit to the fullest.

Breakthrough

Despite the wealth of progressive film design work underway in both Europe and America by the early 1920s, it was France in particular that first took advantage of modern architecture's potential for the cinema. Prior to the war, France had led the world in film production, but shortly after the armistice its proportion of the market fell to 15 percent, with Hollywood taking the lead in the number of features produced. But just as decorative artists had revived their prewar plans for an international exhibition (the future Paris exposition of 1925) to reaffirm a battered France's artistic preeminence, so, too, did filmmakers seek to reclaim the country's cinematic leadership, acknowledging that it would be gained on the basis of quality rather than quantity. By 1921, the enthusiasm of the *cinéaste* Louis Delluc led to the formation of the world's first film art association, the Club des Amis du Septième Art, or CASA. Delluc was able to assemble in CASA filmmakers Marcel L'Herbier, Jean Epstein, Germaine Dulac, and Abel Gance; architect Robert Mallet-Stevens; artist Fernand Léger; musicians Erik Satie and Maurice Ravel; and poets Blaise Cendrars and Jean Cocteau. The club's directors vowed to raise the cinema to its rightful place among the established arts and to use the silent cinema, which depended on strong visual communication for its effectiveness, as a means to promulgate new ideas in design. They treated the screen as modern painters did their canvases, and experimented with novel photographic techniques —soft focus, rapid-fire editing, opaque masks, split screens, Gance's famous triple screen for *Napoleon*—and modern decor. A whirl of imagery derived from modern art movements raced before their cameras; Futurism, Expressionism, and Surrealism were absorbed by the French cinema and contributed to its rich tradition. A mark of CASA's achievement was its representation in many of the most important exhibitions during the 1920s, including the *Salon d'Automne* of 1921; the *Exposition de l'Art dans le Cinéma Français* in 1924; and, as previously mentioned, the Paris exposition of 1925, at Mallet-Stevens's cinema studio on the Champs de Mars for the Société des Auteurs de Film.

Robert Mallet-Stevens was well suited to spearhead CASA's architectural crusade. Born in Paris in 1886, into an artistic family, Mallet-Stevens was as a child a frequent guest at the famous Palais Stoclet, the Brussels villa designed for his uncle Adolphe Stoclet by the Viennese architect and designer Josef Hoffmann. The villa's Secessionist style would influence Mallet-Stevens's building designs of the early 1920s and would provide the model for his work in *Le Secret de Rosette Lambert* (1920; Illus. 39), one of his earliest film sets. Within a few years, however, he aligned himself with the modern movement; his 1923 villa in Hyères for the Vicomte de Noailles ranks as one of the first examples of modern architecture in France, and was the subject of artist Man Ray's last film, an avant-garde exploration of the villa, known as *Les Mystères du Château du Dé* (1929). Over the next fifteen years, through his designs for buildings, furniture, decorative objects, and fashion, Mallet-Stevens would become one of modernism's most ardent proponents.

As well as propagandizing for architecture, Mallet-Stevens advocated progressivism in film, and in 1928 wrote the only book to date devoted exclusively to the subject of modern architecture and the cinema, *Le Décor Moderne au Cinéma*. Adopting the pictorial format of such partisan tracts as Gropius's *Internationale Architektur* (1925), the book displayed a series of photographs of prominent examples of Art Deco and modernist sets. Mallet-Stevens's brief, impassioned introduction was a diatribe against reliance on historical styles for contemporary film sets, and complained that modern sets were then being used "exclusively for places of debauchery: nightclubs or boudoirs of the demi-mondaine, which would

allow one to suppose that the admirable efforts and researches of painters, decorators,
and architects are good to surround drunk-
ards or those of ill-repute."[5] It concluded
with praise for those few who regarded the
cinema as a valid means of artistic expression.

Ironically, the debauched settings that
Mallet-Stevens criticized provided much of
the milieu of *L'Inhumaine* (1924), the earliest
film to use modern architecture, and a striking instance of the ability of vanguard
French artists to move with relative ease between the "high" and the popular arts. Directed by Marcel L'Herbier, *L'Inhumaine*
was a conscious if rather pretentious attempt
to promote modern art and architecture via
a highly elaborated mise-en-scène. Although the idea originated with its star,
Georgette Leblanc, who after a recent visit
to the United States had become convinced
that modern decor would increase the film's
popularity overseas, the most powerful impetus behind the film was the French intellectuals' conviction that the silent cinema
required an imagery that would do justice to
its supreme expressive power. *L'Inhumaine*
was the collaborative effort of those whose
work at the Paris exposition the following
year (with the notable exception of Le Corbusier) would define the avant-garde of design: Mallet-Stevens, who created the
exterior decor; Fernand Léger, the machine-
age laboratory; Pierre Chareau, the furniture; René Lalique, Jean Puiforcat, and Jean
Luce, the decorative objects; Raymond
Templier, the jewelry; and Paul Poiret, the
fashions.

L'Inhumaine opens with the concert star
Claire Lescot, the "inhuman one" of the
title, hosting a soiree of international celeb-
rities at her extravagant villa overlooking an
industrial city. The villa's interior decor was
the work of two film set designers still in
their twenties, Claude Autant-Lara and Alberto Cavalcanti. Although their Art Deco

39. *Le Secret de Rosette Lambert* (1920, Raymond
Bernard). Art Director: Robert Mallet-Stevens.

space is the least interesting element of the
film's architecture, it nonetheless points up
Claire's pleasure-seeking existence (Illus.
40). As Michel Louis notes in *Rob Mallet-
Stevens* (1980), the strong contrasts between
black and white in the room's decor and in
the stylized makeup of the star emphasize
the heightened pitch and exaggerated emotions of her character, the moat around the
dining platform her inaccessibility, the African elements her love of the foreign and the
exotic.[6]

One of the guests at the party, however,
clearly does not fit into this rarefied milieu.
The scientist Einar Noorsen (Jaque Catelain)
is present only because of his desperate infatuation for Claire, who cruelly spurns his
attentions by sending him a small, poisoned
knife with the suggestion that he use it to
kill himself. Compelled to test the limits of
Claire's inhumanity, Noorsen feigns his su-

40. *L'Inhumaine* (1924, Marcel L'Herbier). Art Directors (this set): Claude Autant-Lara and Alberto Cavalcanti.

icide in an automobile accident. When the news arrives at the villa, Claire is unmoved, and her friends are shocked to learn that she intends to give the concert she has planned for the following evening. After the performance, she is obliged to go to Noorsen's laboratory and identify the "corpse." She finally expresses her humanity when, confronted with the body, she weeps. Vindicated in his love for Claire, Noorsen steps forward to reveal his ruse and rewards her with a dazzling tour of the technological wonders of his laboratory. Yet Claire's past life still haunts her: On a later trip by car to Noorsen's laboratory, she is poisoned by a jealous lover. She arrives near death, and Noorsen attempts to revive her with his newly invented lifesaving device. The machine succeeds, and Claire rises, expressing her love for her fellowman.

The spirit of modernity infuses every frame of *L'Inhumaine,* from Léger's cartoons of moving machinery backing the credits to the cubist-inspired end title. Throughout, eccentrically angled camera shots and masks create striking abstract compositions. The film opens with a series of rapid camera movements and superimpositions of trees, roads, and bodies. This technique recalled Italian Futurist paintings of the previous decade, not only conveying the subjective experience of traveling in a speeding automobile but also suggesting the accelerated pace of the characters' life-styles. The following sequence begins with a twirling panoramic shot focusing the audience's attention on the villa Mallet-Stevens designed for the heroine (Illus. 41). His design transforms a traditional residence into an asymmetrical sculpture of white cubic volumes pierced by large translucent windows, through which pour enormous quantities of light. The more traditional entrance to the villa features a wide flight of stairs flanked by symmetrical blocks, which lead to a broad pair of double doors decorated with sharply contrasting circles, squares, and diamonds. Recessed floodlighting provides a subtle indication of the theatrical profession and prestige of the villa's owner.

Mallet-Stevens's second design for the film, a laboratory (Illus. 42), was a dynamic, soaring tower that culminates in rooftop mechanical devices, executed in a style influenced by Italian Futurism and Soviet Constructivism. Reflecting the private and secluded life-style of the scientist who inhabits the structure, the exterior's blank facade is relieved by only a single window and by the lab's entrance, an asymmetrical composition of canopy and support at ground level. The decade's romantic idolatry of the machine found further expression in the whirling wheels, arcs, disks, and spirals of the laboratory's interior (Illus. 43), designed and actually constructed by Léger. Echoing mechanical imagery from science fiction sources like Frederick Kiesler's theater decor for Karel Čapek's *W.U.R.* (Werstand Universal Robots) of 1923 as well as his own cubist canvases, Léger's explorations into kinetic abstract forms, movement, and light for L'Herbier continued in his own avantgarde film *Ballet mécanique,* made during the production of *L'Inhumaine.*

Although *L'Inhumaine* failed with the public, it was received enthusiastically by modern architects. Adolf Loos, an Austrian

41. Jaque Catelain (in auto) in *L'Inhumaine* (1924). Art Director (this set): Robert Mallet-Stevens.

42. (OPPOSITE) Jaque Catelain (center) on the set of *L'Inhumaine* (1924). Art Director (this set): Robert Mallet–Stevens.
43. (ABOVE) *L'Inhumaine* (1924). Art Director (this set): Fernand Léger.

architect whose strictures against applied ornament Mallet-Stevens's decor obeyed, described it as a "stunning poem to modern technique. This entire visual production is musically oriented and Tristan's cry has become reality: 'I hear the light! . . .' The last images in *L'Inhumaine* surpass the imagination. On leaving the theater one has the impression of having witnessed the birth of a new art."[7] When the film had its American premiere in March 1926, under the aegis of The Film Associates, Inc. (a group whose membership included modernists Sheldon Cheney and Frederick Kiesler), it was promoted as "a striking example of what a synthesis of the arts can accomplish when enlisted in the service of the modern cinema" and "a moving picture holiday for those who are weary of Hollywood."[8]

L'Inhumaine is one of the most successful realizations of the technological optimism that underlined so much of the art of the 1920s. It is also a dazzling piece of moviemaking, testament to the skill and aspirations of its director, L'Herbier. Poet in the style of Oscar Wilde, playwright, and screenwriter, L'Herbier had turned to filmmaking in 1918, and until 1928, when commercial constraints finally became prohibitive, his audacious films were important showcases for modern French art and architecture. *Le Carnaval des Vérités* (1920) featured Art Deco sets by Autant-Lara and decorative artist Michel Dufet. In 1921, *Villa Destin* was designed by the fashion illustrator Georges Lepape in the Art Deco style of his mentor, Paul Poiret. Cubism influenced 1923's *Don Juan et Faust*. *Le Vertige* (Illus. 44, 45) of 1926 reunited many of the *L'Inhumaine* team, as well as the modern architect André Lurçat and the artists Robert and Sonia Delaunay.

As the director of a modern work of art like *L'Inhumaine,* L'Herbier valued as a matter of principle both efficiency and collaborative effort. The modern film, he believed,

44. Jaque Catelain in *Le Vertige* (1926, Marcel L'Herbier). Art Directors: Robert Mallet-Stevens, Lucien Aguettand, André Lurçat, and Robert and Sonia Delaunay.

should be constructed in the same spirit as Mallet-Stevens's Pavillon du Tourisme at the Paris exposition of 1925, whose virtues he described in a speech in 1926:

Let us compare this "Tour de Tourism," which you admired at the Decorative Arts Exhibition, this smooth, bare tower which shoots skyward in long flat surfaces devoid of sculpted motifs, stucco or any of the ornamentation which in a classical monument can be compared to chests where bundles of Time lie dormant, earning no interest; and then let us compare it with the Tour Saint-Jacques, a magnificent piece of bravura, where it is clear that the architect had an enormous capital of Time to play with, a capital which he buried unproductive in dainty embellishments added to the mass. Let us compare these two symbols of two contrary rites of construction and conclude that if the architectural mind of today conceived the tower which can be erected in a *month* instead of a tower which takes a *century* to construct, it is because he felt, poor fellow, that Time was lacking![9]

L'Herbier's infatuation with modernity carried over into his personal life as well as

45. *Le Vertige* (1926).

defining the style of his films. His modern offices on the rue Boissy-d'Anglas in Paris were completed in 1923, and a prominent feature of his apartment on the avenue Émile-Deschanel (1924–31) was its game room, complete with exercise equipment and punching bag. The modern film director, like the progressive scientist Einar Noorsen and the ideal inhabitants of a Corbusian villa, would have to prepare to enter the future healthier and stronger than his predecessors.

With his new living quarters under way and a series of celebrated modern films behind him, L'Herbier turned his attention to *L'Argent* (1928). Updating the setting of Émile Zola's nineteenth-century novel to the 1920s, L'Herbier's epic canvas pits the greed of unscrupulous financiers, money-hungry speculators, and decadent aristocrats against the idealism of a Lindberghesque aviator, a "modern" man not unlike *L'Inhumaine*'s Einar Noorsen. The apartment dwelling of *L'Argent*'s Baroness Sandorf—played by the twenty-year-old Brigitte Helm—is the film's best design by Lazare Meerson and André Barsacq. Its luxurious black lacquers, leathers, chrome, and animal skins, which temper the set's hard-edged cubist geometry, were a remarkable anticipation of Paul Ruaud's 1932 apartment for couturière Suzanne Talbot, as was the incomparable luster generated with indirect lighting. The triangular pilasters in the raised game room (Illus. 46), the chevron wall decoration in the living room, the translucent wall enclosing an aquarium, and even the gambling table are lit from within.

L'Herbier with notable success uses light as a dramatic device in *L'Argent,* particularly for the confrontation between wealthy banker Nicolas Saccard and Sandorf, his ex-mistress, during a wild party. Sandorf's feline stalking (Illus. 47) around Saccard's lumbering figure reaches a climax when,

trapped, she finally throws herself on a daybed, its animal skins accentuating the iridescence of her dress, cloche, and shoes. Suddenly, she lunges into space; the moving camera, tracking her closely, captures the shift of every muscle under her silvery gown until, once again, she falls onto a low, curving sofa (Illus. 48), where the final recriminations occur. Sandorf writhes under Saccard's pressure, while beyond and above them the frenzied shadows of the gamblers flicker on the parlor ceiling.

L'Argent's attention to kinetic detail displayed another facet of film's potential that was exploited during the 1920s—namely, the ability to use movement as a dynamic element in composition. One of the first movies to use costumes and decor responsive to the range of human movement was a Russian production. *Aelita* (1924), a science-fiction fantasy set mainly on Mars and directed by Yakov Protazanov, featured sets and clothing designed by Alexandra Exter, a pioneer in Soviet Constructivist stagecraft, Sergei Kozlovsky, Isaac Rabinovich, and Victor Simov. An enormous success with the general public, *Aelita* brought Constructivism to the screen (Illus. 49). Its designs also show the influence of French cubism and Italian Futurism; Protazanov had lived in Paris before making *Aelita,* while Exter had maintained extensive contacts with the Western avant-garde since 1908. Two especially striking conceptions of Exter's are a vibrating headdress of metal sticks and a skirt of hinged metal bars attached to the waist and ankles, which give clear expression to the dynamic force field generated by the body in motion (Illus. 50).

Perhaps the most outstanding examples of kinetic design during the period were the costumes and setting prepared by one of Exter's fellow Russians in France, Sonia Delaunay, working with her husband Robert, for René Le Somptier's serial *Le P'tit Parigot* (1926; Illus. 51). Sonia Delaunay's openness

46. (ABOVE) *L'Argent* (1928, Marcel L'Herbier).
Art Directors: Lazare Meerson and André
Barsacq.
47. (ABOVE RIGHT) Pierre Alcover and Brigitte
Helm in *L'Argent* (1928).
48. (BELOW RIGHT) Pierre Alcover and Brigitte
Helm in *L'Argent* (1928).

to influence from every artistic endeavor—
from painting to the decorative arts, book
illustration, fashion, and even the geometric
appliqué used to decorate automobiles (see
page 8)—inclined her to treat movie design
seriously. What better means was there than
the cinema to explore movement or, in the
specific terms of the Delaunays, "simultaneity," a concept they formulated to express
the spirit of the dynamic and kaleidoscopic
machine age? "Our era is above all mechanical, dynamic, and visual," she wrote. "The
mechanical and the dynamic are the essential
elements of the practical dimension of our
time. The visual element is the spiritual
characteristic of it."[10] By juxtaposing geometric patterns and shapes within a vast
space of open galleries and raised levels, Delaunay in the decor for *Le P'tit Parigot* forms
a dynamic background for mobile groups of
actors, many in fashions she designed. More
than merely fashion is the costume for a
dancer, an abstract sculpture with zigzag
leggings and disk-shaped collar, a design in-

51. (OPPOSITE TOP) *Le P'tit Parigot* (1926, René Le Somptier). Art Directors: Robert and Sonia Delaunay.
52. (OPPOSITE BOTTOM) *Le P'tit Parigot* (1926).

49. (ABOVE) *Aelita* (1924, Yakov Protazanov). Art Directors: Alexandra Exter, Sergei Kozlovsky, Isaac Rabinovich, and Victor Simov.
50. (RIGHT) *Aelita* (1924).

tended, like Exter's, to emphasize the movement of the body (Illus. 52).

Although finally more successful as a showcase for the Delaunays' talents than as architecture, the decor for *Le P'tit Parigot*—paintings, furnishings, clothing, fabrics—was a brilliant résumé of the activities of the French pioneers, work that convinced the film mainstream of modernism's potential as a viable style for the broader art of the commercial cinema.

The Modern Moment

Although it was primarily the example of the French cinema that spurred the widespread adoption of modern architecture for film sets in the mid-1920s, other influential secondary sources existed. As modernism grew more familiar and widely accepted, modern architects acquired more commissions, and journalistic coverage of the style spread from avant-garde manifestos and small magazines to the popular press. More and more books on modern architecture began to appear, and publicity from exhibitions like the Paris exposition of 1925 generated a great deal of public interest. Modernism was in the air, promoting the value of a progressive life-style to an era obsessed with progress.

While modern film design would achieve its greatest triumphs and visibility during the ten-year period between 1928 and 1938, two fundamental changes occurred in the field in the process of this popularization. First, the responsibility for creating modern film sets shifted from the avant-garde architect to the film design specialist. Second, the intellectual and propagandistic goals of the French pioneers were not taken up by its new practitioners: Modern film decor no longer had a mission to convince the public of modernism's value. Instead, the focus was primarily on the visual and connotative aspects of modern design. Ideologues like Mallet-Stevens were no longer essential for the creation of modern design at film studios.

In France, the principles of modernism appeared in the work of Robert Gys, a protégé of Mallet-Stevens, who designed *Le Duel* (1928) for director Jacques de Baroncelli. At the same time L'Herbier hired Robert-Jules Garnier, a veteran set designer who had worked in the French cinema since shortly after the turn of the century. Garnier's success in absorbing the essence of modernism can be seen in his designs for L'Herbier's *Le Diable au Coeur* (1928), especially in the film's nightclub, which is surrounded with backlit glass walls, ceiling soffits, and floors (Illus. 53). (The set may also have influenced architect and designer Pierre Chareau—who had collaborated on L'Herbier's *Le Vertige*—in the design he created with Bernard Bijvoet for the famous Maison Dalsace, the "Maison de Verre" (1928–32). Its exterior walls of glass were lit from the outside by industrial lighting.)

L'Herbier also collaborated with designers from outside the architectural avant-garde, Lazare Meerson and André Barsacq, on *L'Argent*. Barsacq had created another striking modern design with his ocean liner for director Jean Grémillon's *Maldone* (1928) (see page 145). But it was Meerson, more than any other French designer, who brilliantly extended the visual legacy of pioneers like Mallet-Stevens into the 1930s.

Born in Russia in 1900, Meerson was educated as an architect. He emigrated to Germany after the revolution and then, in 1924, to France. Like many of the Russian film emigrés who flocked to France, Meerson gravitated to the Albatros studios at Montreuil, where he worked first as a scene painter and then as an assistant to Alberto Cavalcanti on L'Herbier's *Feu Mathias Pascal* (1925). Meerson's solo design debut at Al-

53. *Le Diable au Coeur* (1928, Marcel L'Herbier). Art Directors: Robert-Jules Garnier, Claude Autant-Lara, and Louis Le Bertre.

batros took place the same year, in Jacques Feyder's *Gribiche* (see page 118). His sets' elegance established him almost overnight as France's leading film designer, a position that he maintained for the next decade, during which he worked for many of the country's leading directors and studios. Although his premature death in 1938 at the age of thirty-eight, two years after moving to England at the request of producer Alexander Korda, cut short a remarkable career, his influence is felt even today in the work of his many disciples.

Meerson's sets evolved organically from the most ephemeral Chagall-like sketches and collages to final constructions of iron, cement, and glass. Because his exacting standards would leave nothing to chance, he took responsibility for every aspect of a film's design and supervised every detail. (Even at the height of his career, Meerson would take a set's measurements himself.) During the process of design and execution he never hesitated to change details to improve and sharpen his conceptions. As Léon Barsacq noted in *Caligari's Cabinet and Other Grand Illusions,* Meerson's highly refined methods left the viewer in awe of "the sense of quivering life, the aerial quality of his designs, which seem never to be fixed, but to pulse with the same rhythm as their films."[11]

Meerson discussed his theories in a 1927 article in *Ciné-Magazine,*[12] where he described film design as the art of abnegation and reduction. The film designer had constantly to efface himself to allow the major elements of the film—the direction, subject matter, and interpretation—to emerge clearly. Design should never be placed above the work itself, he argued, and in an attack that was most likely directed at the cerebral aestheticism of the Mallet-Stevens and L'Herbier collaborations, he criticized a cinematic "super-architecture" that, by attracting attention to itself, detracted from the sense and import of the script. Instead he advocated a film architecture of atmosphere and ambience, one that would harmonize with the film and pass unperceived except in its ability to reinforce a scene.

To achieve this goal Meerson fused the two principal modes of film aesthetics—the realism of the Lumière brothers and the studio artifice of Méliès—in equal parts. Meerson's was a minimalist aesthetic of plain surfaces; strong, abstract geometry; and light-filled spaces. His designs were stylized, but not as exaggeratedly as the dark, brooding decor of German Expressionism, with its shallow depth and obvious distortions. Although all of Meerson's work was characterized by a precise geometric clarity, his modern film sets provided him the opportunity to give his flair full vent. His sparest sets, those for Julien Duvivier's *David Golder* (1930), were created in keeping with Mies's philosophy of *beinahe nichts,* "almost nothing."[13] The space of the industrialist Golder's living room, for example, is more suggested than circumscribed by the use of subtly stepped levels, a few pieces of modern furniture, and an enormous glass wall. Outside the window of an executive's office, Meerson's painted backdrops capture the spirit of industrialism with the economy of a Japanese illustrator.

Meerson's deference to a film's spirit made him the favorite collaborator of many directors. Although he worked with Marcel L'Herbier and Julien Duvivier, it was Meerson's position as *architect du roi* to René Clair and Jacques Feyder, for each of whom he designed seven films, through which he achieved his greatest successes. His refusal to impose an *a priori* style on any film project enabled his decor to harmonize with the romantic, often fatalistic realism of Feyder and the whimsical humanism of Clair.

For Jacques Feyder's *Les Nouveaux Messieurs* (1928; Illus. 54), Meerson created an interior whose design was reminiscent of the interlocking solids and voids of Le Corbusier's Villa La Roche-Jeanneret (1923–24). (The film itself indicated that the house was located on the nearby rue Mallet-Stevens, the site of Robert Mallet-Stevens's own recently completed ensemble of urban villas, suggesting that Meerson's skillful treatment also contains elements of parody: The modern setting may be as much a satire of the cinematic aspirations of Mallet-Stevens as an aesthetic device.) Glass walls and an open plan—exaggerated by the use of false perspective—enhance the illusion of depth. Indirect lighting and a monochromatic palette clarify the formal geometry. Even minor details echo Corbusian motifs: The asymmetrically placed sculpture shelves had been used by the architect for his Pavillon de l'Esprit Nouveau at the Paris exposition of 1925.

Meerson did his best modern film work for René Clair's *A Nous la Liberté* (1931; Illus. 55) by combining constructed sets with space-expanding backdrops. The factory that is the setting for the film is designed in the formal language of the modern movement, and all the elements that modern architects insisted be features of industrial architecture—ease of movement, hygiene, efficiency, airiness, and open space—are included in Meerson's plan. Echoing J. A. Brinkman and L. C. Van der Vlugt's 1928 Van Nelle factory in Rotterdam, the exterior of *A Nous la Liberté*'s phonograph factory was erected at full scale on the set of the Tobis studio lot at Épinay, using architectural materials. To enhance the illusion of the vast space of the building's interior,

54. *Les Nouveaux Messieurs* (1928, Jacques Feyder). Art Director: Lazare Meerson.

Meerson employed false perspective not only for the structure itself but also for the workers who populated it, placing taller to shorter adults in the foreground and middle ground of a long table of laborers, and children in the background (Illus. 56).

A Nous la Liberté is also a striking example of the tendency of moviemakers to adopt modernism's most vanguard aesthetic features while ascribing connotations to them that were often directly opposite from what modern architects intended. Although throughout the 1920s and '30s the connotations were typically positive, though not egalitarian, in *A Nous la Liberté* they became negative and threatening. The rationally organized factory is clearly equated with the prison from which the two protagonists escape at the beginning of the movie. The long, clean lines of the architecture are used to suggest regimentation (Illus. 57); the concern for hygiene, sterility. Such recurrent

55. *A Nous la Liberté* (1931, René Clair). Art Director: Lazare Meerson.

motifs as horizontal windows, stairways, and open vistas, typically used by modernists to express freedom of movement, function here not as an integral part of the structure's design but rather as an ironic counterpoint to the closed world of the factory/prison.

A Nous la Liberté was the best modernist decor of Meerson's considerable output—approximately thirty films, of which more than one third contained modern sets. While being neither partisan nor propagandist for the modern movement, Meerson nonetheless set before the public a film design that fulfilled Le Corbusier's aesthetic ideal of an architecture that displayed "plastic facts,

clear and limpid, giving rest to our eyes and to the mind the pleasure of geometric forms."[14]

While French film benefited from the presence of so many talented designers at work during the '20s and '30s, German cinema during the same period had not only one of the medium's outstanding directors in Fritz Lang, but also the fertile soil of Weimar culture in which to grow. In the realm of design, especially, Germany was fortunate to have the many talented artists of the Bauhaus, which throughout this period proved to be a rich source for modern film decor.

Lang's films of this era are as indicative of

studio that *Metropolis* required, and show the stages in the evolution of a fantastic city that combines the last stages of Expressionism with emerging strands of modernism. One sketch (Illus. 59) features an all-glass tower that recalls both a similar structure proposed by Mies in 1922 (Illus. 60) and the sleeker, though no less energetic, Schocken Department Stores designed by Erich Mendelsohn during the second half of the 1920s. Many of the film's multilevel urban schemes echo designs produced by Italian Futurists Antonio Sant'Elia and Virgilio Marchi; even Kettelhut's dynamic, graphic style in rendering the *"Herzmaschine"* (Illus. 61), power center of the lower city, recall that of Sant'Elia. While the aesthetic theories of the Futurists found their most powerful cinematic realizations in the French films of the '20s, the actual architectural designs they proposed were most convincingly carried out in *Metropolis.*

The centerpiece of Kettelhut's design is a gigantic tower, 150 stories tall and topped by a landing platform for airplanes. Gossamer bridges supported by slender, truss-braced legs span the canyons of the lesser skyscrapers. The settings are animated with special effects, especially the recently invented Schüfftan process of using mirrors to combine miniatures and live action.

The most extraordinary of Lang's films after *Metropolis* was another ambitious science fiction epic, *Die Frau im Mond* (1929), a three-hour space opera dramatizing man's first voyage to the moon. In contrast to the mysticism that colored much of *Metropolis, Die Frau im Mond* rigorously adopted a scientific, documentary-like realism, and as such represented a filmic example of the architecture, photographs, and industrial design produced under the Neue Sachlichkeit ("New Objectivity") approach to art. Less a movement than a consensus among artists of which the Bauhaus was a leading institution, Neue Sachlichkeit proposed the crea-

58. *Dr. Mabuse der Spieler* (1922, Fritz Lang). Art Director: Otto Hunte.

tion of rationally directed, functionalist art, one that unequivocally embraced industrialization and technology as significant realities of the twentieth century. In *Die Frau im Mond,* Lang confronts the realities of moviemaking with equal rigor by the use of a clear visual language that lets the audience *see* the story (virtually without having to read the subtitles) and through his unleashing of UFA's formidable technical know-how.

The design of the film was the effort of artists and scientists, a model of the collaboration between art and industry encouraged by German design organizations from the Deutscher Werkbund to the Bauhaus. For their decor (Illus. 62), Emil Hasler, Vollbrecht, and Hunte worked with the German missile experts Hermann Oberth and Willy Ley as technical advisers for the film's intricate models of rockets. While the decor of the hero's apartment follows that seen in Lang's *Spione* (1928), *Die Frau im Mond*'s great steel-and-glass space center afforded Lang a novel and challenging cinematographic opportunity. The aerial scenes of the center, seen as if from an airplane, are as dazzling as anything in *Metropolis.*

59. (OPPOSITE) City of the future, drawn in 1925 for *Metropolis* (1927, Fritz Lang). Delineator: Erich Kettelhut.
60. (LEFT) Model of a proposed skyscraper (1922, Ludwig Mies van der Rohe).
61. (BELOW) Drawing of the *"Herzmaschine"* for *Metropolis* (1927, Fritz Lang). Delineator: Erich Kettelhut.

Die Frau im Mond was Lang's last silent film, and like *L'Argent,* Marcel L'Herbier's penultimate silent feature, it crystallized a moment in the cinema's involvement with modern architecture during the 1920s. While *L'Argent* was the culmination of the decade in which French pioneers injected modernism into the mainstream of film design, *Die Frau im Mond* was a work of art that embodied the objective, pro-technology spirit at the heart of Weimar culture. Taken together, the two films represent a twilight of silent cinema, when the visual poetry of the pure image burned brightest before its extinction.

Modern film decor itself was far from extinguished as the German cinema entered the sound era. After the extravagance of his science fiction films, Lang turned to more restrained modern designs. Vollbrecht and Hasler collaborated on the housing complexes for *M* (1931) and *Das Testament des Dr. Mabuse* (1933; Illus. 63). The exterior of the latter shares many architectural features —cubic massing, smooth white facades trimmed in masonry, horizontal fenestration —with residential units designed by modern architects in Germany such as those in the Zehlendorf section of Berlin (1927; Illus. 64) by Bruno Taut.

Another vanguard influence in German film was the designer Franz Schroedter, who was as adept as Lang's team in creating modern film decor. Born in 1897 in Berlin, Schroedter, an architect, designed for the German cinema from 1919 until the 1950s, when he retired from film work. His first modern set was the artist's studio (Illus. 65)

62. (TOP) *Die Frau im Mond* (1929, Fritz Lang). Art Directors: Emil Hasler, Otto Hunte, and Karl Vollbrecht.
63. (MIDDLE) Drawing of an apartment building for *Das Testament des Dr. Mabuse* (1933, Fritz Lang). Delineator: Emil Hasler.
64. (BOTTOM) Housing development, Berlin (1927, Bruno Taut).

in *Angst* (1928), for which he borrowed elements from Le Corbusier's 1922 studio-house for the artist Amedée Ozenfant. *Angst*'s protagonist lived and worked in an ascetic, one-room space, sparsely furnished, its bare walls decorated with only a few contemporary artworks. Schroedter reworks Le Corbusier's sculptural grouping of forms around an open-riser stair, but regrettably excludes the dramatic corner window of Le Corbusier's scheme. Rectangular panels perforated with circles had been used similarly by Le Corbusier in a house he designed at Vaucresson in 1922. Like most German set designers of the time, Schroedter had a predilection for the tubular furniture of the Bauhaus masters, and prominently displays Marcel Breuer's 1925 Wassily lounge chair. The most interesting element in *Angst*'s design, and one that may in fact be an original contribution by Schroedter, is the freestanding workstation, an asymmetrical tubular structure integrating two tables at different heights, a screen, and two lighting fixtures.

The Bauhaus also inspired Schroedter's most notable design, the automobile factory in *Die Nacht gehört uns* (1929), one of the first German sound films. Here Schroedter

65. *Angst* (1928, Hans Steinhoff). Art Director: Franz Schroedter.

adopts the Bauhaus's industrial-style glass walls in metal frames, undecorated walls, and pipe railings. In Schroedter's sketch (Illus. 66) the horizontality of an apparently endless glass wall works in unison with equally powerful diagonal and vertical elements. Schroedter uses a cubist vocabulary for the office interiors (Illus. 67), in which he experiments with designs for industrial objects, lighting, and especially tubular furniture. While many of the tubular chairs in his sketches are designs recognizable as those of Mies van der Rohe and Marcel Breuer, a plan for a slab desk cantilevered off a wall on one side and supported by an orthogonal tubular frame on the other is an impressive invention.

Schroedter's interest in industrial design was shared by Robert Neppach and Jack Rotmil, who created a number of novel sets using artificial illumination. Neppach's facade for the gourmet shop in *Delikatessen* (1930; Illus. 68) unites door, shopwindow, and sign with a wide band of translucently lit glass trimmed with continuous strips of tubular lighting fixtures, anticipating on a smaller scale the facade of the Bioscoop Vreeburg Cinema (1936) in Utrecht by Gerrit Rietveld. In *Vom Täter fehlt jede Spur* (1928), Jack Rotmil's undulating lines of exposed light bulbs accentuate the curving spandrels and ribbon windows of a Berlin amusement park. Many of Rotmil's designs of the late 1920s feature curving spandrels of translucent glass, chrome railings, and white, streamlined forms; all were trademarks of Erich Mendelsohn, and all would become clichés of commercial architecture for the next several decades.

The high quality of the decor in German films of the era (and the number of Bauhaus pieces used to furnish commercial establishments in scores of films) attest to the Bauhaus's great influence on designers as well as its success with the German public. Yet even without the benefit of such a force, countries outside Germany eventually began to be exposed to modernist trends. In Italy, where little in the way of architectural innovation had occurred during the 1920s, modern Italian architects campaigned in the early 1930s to convince the Fascist regime to adopt modernism as the official state style. Italian movies of the decade, however, continued to use modern architectural decor for less exalted purposes. Such design was concentrated almost totally at the Cines studios, where filmmakers turned to modern settings to add a glamorous sheen to the studio's romantic comedies and society dramas. These imitated the proven formulas of contemporary Hollywood and Berlin films, particularly the Cinderella scenarios, the posh tone, and the wealthy characters of the German and American films. It was the studio's head of set construction from 1929 to 1933, Gastone Medin, who provided most of the appropriately deluxe modern decor. If the short-lived Futurist movement of the teens had no real avant-garde successor in the Italian cinema of the 1930s, film designers like Medin at Cines did nonetheless produce a series of striking modern designs that attest to the internationalism of the cinema's "modern moment."

Although only in his early twenties when he made his debut with Alessandro Blasetti's film *Sole* in 1928, Gastone Medin played an important role in the revival of Italian film design. By 1932, Medin's work had become skilled in the modern vocabulary as displayed in his Roman residence for the automobile businessman in *Due Cuori felici* (1932) and the airport interiors for a film putatively titled *La Dinamo dell'eroismo*. In *Due Cuori felici,* suites of rooms (Illus. 69) flow gracefully into one another: Only wide, sliding glass doors distinguish a spacious living room/study from an equally generous dining room. Along one wall of the living area Medin assembles an asymmetrical composition of built-in furniture

66. Drawing of a factory for *Die Nacht gehört uns* (1929, Carl Froelich). Delineator: Franz Schroedter.

and hidden lighting. Textures, fabrics, and carpeting are shrewdly used to highlight the room's harder finishes. In *La Dinamo dell'eroismo*, Medin includes an exceptionally noteworthy detail in the tubular mezzanine railing infilled with panels of wire mesh (Illus. 70).

Illustrated by numerous set stills, both films were prominently featured and praised for their designs in *La Casa Bella*,[15] one of the modern movement's leading magazines. *La Casa Bella* also displayed film designs by modern architects Enrico Paulucci and Carlo Levi for *Patatrac* (1931), the Cines stu-

dios' romantic comedy about an aristocratic dandy.[16] While the bedroom (Illus. 71) of *Patatrac* is a theatrical mélange of patterns and textures, the film's decor for the Almaier jewelry shop ranks as one of the cinema's most elegant, restrained creations. Only a thin horizontal display window and metallic lettering relieves the shop's severe, almost blank facade, a striking conception that suggests the immense value of the contents displayed inside (Illus. 72). The vault, a black square incised into gently curving walls, was opened via controls as painstakingly crafted as the shop's precious artifacts. The tubular chairs were German designs by the Luckhardt brothers.

The film decor of the architect Giuseppe Capponi for Guido Brignone's *La Voce lontana* (1933), another Cines production, and Max Ophüls's *La Signora di Tutti* (1934) are notable for a dynamic sense of space and movement. Although these qualities were absent from Capponi's most famous building, the rectilinear Institute of Botany and Pharmaceutical Chemistry at the University of Rome, his originality seems to have been liberated by the freedom of cinema design. "The duty of an architect in a film," Capponi wrote, "is not as the preparer of backdrops, but as the *director of the silent elements of the scene* (objects, lights, architecture). Inasmuch as they ought to live, to express themselves in their very rapid and synthetic language, they ought to *perform* like the actors."[17]

With their implication of movement, stairways were important elements in Capponi's film architecture. The hall of the professional school in *La Voce lontana* (Illus.

67. (TOP) Drawing of an office for *Die Nacht gehört uns* (1929).
68. (MIDDLE) *Delikatessen* (1930, Geza von Bolvary). Art Director: Robert Neppach.
69. (BOTTOM) *Due Cuori felici* (1932, Baldassare Negroni). Art Director: Gastone Medin.

73), for example, is dominated by an expansive double-flight stairway, its forceful diagonal thrust punctuated by a row of freestanding columns and the pronounced horizontality of an open mezzanine. A helical stair in the radio station lobby (Illus. 74) of the same film suggests spiraling motion. Walls of luminous glass in the background accentuate the powerful lines of both sets of stairs by placing them and actors into stark silhouette.

The Italian cinema's apolitical appropriation of architectural modernism was typical of the European cinema in general, which had come to value modern architecture for its stylishness rather than on any ideological grounds. However, as a footnote to the modern movement as it was represented in European film architecture, mention should be made of the Soviet Union, and one film in particular that has become a landmark in the cinema of the period. For many Soviet filmmakers of the 1920s, architecture was a potent symbol of the new Communist society that was the legacy of the revolution of 1917. Even had the cost of building elaborate sets on soundstages not been economically prohibitive, many filmmakers would likely have chosen to film outdoors, where both construction sites and new Soviet buildings provided suitable backdrops to the drama of Soviet life being played out in the streets. The spirit of modernism runs throughout the work of the Soviet director Sergei Eisenstein, whether in the Constructivist-inspired posters that graphic designers created for the films, or in his own rapid-fire editing, which captured the speed and immediacy of modern life. In 1928, in response to the Communist Party's decision to collectivize farms and build up heavy industry, Eisenstein began preparations for an inspirational movie later entitled *Staroye I Novoye (Old and New)*, and commissioned the young architect Andrew Burov to design the film's outdoor sets (Illus. 75). "I

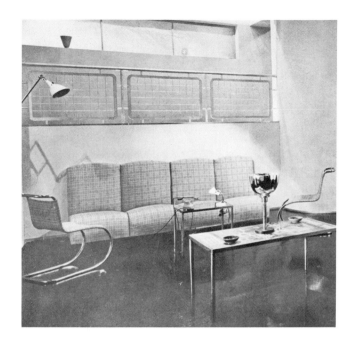

70. (TOP) *La Dinamo dell'eroismo* (early 1930s). Art Director: Gastone Medin.
71. (BOTTOM) *Patatrac* (1931, Gennaro Righelli). Art Directors: Enrico Paulucci and Carlo Levi.

aimed to produce not merely decorative effects," Burov stated, with a socialist zeal, "but, by means of the film, to introduce new methods of industrialized agriculture and to design buildings built with new materials and by modern methods. . . . I see (in the cinema) above all an excellent means

72. (OPPOSITE TOP) *Patatrac* (1931).
73. (OPPOSITE BOTTOM) *La Voce lontana* (1933, Guido Brignone). Art Director: Giuseppe Capponi.
74. (ABOVE) *La Voce lontana* (1933).

of spreading among the masses the great ideas of our time. . . . The cinema should . . . show what is, as well as what ought to be."[18] In one remarkable scene indicative of Soviet optimism, a young peasant girl envisions a mechanized future of modern agricultural buildings, their stark white forms boldly profiled against the sky.

So accomplished were Burov's sets for *Old and New* that they earned uncharacteristic praise from two leading modernists. Le Corbusier viewed segments of the unfinished film during a 1928 trip to Moscow and

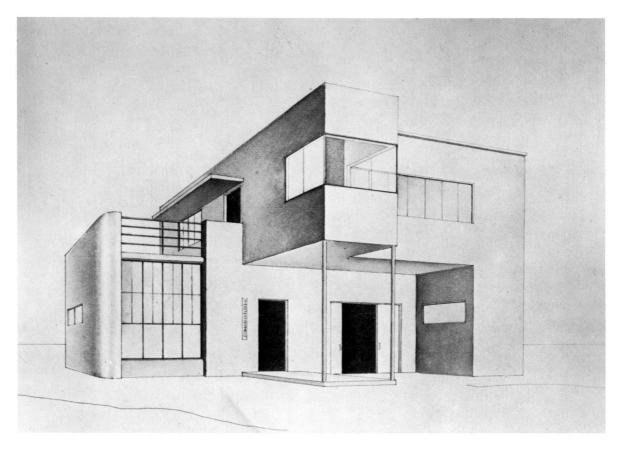

75. Drawing of an industrialized farm building for *Old and New* (1928, Sergei Eisenstein). Delineator: uncredited.

was particularly impressed with its promotion of buildings so similar to his own model houses at Stuttgart the previous year. Nor did the similarity elude Alfred Barr, the first director of New York's Museum of Modern Art. Claiming that the film sought to inspire a hundred million peasants to undertake modern farming, Barr praised the dairy as "the finest of modern Russian buildings in its severity and elegance. The slender supports . . . are even more daring than those used by Corbusier in his larger house at Stuttgart."[19]

The propagandistic use of modern architectural sets for *Old and New* were finally an anomaly within the popular cinema, where most filmmakers ignored the modern movement's more radical underpinnings. It would remain for the American cinema to dissociate modernism most strikingly from its egalitarian visions. There modern decor would achieve its widest dissemination, aided by the Hollywood studios' unparalleled publicity and marketing machines. While like *Old and New* Hollywood's films looked forward to a world transformed, its utopias were visions of individual affluence rather than of collective well-being—distinctly American dreams, but dreams all the same.

CHAPTER 4
Hollywood Unlimited

I went to the land of the Moviemakers and saw them at work. As I go back over the weeks I spent within the innermost walls of those great studios and watched the master minds and ·master hands at their appointed tasks I am filled with the wonder of it all. I thrill at the miracles performed before my eyes; at the sight of a thousand threads in a tangled skein wrought into a fabric of exquisite design.[1]

John J. Floherty's 1935 book, *Moviemakers,* from which the passage above is taken, captures the marvel of the Hollywood studios at their zenith, a spectacle to which even more sophisticated and jaded writers than the excitable Floherty would succumb. In F. Scott Fitzgerald's unfinished novel about doomed movie mogul Monroe Stahr, *The Last Tycoon,* his narrator described the spell the studio cast even at night: "Under the moon the back lot was thirty acres of fairyland—not because the locations really looked like African jungles and French cha-

teaux and schooners at anchor and Broadway by night, but because they looked like the torn picture books of childhood, like fragments of stories dancing in an open fire. I never lived in a house with an attic, but a back lot must be something like that, and at night of course in an enchanted distorted way, it all comes true."[2]

The Hollywood myth that so enthralled Floherty and Fitzgerald was equally powerful for the moviegoing public, a fact reflected in the movie capital's enormous economic success. During the 1930s, Hollywood films dominated Western screens. In 1933 alone, the industry made nearly five hundred features, a figure that represented almost half the films made in the West and two and one half times as many films as its next Western competitor, England. This level of output was made possible by the strong corporate organization of the Hollywood studio system, a vertically structured network that connected the essential functions of production (at the studios' soundstages, back lot, and backstage departments), exhibition (its chains of movie theaters), and distribution.

The potentate at the center of the studio empire was the Hollywood producer, who was responsible not only for the financial backing of the film but also for the selection of its stars, writers, director, designer, and all other key personnel. Of the same working-class or middle-class origins as the majority of their audience, many producers had early careers in the fashion trades: Samuel Goldwyn had been a glove salesman, Paramount's Adolph Zukor a furrier, and David O. Selznick's father was a jeweler before he became a producer. As Robert Sklar notes in *Movie-Made America,* this background was a significant factor in Hollywood moguls' respect for the financial value of design.[3]

By the late '20s, the "modern look" affected every facet of the typical Hollywood feature, from film production values to advertising layouts to movie house designs. Among the results of Hollywood's enthusiastic adoption of modernism was the influence it came to wield on couture via movie costuming. Movie stars' film wardrobes were inevitably glamorous—the latest in chic apparel, a look to be emulated. Because a movie would generally take a year in production and would be in circulation for a year or even more, it was necessary to anticipate trends to keep the film's style up-to-date for as long as possible. A film that featured clothes and hair *à la mode* would be more likely to attract audiences eager for advice on style, and would hence have a longer shelf life.

Once movie producers realized the economic advantages to be gained from treating design as a serious consideration in the preparation of a film, Hollywood quickly rose to a commanding position not only as a popularizer of fashion trends but also as an initiator of them. In 1921, British novelist and fashion arbiter Elinor Glyn had been shocked by the backwater condition of Hollywood costuming and recommended copying Paris couture as the only remedy. By 1933, however, the editors of *Vogue* conceded that fashion now originated simultaneously in Paris *and* Hollywood. So effective did Hollywood become at consumer trend-setting that canny retailers turned enormous profits by producing entire lines of movie-inspired fashions, and leading studio costumers, like MGM's Adrian, became successful entrepreneurs outside the studio.

Hollywood's recognition of its ability to supply women with fashion advice—and thereby keep them coming to the theaters for more—seems to have sparked similar attempts in the area of interior decoration. That a woman's home was as important to her as her clothes was the reasoning presented by the head of MGM's art department when he convinced the studio to launch its Art Deco decor in the late 1920s.

Its pursuit of stylish and *au courant* decor led Hollywood, in its own inimitable way, to feature by 1930 adaptations of modern designs by a number of the architects who would be shown at The Museum of Modern Art's landmark exhibition two years later. This fact refutes the general belief among architects that the Museum's exhibition was responsible for introducing modern architecture to the American public. For example, in its decor for *Paid* (1930; Illus. 76), released only three months after *What a Widow!,* MGM borrowed heavily from Otto Haesler's design for a school in Celle, Germany (Illus. 77). For the sets of the musical comedy *Palmy Days* (1931), Samuel Goldwyn designers Richard Day and Willy Pogany reworked the Philadelphia Saving Fund Society Building. The film's Clark Bakery skyscraper replicates not only the exterior of the PSFS but also its multifunctional interior, combining factory, restaurant, and offices in a single structure. At the

same time, *Palmy Days* satirized the health-conscious fervor of the new architecture by having its protagonist, a progressive industrialist, insist that his employees exercise in the building's rooftop steel-and-glass gymnasium (Illus. 78).

But however many requests studios eventually received for pictures of their modern sets, to claim that Hollywood films were as effective a source of interior decoration ideas as they were of fashionable clothing would certainly be an overstatement. Women who willingly dyed their hair blond like Jean Harlow's or wore "Juliet caps" in imitation of Norma Shearer in MGM's version of Shakespeare's play were understandably reluctant—or, more likely, unable—to undertake the expensive redecorating schemes featured in popular films. If the movies of this period did not actually initiate design trends, they did provide conspicuously attractive settings for their scenarios, and, more important, anticipated and virtually defined for the general public modern architectural trends then only barely perceptible on the design horizon.

From the studio's perspective, modernist decor provided the further economic benefit of helping distinguish its products. Three out of every four American movies were produced by one of eight major studios: Metro-Goldwyn-Mayer, 20th Century–Fox, Paramount, Warner Bros., RKO, Columbia, Universal, and United Artists. These films required differentiation within the vast international marketplace, and to accomplish this the studios developed a variety of marketing tactics. Stars ranked as a

76. (TOP) *Paid* (1930, Sam Wood). Supervisory Art Director: Cedric Gibbons.
77. (MIDDLE) School, Celle (circa 1929, Otto Haesler).
78. (BOTTOM) *Palmy Days* (1931, Edward Sutherland). Art Directors: Richard Day and Willy Pogany.

studio's most visible standard-bearers. Shaping a star's onscreen persona was the responsibility of staff writers, producers, and directors, while publicists, aided by widely read fan magazines, manufactured a comparable public persona—often with considerable license. Moviegoers knew that Clark Gable, Joan Crawford, and Greta Garbo represented MGM, the studio that by the late 1930s could boast of having "more stars than are in the heavens." Carole Lombard and Marlene Dietrich carried Paramount's banner; Astaire and Rogers, RKO's. Another public-recognition factor was specialization in a genre. Universal dominated the great horror films of the decade; Warners created the best gangster films; Paramount the most worldly comedies.

Costuming and design likewise played a part in the creation of a studio's image. The importance a studio attached to its set designs is evident in the share they were allotted of a typical Hollywood film budget. In a million-dollar production of the late 1930s, for example, the direct cost of the sets and related personnel salaries accounted for 12.5 percent of the total budget—exceeded only by the 30 percent devoted to the salaries of the performers.[4] At the head of the studio's design personnel was the supervisory art director. In his offices the initial meeting to establish the film's schedule and budget took place, involving the director, writers, producer, and all other important employees. Supervisory art directors also oversaw the studio's art department, which could employ as many as forty-five staff members.

The atmosphere at the great art departments of the 1930s was one of terrific bustle. Paramount's art department, for example, produced enough designs to keep three eight-hour shifts of set builders active on a dozen soundstages, from which about forty films a year emerged. Many of the younger members of the department were graduates of architecture schools, especially the University of Southern California. Not only was the pay at the studios traditionally better than at architectural offices, but during the darkest days of the Depression, it was the *only* pay available. Without the specialization that came later with unionization, many design personnel in the 1930s found themselves doing a variety of different jobs —as sketch artist, construction supervisor, assistant art director—in a fluid and efficient environment, almost an atelier, that nurtured highly talented designers.

The enormous production schedules of the Hollywood studios from the 1930s through the '50s required a system of preparing sets quite different from that in Europe, where a designer like Meerson would himself have initiated the design and presided over the creation of drawings and construction. Hollywood, in contrast, used a two-tier system that divided responsibility between a supervisory art director, who established the set's tone or concept, and a unit art director, who carried out the design and oversaw its construction. During the 1930s, a major studio like MGM, for example, had a design staff of one supervisory art director, eight or nine unit art directors, thirty draftsmen, and five or six illustrators.

At three studios in particular—Paramount, RKO, and MGM—producers assigned set designers the task of creating a distinct modern architectural "look," just as studio musicians were responsible for a distinct sound and costume designers a particular silhouette. These companies' receptivity to modernism was to some degree a reflection of the genres in which they specialized: Modern decor was a particularly appropriate backdrop for their society comedies and dramas and lavish fairy-tale musicals. These companies created a cohesive body of work, representing the best, most consistent modern design that dominated the cinema of the 1930s.

Paramount

During the decades between the wars, Hollywood was flooded with European émigrés, prominent figures from the arts who had been attracted to America by its greater opportunities. For those who arrived in the 1920s, like Ernst Lubitsch, the lure was primarily the artistic and economic potential of Hollywood's superb physical plant and phenomenal world market; in the 1930s, for Fritz Lang and others, the political refuge the United States offered was a more considerable motivation. Germans were the majority in this emigration, if only in terms of the number of actors, directors, writers, producers, and designers who settled on the West Coast. The designers in this group would prove to exercise as substantial an influence on Hollywood's set design as German and Austrian architectural émigrés like Richard Neutra, Walter Gropius, and Mies van der Rohe were to have on American architecture the following decade.

The German presence was strongest at Paramount, whose art department was under the direction of Hans Dreier. Born in Germany in 1885, Dreier studied architecture in Munich and supervised architectural projects for the German government in West Africa. He designed for UFA from 1919 until 1923, after which he came to Paramount at the invitation of director Ernst Lubitsch. Promoted to the position of supervisory art director in 1932, Dreier remained at the studio until his retirement in the early 1950s. He died in 1966.

Under Dreier's supervision the Paramount art department became a Bauhaus-like workshop of local architectural school graduates and fellow émigrés, most notably two of southern California's leading modernists, Jock Peters and Kem Weber. Prior to World War I, Peters had worked in the Berlin office of Peter Behrens, where Gropius and Mies had also apprenticed. In 1923, he left Germany for Los Angeles and designed movie sets for Famous Players–Lasky (where Frank Lloyd Wright's son Lloyd was also employed as a designer) until 1927, when he started his private architectural practice. His best-known work during the period was the luxurious Art Deco interiors for the Bullocks-Wilshire Department Store (1929) in Los Angeles.

Berlin-born Kem Weber, who had been sent to America by the German government to oversee the installation of the German exhibition at the Panama Pacific Exposition of 1914, had a more diversified career, having worked as an architect, a teacher, and a furniture and industrial designer. Weber's Airline Chair (1934–35), with its striking contrast between boldly profiled side supports and two thin sheets of wood that act as an integral seat and back, remains one of the decade's most beautiful and original designs.

When the number of professional clients began to decline in the early years of the Depression, both Peters and Weber turned to the booming movie industry, employment that they viewed as a mixed blessing. Although Peters, in particular, was attracted by the quick realization of architectural design that the movies made possible, both men yearned for the permanence of actual buildings.[5] While credited examples of these designers' cinematic efforts are few—one of the most beautiful is Weber's design for the nightclub from *The Big Broadcast* (1932; Illus. 79)—the fact that Dreier sought their expertise confirms Paramount's commitment to modernism.

Paramount's modern of the 1930s was the studio style most closely aligned with the Bauhaus repertory: White, unadorned surfaces; horizontality; and elegant simplicity are hallmarks of both styles. In *A Bedtime Story* (1933; Illus. 80), a dramatic use of space distinguishes the Paris apartment of

79. (ABOVE LEFT) Drawing of a nightclub for *The Big Broadcast* (1932, Frank Tuttle). Delineator: Kem Weber.
80. (ABOVE RIGHT) *A Bedtime Story* (1933, Norman Taurog). Supervisory Art Director: Hans Dreier.
81. (LEFT) Dorothea Wieck in *Miss Fane's Baby Is Stolen* (1934, Alexander Hall). Supervisory Art Director: Hans Dreier.

the sophisticated bachelor played by Maurice Chevalier. Thin metallic columns support a curving drum in the double-height section of an expansive living space. A terrace containing a white helical stairway opens off a tall glass wall sheathed in sheer draperies. A notably progressive element of the design was the decision to allow area carpeting, furniture, and freestanding screens to demarcate space. The large table of asymmetrical shelving recalls contemporary, De Stijl–inspired furniture by local architect Rudolph Schindler.

A specialty of Paramount designers was the predominantly white set, such as that designed for the movie star's villa in *Miss Fane's Baby Is Stolen* (1934; Illus. 81). Photographing pure white in films became possible only in the early 1930s, as the result of technical developments in film stock and lighting.[6] Recent aesthetic trends in architecture made these monochromatic sets fashionable, especially the construction of white buildings like Richard Neutra's Lovell House in Los Angeles. Interior decorators had also begun experimenting with white decor, and, as had been the case with clothing fashions, influenced Hollywood only to be influenced by it. While the fashionable decorator Syrie Maugham (author Somerset Maugham's wife) may not have originated the vogue for all-white rooms, her much-publicized living room of 1933, with its sofas upholstered in beige satin and Louis XV chairs painted white, combined modern and classic elements so adroitly that it caught the eye of fellow decorators and movie designers alike. But as Martin Battersby has shown in *The Decorative Thirties,* the all-white craze had actually peaked the previous year: 1932 had seen Oliver Messel's all-white theater decor for *Helen,* Max Reinhardt's sensational London production of Jacques Offenbach's operetta *La Belle Hélène,* and Hollywood's unveiling of its newest star, Jean Harlow, whom Battersby describes as being composed of equal parts of "snow, marble and marshmallow."[7]

The most remarkable feature of these Paramount sets was their diffused lighting, which lent them a lambent glow previously unseen in film. This effect was accomplished through the free use of chrome elements and diaphanous, translucent walls. Diffuse lighting is seen at its best in Dreier's and Robert Usher's design for the Brewster Advertising Agency in Raoul Walsh's *Artists and Models* (1937; Illus. 82). Reminiscent of a Japanese residence with its softly glowing rice-paper screens, this very economical set achieves a luminous quality from its embossed translucent glass or plastic panels, which also ingeniously double as the exterior wall of the reception area and as a low semicircular wall that both conceals the secretary's workstation and helps direct visitors. For the exterior wall of the executive office the designers slid a strip of clear glass between a spandrel of translucent material and a soffit of white plaster. Combining translucent and clear glass in a single plane was a problem that challenged architects of the decade, which

was enamored of glass bricks, and one that Dreier and Usher handle with considerable finesse. Equally sophisticated is the design for the agency's poster stands, supported by thin frames (Illus. 83). The curved "wall" formed by freestanding panels defines a thin layer of space, and mirrors the low semicircular wall in the reception area.

Modern design was superbly integrated into the work of one of Paramount's most famous directors of the 1930s, Ernst Lubitsch, where it contributed *grande luxe* luster to sparklingly witty comedies of upper-class sophistication. One of the film industry's most prized émigrés, Lubitsch settled in America in 1924 after the successes of his exotic German spectacles had attracted the attention of Hollywood. Comedies of manners, full of romantic triangles, which were to become Lubitsch's specialty, had been introduced to Hollywood by Erich von Stroheim. Lubitsch's lighter, less mordant tone and his comic skills (the famous "Lubitsch touch") gave them a polish that transformed them. In addition, his greater adaptability to working within the studio system ensured him a long and prosperous career as a director, almost half of which was for Paramount.

One of the first of Lubitsch's films to contain modern decor was *One Hour with You* (1932). Here, Maurice Chevalier and Jeanette MacDonald are teamed in a Parisian apartment setting reminiscent of Jock Peters's Art Deco commercial work of the late 1920s in its shallow cubist massing and geometric patterning. Later that same year, Paramount's modernism reached its peak in the designs for Lubitsch's own personal favorite among his films, *Trouble in Paradise.*

Directed by Lubitsch at midcareer, *Trouble in Paradise* balances European, almost Mozartean insights into romantic relations with quick American pacing and verve. The film's slightly tart quality is a result of the director's oblique rendering of sex, a device

82. Gail Patrick (right) in *Artists and Models* (1937, Raoul Walsh). Supervisory Art Director: Hans Dreier; Unit Art Director: Robert Usher.

that lay at the heart of the "Lubitsch touch." Lubitsch achieves this subtlety by treating objects almost as minor characters who comment ironically on the erotic confusion of the all-too-human major ones. As a typical example, the Lubitsch camera often focuses discreetly on doors that mask the antics behind, which are tactfully left to the audience's imagination.

One especially memorable sequence is composed of vignettes, each showing a different Art Deco clock marking the passing of time during an evening-long tryst (Illus. 84). Only offscreen do voices convey the anticipation, evasion, and finally disappointment of a mating game. Later in the film, Lubitsch delicately mocks Hollywood's sexual taboos when he reveals the same pair's first embrace as a reflection in a mirror, and finally as an entwined shadow on the satin coverlet of a double bed.

Trouble in Paradise's amorous contest takes place in what is the design centerpiece of the film, the villa of the wealthy widow of a perfumer, set in Paris. A low entryway opens onto a two-story room which is connected to a second floor by a giant circular stairway placed against a glass wall. One segment of the wall leads out to stepped terraces and gardens; another section is divided

83. Jack Benny in *Artists and Models* (1937).

84. Kay Francis and Herbert Marshall in
Trouble in Paradise (1932, Ernst Lubitsch).
Supervisory Art Director: Hans Dreier.

into vertical panes of glass above a long
built-in sofa.

In *Trouble in Paradise,* all the elements of
decor are designed of a piece and help impart
a chic modern sheen to the film, one of the
most brilliant Hollywood comedies of the
Depression. The architecture of *Trouble in
Paradise*—pristine, white, filled with light—
closely approximates the designs of Neutra,
then Los Angeles's leading modern architect. Ironically, Neutra wrote despairingly
of movie design, suggesting that it was responsible for the propagation of mediocre
historical styles. "Motion picture sets,"
Neutra wrote in 1941, "have undoubtedly
confused architectural tastes. They may be
blamed for many phenomena in this landscape such as: Half-timber English peasant
cottages, French provincial and 'mission-

bell' type abodes, Arabian minarets, Geor-
gian mansions on 50 by 120 foot lots with
'Mexican Ranchos' adjoining them on sites
of the same size."[8] In his assessment of the
movies' influence, Neutra perhaps gave
them more than their due; in his condemnation of their designs, especially in light of
Paramount's achievements, he surely gave
them less.

RKO

With their flat, undecorated planes and
weightless volumes set into asymmetrical
compositions, the modern sets created at
Paramount studios during the 1930s shared
architectural characteristics with many of
the buildings the European avant-garde presented at the Deutscher Werkbund exhibition of 1927 and The Museum of Modern
Art exhibition of 1932. In contrast, designers at RKO studios invented their own fanciful and decorative amalgams of modern
architecture, streamlined Art Deco, and
neo-classicism.

The RKO style was most consistently
seen in eight of the nine musicals that the
studio made starring Fred Astaire and Ginger Rogers (their last film for RKO, *The
Story of Vernon and Irene Castle* (1939), was
set before and during World War I). The
decor of the team's fourth outing, Mark
Sandrich's *Top Hat* (1935), displays the style
at its most exuberant. As Arlene Croce ob-
serves in *The Fred Astaire and Ginger Rogers
Book,* movie musicals of the 1940s and '50s
were democracies where every member of
the hoi polloi with a song in his or her heart
got a chance to sing, dance, and cavort.[9]
While some musicals of the Depression did
extol "the Forgotten Man," moviegoers of
the class-conscious 1930s were more likely
to respond to escapes into the *très riche* world
of Daddy Warbucks. *Top Hat* fulfilled that
desire unequivocally, with Astaire, in white

tie and tails, and Rogers, a bird of paradise in satin and feathers, dancing through swank decor of svelte greyhounds, prancing harlequins, and furling banners. Stylization and artifice were *Top Hat*'s keynotes. Venice inspired the film's design *capolavoro,* a two-soundstage expanse of balconies, terraces, and piazzas linked by a serpentine canal dyed black for the occasion and crossed by three high-kitsch bridges. It was on this set that Astaire and Rogers performed the elegant "Cheek to Cheek" and the "Piccolino."

Later that year, RKO would provide equally fanciful, if less extravagant, decor for the salon of the eponymous heroine of *Roberta* (1935)—a neo-rococo confection of crystal chandeliers, polished floors, lattice, and curvilinear moldings derived from no known classical repertory but created nonetheless with the precision of the architect's drawing tools.

Streamlining runs as a leitmotif throughout many of the Fred Astaire–Ginger Rogers films: in the shallow curves of the balcony and stairs in the hotel esplanade of Sandrich's *The Gay Divorcee* (1934; Illus. 85), in the teardrop shape of the ocean liner windows in Sandrich's *Shall We Dance* (1937; Illus. 86), and in the graceful sweep of the double stairway in the Silver Sandal Club of George Stevens's *Swing Time* (1936; see page 136), where the stairs' gentle curves are all the more pronounced against the zigzag angularity of the treads and risers themselves.

A more subtle expression of streamlining are the high-gloss surfaces, in their support of frictionless movement, that were essentials of the decor of all the Astaire and Rogers musicals. Croce writes that the film's dance floors were usually wooden, covered for the more elaborate sets (like *Top Hat*'s Venice) with Bakelite, a plastic product favored for its modernity by architects as well. New industrial materials like Bakelite, Formica, and vitrolite—a heavy black glass

85. (TOP) *The Gay Divorcee* (1934, Mark Sandrich). Supervisory Art Director: Van Nest Polglase; Unit Art Director: Carroll Clark.
86. (BOTTOM) Ginger Rogers and Fred Astaire in *Shall We Dance* (1937, Mark Sandrich). Supervisory Art Director: Van Nest Polglase; Unit Art Director: Carroll Clark.

—enjoyed a vogue during these years. Modernist designer Paul Frankl, beside himself with praise for these products, wrote in *Form and Re-Form* (1930) that "industrial chemistry today rivals alchemy. Base materials are transmuted into marvels of new beauty."[10] Retaining the pristine state of these glossy surfaces proved as difficult in film as it did in architectural usage. Cardboard covered the Bakelite floors at RKO during camera rehearsals, and individual takes were separated by long delays as scratches were removed with Energine (oil would have been quicker, but would have made the floors too slippery for dancing). Astaire and Rogers had to seem to glide through space on thin cushions of air, their feet never touching the ground—an illusion that would have been destroyed by any blemishes on the surface.

Hollywood had established a connection between streamlining and frictionless movement as early as 1931, when *Silver Screen* magazine published an article entitled "Streamlined Ladies," which proclaimed: "This is the speed age. Motion picture stars, like motor boats, aeroplanes and racing cars, are built on greyhound lines. . . . A few years ago screen beauties were more generous in build than today. Now, diet, exercise and masseurs play important parts in the demand for faster figures."[11] The quick rise to fame of Jean Harlow, the prototype of this new star, was attributed to "the speedy lines of her body design."[12]

Streamlining's uninterrupted lines were expressed most poetically in the seamless dance routines of Astaire and Rogers. Many of these sequences were shot by mounting the camera on a special wheeled vehicle nicknamed "the Astaire dolly," which could follow the pair's every move. The dolly's keeping as tight as possible to the action allowed each member of the audience to travel vicariously with the stars along radiant curving walls and up streamlined stairways. Through the enormous popularity of their films and the universal attempts to mimic their every detail, streamlining became the "look" of the musical genre in every movie capital of the 1930s.

Assigning the proper credit for the creation of RKO's modern design is difficult. Brooklyn-born Van Nest Polglase, the supervisory head of RKO's art department during the 1930s, is the individual to whom the conception of the style is most often attributed. Born in 1898, Polglase studied architecture and interior design and practiced the former in New York prior to World War I. In 1919, he began designing for Famous Players–Lasky, where he might have come in contact with Paul Iribe, who was the designer of the Art Nouveau sets of De Mille's *The Affairs of Anatol.* He relocated to Hollywood in the late 1920s and quickly established a reputation for his skill in modern design during short stays at both Paramount —where he reputedly introduced the notion of the "all-white" set—and MGM. At the invitation of David O. Selznick, a producer with an eye for topnotch production values, Polglase joined RKO in 1932, the year before the release of *Flying Down to Rio,* the first Astaire and Rogers musical, and probably the only one designed by him personally. Afterward, even firsthand accounts of the degree of Polglase's involvement differ. Maurice Zuberano, an illustrator with the design department during the 1930s, has ascribed the development of the RKO style largely to the brilliant unit art director Carroll Clark, assisted by chief set designer Allan Abbott, whose sketches were the sets' genesis.[13] Throughout the 1930s, Polglase's design involvement diminished as his duties became primarily administrative, until his retirement from the studio in 1942. He died in 1968.

RKO's art department could, in addition to supplying such bravura shows of excess as *Top Hat,* prove itself to be a master of understatement, creating modern interiors that contained only slight suggestions of

87. *Shall We Dance* (1937).

neo-classicism. The ocean liner stateroom from *Shall We Dance* is an especially refined example (Illus. 87). In one gently curving wall a deeply recessed niche contains the indirect lighting that is the room's only source of illumination. The niche also defines the beds and, in an unusual and original scheme, leads the viewer's eye to the back of the set, where a black panel decorated with white neo-classical figures hangs above a pair of white settees and a table. The conjunction of the niche and the floating panel is a striking visual opposition: the horizontal white niche recessed in a dark-gray wall contrasts with the square black panel suspended from a light-gray wall. Even the beds are architecturally conceived, their crisply tailored white bedcovers and pillows backed by a low black counter ending in cantilevered night tables.

Just as Paramount had perfected the all-white set, RKO created black-and-white decor with an unmatched flair, using the sharp contrasts of the palette as a counterpoint to the smooth, quiet grace of streamlining. In the hotel esplanade for *The Gay Divorcee,* black-and-white graphics compose the major elements of the film's style—like architecture and decorative motifs—as well as the subtler components of landscaping and the semaphore-like costumes. In *Swing Time,* the weather itself is marshaled into the design concept, with snowy cityscapes and star-filled skies used as sheer white draperies for chic penthouse nightclubs (see page 136). Even the casting played its part. In *The Fred Astaire and Ginger Rogers Book,* Croce asks if there might be an aesthetic rationale for their choice of swarthy Latins as the lovers who are forever pursuing blond ice maiden Ginger Rogers, until the obligatory "happy ending" reunites her with Fred Astaire.[14]

However glamorous, RKO's was the least successful use of design among the three studios that developed distinctive modern styles, because it stressed decorative motifs over the spatial and formal potentials of modern architecture. Yet ironically it was the graphic simplicity of these very motifs —streamlining and black-and-white decor —that made RKO modern the style most recognizable to the public. Then, too, no other studio could hope to find as perfect an embodiment of its look as Fred Astaire and Ginger Rogers.

Metro-Goldwyn-Mayer

"Ars Gratia Artis" ("Art for Art's Sake"), the motto of Metro-Goldwyn-Mayer, which rides above its famous roaring lion, is a statement of high ideals that may not always have guided the company's executives. Yet as America's most prestigious and financially stable studio of the 1930s, MGM did produce Hollywood's largest body of modernist sets, which succeeded on the levels of broad concept, minute detail, and exceptionally well-realized execution.

MGM had been responsive to modern decor since it began operation in 1924. That year, Louis B. Mayer, vice-president in charge of production, took the advice of William Randolph Hearst and hired Russian-born designer Romain de Tirtoff, more commonly known as Erté. Erté's work had been familiar in America since 1915 via his fashion, interior design, and cover illustrations for *Harper's Bazaar,* which he executed while living in France. By the time he ar-

rived in Hollywood in 1925, Erté enjoyed an even more considerable reputation as a result of his Art Deco stage designs for George White's *Scandals,* a series of New York musical revues. On the transcontinental train trip that took the designer from New York to Hollywood, the American press treated him as a major celebrity and sought his opinion on every aspect of fashion.

Expectations of success in Hollywood were high on both Erté's and Mayer's parts. Erté aimed to revolutionize Hollywood costume and set design, raising it to the exalted position of *The Cabinet of Dr. Caligari,* the film that, by Erté's own admission, had sparked his interest in the design possibilities of the film medium.[15] Mayer, who to pamper the artist went as far as recreating his Paris studio on the MGM lot, intended to attract as much publicity as possible with his new prize. Regrettably, art and commerce collided, and the relationship lasted only the year. The individualistic and temperamental Erté found it impossible to work with the equally headstrong but more powerful stars, the endless delays, and the concessions to mass taste that he considered hindrances to his creativity.

Costumes and pageantry displays constitute the executed legacy of Erté's stay in Hollywood, and his set designs unfortunately remain only in a series of exciting but unrealized sketches. The building types that Erté deployed for MGM designs artfully epitomized the sophisticated, *très* snob world of stage stars and couturiers, nightclub trysts and glamorous boudoirs. Outstanding among them are the set sketches for *Paris,* one of the films Erté had initially been hired to design (its inane treatment of the Parisian *haute monde* precipitated his flight from Hollywood). The nightclub for *Paris* is a triangular space, its geometric imagery and setback profiles anticipating by several years the Art Deco style that would be used for skyscrapers in the United States. Red and gold dominate the color scheme, a palette Erté chose carefully since the studio intended to shoot the film's most important scenes in the early Technicolor process. Pairs of female nudes used as drapery pulls reveal Erté's penchant for a somewhat perverse sexual exoticism, reminiscent of a similar inclination in the Ballet Russe. The equally exotic home of the film's hero, originally intended to be a French couturier, is described vividly by Erté in his autobiography.[16] Its drawing room—all in black and white—has one wall sheathed in an ermine curtain. Fox fur cushions cover the furniture, especially the requisite divan, also in ermine, for flirtatious lounging.

In marked contrast to the jagged faceting and languid curves of the *Paris* settings, the dressing room as sketched for *A Little Bit of Broadway* (Illus. 88) was designed in a remarkably restrained, severely orthogonal style that recalled the geometric precision of the work of the Viennese designer Josef Hoffmann. Erté composed walls, furniture, and decorative accessories as flat, abstract planes divided into sharply defined rectangles; a single stylized floral motif unifies drawers, doorjambs, and furniture. In Erté's sketch the furniture and doors are lavender, the walls gray, dadoes and carpet black, and the bowl of flowers brilliant vermilion.

After Erté's departure from Hollywood, Cedric Gibbons, then supervisory head of the studio's art department, rose quickly to become the driving force behind the use of modern architectural decor at MGM. Mayer's disastrous experience with the *artiste* Erté may have convinced him to consolidate the art department under Gibbons, a more corporate-minded designer. Austin Cedric Gibbons was born in Brooklyn in 1890. His father, Patrick Gibbons, had had a successful architectural practice in New York. It was assumed that the young Gibbons would continue in the family business—his grand-

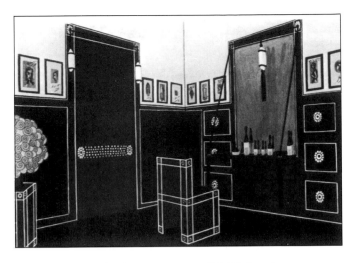

88. Drawing of a dressing room (1925) for *A Little Bit of Broadway*. Delineator: Erté.

father had also been an architect—but Cedric inclined more toward painting and sculpture than architecture, and he enrolled in the Art Students League in New York. He became a draftsman in his father's office after graduation, circa 1911, but soon resigned to work for Hugo Ballin, a muralist and designer for theater and film. Gibbons moved to California shortly after World War I and designed sets for Samuel Goldwyn. He became the first head of MGM's art department when the studio was formed in 1924, a position he held until retirement in 1956. He died four years later.

As an executive of the world's largest film studio, Gibbons was a prominent figure on the Los Angeles social and cultural scene. The designer of the "Oscar" statuette, he cut a striking figure and lived as lavishly as any Hollywood star. He would drive to the studio in his gleaming white Duesenberg, wearing a fresh pair of white gloves (which, some reported, stayed on for much of the day). Los Angeles's lack of cultural inhibitions encouraged Gibbons to be daringly inventive, just as it had Richard Neutra and Rudolph Schindler. Armed with a propaganda organization the like of which no architect could ever call into service, Gibbons viewed himself not as a slavish imitator of his more exalted brethren, with whom he exhibited designs in Los Angeles, but as an equal partner in the promulgation of modern architecture in the United States. Writing about set design in the *Encyclopaedia Britannica,* Gibbons urged that movie decor move beyond the commercial framework of the popular cinema: "If realism can be abandoned," he stated, "we may look for a setting which in itself will be as completely modern as is modern painting or sculpture."[17]

If Gibbons's actual design input at MGM has often been open to speculation, his ability to shape a distinct studio style and to assemble the best design talent available for MGM is uncontested. During the years around 1930, the studio's cadre of top designers was at its peak and included Van Nest Polglase; Mitchell Leisen, then costumist and set designer for De Mille, among others; and Merrill Pye, furniture designer and architect.

The outstanding member of Gibbons's team was Richard Day, born in Canada in 1896. Although his father was an architect, Day, like Gibbons, received no formal education in the profession; in fact, he was largely self-taught. Day began his half-century career by designing for director Erich von Stroheim at MGM in the early 1920s, and spent a total of seven years at the studio. In *The Art of Hollywood,*[18] John Hambley and Patrick Downing credit Day with designing at least forty-eight films during this period, including *Our Dancing Daughters* (1928), one of Hollywood's first films to show the influence of the Paris exposition of 1925. In 1930, secure in his reputation but dissatisfied with designing in Gibbons's shadow, Day moved to the Samuel Goldwyn studios. Over the next eight years, until he became the supervisory head of the

art department at 20th Century–Fox, he would design superior examples of cinematic modern architecture, most notably the multifunctional skyscraper in *Palmy Days* (1931; see page 77), the research institute in *Arrowsmith* (1931), and the automobile factory in *Dodsworth* (1936; see page 130).

From the time of their earliest projects, Gibbons and his "architecture and engineering department," as he preferred to call it, displayed an exceptional talent for creating modern movie decor. Their preoccupation with geometric form and movement within a set was fully evident in the Art Deco designs for *Our Modern Maidens* (1929), the middle film of MGM's trilogy about "youth, mad, pulsating, intoxicated with reckless abandon"[19] that began with *Our Dancing Daughters* in 1928 and ended with *Our Blushing Brides* in 1930. In the living room of *Our Modern Maidens* (Illus. 89) huge arched openings trimmed with serrated moldings suggest the moving gears of an immense machine. The most extravagant element in the room is the faceted staircase that spirals around the fireplace and leads to a circular balcony supported by a giant serrated bracket. Although it is a much larger and baroque treatment of the subject, the MGM stair resembles a number of Le Corbusier's designs during the same period: Consider the roof-garden stair for the Paris apartment of Charles de Beistegui (1930).

An unusual and glamorous product of the studio's Art Deco phase was Richard Day's monumental dining table (Illus. 90), a trademark of MGM's decor around 1930, and one that appeared in many of its films. Designed in a style that updated classicism with "machined" finishes, Day's table features a pair of white triglyphs extracted from their typical context in a Doric frieze, which gives vertical emphasis to its stocky black piers. Flouting the classical precedent of having deep lintels borne on slender posts, the ta-

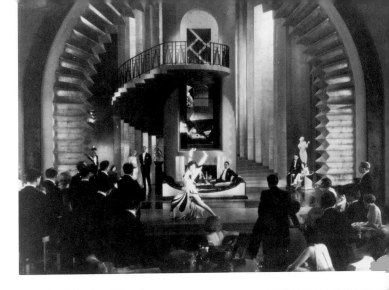

ble's wide piers support only the thinnest sheet of highly polished glass, itself almost dematerialized into a blaze of light by hidden sources of illumination.

Shortly after the release of *Our Dancing Daughters,* Cedric Gibbons began to design his own house in Santa Monica Canyon, into which he later moved with his wife, the film star Dolores del Rio. Created in collaboration with Douglas Honnold, a local architect working at MGM, the Gibbons home on Kingman Avenue has the forbidding aspect of a soundstage: An almost windowless facade opens through a solid gun-metal gray door to an interior of fantasy and theatricality. In surprising contrast to the opaque front facade, the rear one, which is visible as one enters, is constructed entirely of glass and affords a view of the garden's lush landscaping, pool, and tennis court. Running along this glass wall is a gently rising stairway that leads up to the house's main public spaces: a twenty-five-foot-wide by forty-five-foot-long room which Gibbons furnished with freestanding curvilinear bookcases and sofas swirling off an enormous fireplace made of black terrazzo and silver nickel (Illus. 91). To this magnificently proportioned space Gibbons added two whimsical details: water sprinklers on the copper roof above to create the sound of rain, and a recessed light projector to cast the illusion of moonlight on a wall opposite.

However fanciful, the house is far more than merely a cinematic folly. So successful

89. (TOP) *Our Modern Maidens* (1929, Jack Conway). Supervisory Art Director: Cedric Gibbons; Unit Art Director: Merrill Pye.
90. (MIDDLE) Greta Garbo and Anders Randolf in *The Kiss* (1929, Jacques Feyder). Supervisory Art Director: Cedric Gibbons; Unit Art Director: Richard Day.
91. (BOTTOM) Dolores Del Rio and Cedric Gibbons in their residence, Los Angeles, circa 1930.

is the modernist sense of space displayed in its layout that it flatly belies the characterization of Gibbons as a purely supervisory art director with more ability to spot talent than talent itself. A particularly telling example of Gibbons's skill, reminiscent of Le Corbusier's *promenades architecturales,* is the ascent from the entrance foyer up to the living room, a stairway filled with shifting views of the interior and exterior, which culminates in a vista of the distant horizon of the Pacific Ocean. Another unusual feature is Gibbons's use of lustrous materials and indirect lighting to allow the house's setback forms to sensuously shape and define interior space.

The Gibbons house demands our attention not only as a testament to the designer's gifts, however, for in its conflation of styles it serves as a bridge between two phases of the history of modern decor at MGM. While on one hand the house is a résumé of the decorative Art Deco sets of the late 1920s, like those for *Our Modern Maidens,* on the other hand it also anticipates the series of spatially innovative sets that would become the distinctive element of the studio's style during its peak years from the early to mid 1930s.

MGM's use of open planning in these designs look back to the great American master architect, Frank Lloyd Wright, who had decisively expanded interior space beyond the confined residential block with his Prairie Houses in the Midwest early in the century. The Robie House (Illus. 92) of 1908 is the masterpiece of this phase of Wright's long career. Built for a twenty-seven-year-old bicycle manufacturer, the house stands on a small corner lot some eight miles south of Chicago's business district. *Stands,* though, is hardly a worthy description for Wright's radical plan for a grouping of long and low horizontal walls, terraces, and roofs that appear to float by one another freely and asymmetrically, anchored to the ground by

only the strong vertical fireplace block. The exterior plan is also reflected in the interior, which contains one of the most remarkable spaces in modern architecture. On the upper floor, one rectangular volume housing the private functions of kitchen and servants' quarters is staggered against the public sector of living and dining rooms. Not only does the occupant have a sense of free and easy movement from the living and dining rooms around the fireplace and stair, he also experiences a vivid impression of being led outward, an illusion heightened by the thrust of the broad roof eaves which extend the room's ceiling plane through the glass doors and onto the terrace.

Shortly after the completion of the Robie House, the European publisher Wasmuth began issuing volumes of Wright's designs executed in simple, powerful drawings. The range, inventiveness, and rich detail shown in these works, which had been created by an architect only in his forties—traditionally considered to be the time an architect *begins* the most fruitful phase of his career—were astonishing, and their impact on European modernists was profound.

Wright's influence was especially strong on the Dutch avant-garde painters, architects, and sculptors known collectively as the De Stijl group, which included the painter Piet Mondrian. While the De Stijl architects adopted the spirit of Wright's formal and spatial concepts, they substituted for his traditional building materials—wood, stone, and brick—ones that they felt more suitably conveyed the precision and high finish of the machine—smooth stucco, steel, glass in metal frames. Architect and furniture-maker Gerrit Rietveld's 1923 Utrecht house for Mrs. Truus Schröder-Schrader (Illus. 93) retained the Wrightian concept of open planning in its asymmetrical, interlocking spaces and hovering horizontal planes, but cast them in a more cubic form and clad them in "machined" materials and primary colors. Although its almost violent juxtapositions of geometric shapes was an exaggeration in comparison to the more contained volumes of later modern works, the Reitveld house was the archetype for a style employed during subsequent years in both building and set design.

In *The Easiest Way* (1931), for example, MGM designers created a fully realized illustration of these formal and spatial concepts. Like the Schröder-Schrader House, MGM's office for *The Easiest Way* (Illus. 94) is a dynamic composition of masses and planes floating independently of one another, apparently suspended in space. Both Rietveld and MGM rejected traditional modes of construction: Instead of expressing their usual function as load-bearing and support elements, the beams, columns, and wall piers seem to defy gravity. Corners, which normally provide structural rigidity, are replaced by non-load-bearing glass walls. In the film design, the glass corner expands from the perimeter of the room, as it had in the glass-enclosed, circular stair towers at Walter Gropius's and Adolf Meyer's model factory at the 1914 Deutscher Werkbund exhibition in Cologne. The asymmetrical pattern of the mullions suggests Gibbons's familiarity with Rudolph Schindler's Howe House.

The same year that *The Easiest Way* was released, MGM also produced a vehicle for Greta Garbo, Robert Z. Leonard's *Susan Lenox: Her Fall and Rise,* which featured the studio's best modern design of the decade. During the late 1920s and '30s, the screen persona of Garbo had been developed by MGM into that of a modern, intelligent, and often free-spirited woman who flouted the accepted conventions of society—at least until the last reel, when the mandatory moralistic ending demanded either her reformation through marriage or retribution through death. Her films' designers had selected Art Deco decor and furnishings to es-

92. (TOP) Robie House, Chicago (1908, Frank Lloyd Wright).
93. (BOTTOM) Schröder-Schrader House, Utrecht (1923, Gerrit Rietveld).

tablish the sophisticated, affluent milieus of Diana Merrick, Garbo's wanton millionairess in *A Woman of Affairs* (1928); of Arden Stuart, torn between the bliss of a family and the passion of an affair in *The Single Standard* (1929); and of Irene Guarry in *The*

94. Constance Bennett and Adolphe Menjou in *The Easiest Way* (1931, Jack Conway). Supervisory Art Director: Cedric Gibbons.

Kiss (1929), who was extricated from a love-less marriage by murder. By the time of *Susan Lenox,* these more decorative settings had given way to the cleaner, starker style of the modernists, which provided Garbo with her most striking backdrops.

Susan Lenox opens with Rodney Spencer (Clark Gable) saving Susan from being virtually sold into marriage by a heartless uncle, and ends with his shunning her be-

cause of his mistaken belief that she has become the mistress of a circus promoter. Years pass. In part two—the "Fall" of the title—Garbo has become the fallen woman she had been wrongly accused of being, the mistress of a wealthy but shady politician. One evening, Rodney attends a party at Susan's ultramodern penthouse, during which she realizes that she still loves him. She repents her wanton ways and, in part three, follows Rodney to the jungle, where they are reunited and live happily, if poorly, ever after.

Bracketed between the earthbound decor of the outer segments, Susan Lenox's lofty penthouse was clearly gained at the expense of her morality—a sacrifice that nonetheless allows her to live at the height of material luxury. American audiences of the Depression, inculcated with a Puritan ethos of "forbidden fruit is always sweetest," probably viewed the trade as a good one.

Susan Lenox's was one of a growing number of penthouses appearing in movies made around 1930, paralleling the construction of a group of luxurious residential towers in Manhattan which captured the public's imagination with the allure of high-rise living. Because of new building methods, large areas of glass windows could be wrapped around a structure's exterior corners, affording spectacular skyscraper-filled views from many apartments, as, for example, in the Majestic of 1931. Susan Lenox's apartment not only exaggerates this innovation to remarkable proportions, but also brilliantly blends four modern architectural elements that surface in various settings—nightclubs, hotels, and residences—in MGM films throughout the late 1920s and early 1930s: a white fireplace block of setback faceting (here, fronted by andirons in the shape of modernistic skyscrapers); a glass wall subdivided into horizontal panes by thin mullions; broad, stepped platforms; and a giant version of a circular ceiling beam. These features are unified along a diagonal axis that originates at the center of a circular, glass-enclosed foyer, its dropped ceiling beam washed with indirect lighting (Illus. 95).

In the beautifully fluid sequence that introduces the apartment, cinematographer William Daniels's camera glides along this diagonal axis and draws the viewer gracefully through the semicircular glass wall of the foyer, into the living room. After traveling for some distance, the camera finally stops with a gently curving motion, bringing into view the entrance of Garbo from the terrace, beyond which lies infinite space, an illusion created by the lights of distant skyscrapers on the horizon.

For the sequence that takes place in the apartment, lighting, materials, and finishes are carefully chosen to indicate unequivocally the luxury of the setting. Metallic finishes dominate: the black-and-silver facets of the piano, the satiny sofa in an indirectly lit niche of mirrors, and the metal-and-glass curtain wall softened only by vertical panels of sheer draperies. Even Garbo herself (Illus. 96) is brought into the harmony of the decor, her every move made incandescent by the myriad reflections of her silvery dress, while the curving lines of a metal tubular chair (reminiscent of Mies's MR chair) trace her seductively languid contours. (Two decades later, Judy Garland would pay similar homage to Mies's Barcelona chair when in *A Star Is Born* (1954) she removed its back cushion and played its leather straps like the strings of a harp.) Rarely have fashion, architecture, and star persona been combined into so crystalline an image.

In addition to its purely decorative function, the set for Susan's apartment was used in a novel way as a framing element that could, in effect, change the parameters of the available screen space. The filmic space of typical feature films of the periods was of a squarish proportion—1.33 : 1, or an image one and a third times as wide as it was high. By the deployment of devices such as dropped beams and ceilings, however, set designers were able to "block out" a section of the screen, reshaping it to the even more horizontal proportions that are a hallmark of modern architecture. In the foyer of the Garbo penthouse, a dropped beam occupies the top portion of the screen image, which

95. *Susan Lenox: Her Fall and Rise* (1931, Robert Z. Leonard). Supervisory Art Director: Cedric Gibbons.

consequently brings the background into prominence and increases the depth of field.

Another excellent product of the MGM design department during these years was the Manhattan apartment Gibbons created for the American secretary of state in *Men Must Fight,* a 1933 film concerning the outbreak of a world war in 1940. The wealth and social prominence of the character are immediately discernible from the huge scale of the apartment's living room (Illus. 97, 98). A glass wall to the right of the set leads to a terrace overlooking the street; the apartment's residents enjoy a rooftop terrace as

well. The room's three functional areas— entrance hall, living room, and library— flow in one spatial continuum and are all visible in a single shot. Bedrooms and a study open directly from the living room, without unnecessary linking corridors. A curving built-in unit combining a sofa, bookshelves, and a set-back radio cabinet distinguishes the living room from the library. Freestanding furniture also defines space: Seating groups of modernistic furniture are placed informally throughout the room, while a central ensemble stands on an area rug. The focus of the set, however, is its semicircular, glass-enclosed entrance hall. Having drawn the viewer through the room along a horizontal axis, Gibbons proceeds to redirect the emphasis along a vertical one, defined by a round elevator shaft that is surrounded by a broad spiral staircase. Unlike the staccato movement suggested in the design for the stair of *Our Modern Maidens*, the stairway in *Men Must Fight* sweeps smoothly upward, stressed by continuous spandrels decorated with three chrome moldings.

In the mid-1930s, Frank Lloyd Wright introduced a number of new concepts in open planning. One such scheme opened the building up to a spiraling flow of space, which might be described as a corkscrewing of the structure upward. Developed by Wright as early as the 1925 Sugarloaf Mountain project for Maryland, the spiral motif became increasingly important in his buildings of the 1930s, reaching its culmination in the Morris Gift Shop in San Francisco in the late 1940s and in New York's Guggenheim Museum, completed in 1959, the year of Wright's death.

Alden B. Dow, a disciple of Wright, applied the spiral planning scheme to a domestic context in his John S. Whitman House (1934) in Midland, Michigan, which later inspired a cinematic equivalent in Gibbons's San Francisco house design for the 1936 film *After the Thin Man* (Illus. 99). This modern residence was an ideal setting for the free-spirited personalities of its inhabitants, the sophisticated detective team of Nick and Nora Charles. In contrast to Nora's upper-crust family, with their moribund propriety in a Victorian mansion, the Charleses were progressive and up-to-date, enjoying all-night parties; risqué, pleasure-seeking friends; and the challenges of their unusual occupation as dilettante sleuths.

Both Dow and Gibbons used the open plan vertically as well as horizontally, with intermediate levels connected to the first and second floors by means of double-height halls. In Dow's residence for Whitman, the intermediate level, which contains the sitting room and sun deck, is a separate adjunct space located off the stair's landing. In Gibbons's design for the Charleses, the intermediate level is integrated more fully into the planning scheme of the house. Not only

96. Greta Garbo in *Susan Lenox: Her Fall and Rise* (1931).

97. *Men Must Fight* (1933, Edgar Selwyn). Supervisory Art Director: Cedric Gibbons.

does it function as the entrance hall, it is also a sitting room and connecting landing: one half-level up is a balcony doubling as a library, from which doors lead to bedrooms; one half-level down is the living room. The flow of the *Thin Man* house's spiraling continuum is accentuated by curved enclosing walls, reminiscent of those in Wright's S. C. Johnson and Son Administration Building —a departure from Gibbons's earlier practice of using the interpenetration of trans-

parent and opaque planes to define space, as he had done, for example, in the residence for the 1931 film *Susan Lenox: Her Fall and Rise.*

Under Gibbons's leadership, MGM's sets were the premier showpieces of 1930s films, its designers versatile enough to work in a broad range of contexts, extending from the hard-edged luxury of penthouses for Garbo to the comfortable warmth of the *Thin Man* home. MGM's success ultimately lay in its

98. *Men Must Fight* (1933).

99. *After the Thin Man* (1936, W. S. Van Dyke). Supervisory Art Director: Cedric Gibbons.

ability to combine the elegant architectural sensibility of Paramount with the energetic decorative qualities of RKO. The perfect balance it achieved between the two has left us the most valuable design legacy of any Hollywood studio.

Although MGM, Paramount, and RKO were the only three Hollywood studios to create a large and significant body of modern film work, designers at other studios did use modern decor as well. If these designs tended to be isolated examples and limited in their scope, they were nonetheless often of top quality.

Universal, which produced during the 1930s such now classic horror films as *Dracula* (1931), *Frankenstein* (1932), and *The Mummy* (1932), released in 1934 *The Black Cat,* perhaps the decade's most unusual and eccentric horror feature. Not only were its sensibilities far removed from the standard monster formula of the period, but its decor replaced standard Expressionist ingredients —the creaking doors and dark brooding shadows that were de rigueur for the genre —with modernism.

Charles D. Hall, *The Black Cat*'s designer, and Edgar G. Ulmer, its writer and director, share the credit for this architectural tour de force. Like so many of the film specialists who created excellent modern decor, Hall and Ulmer could claim only tangential connections to professional architectural practice. Hall, who was born in England in 1890, studied at an art school and worked during his teens in an architectural office. Although he created superb Expressionist decor for Universal's shockers like *Frankenstein* and *Dracula* and distinguished himself in modern film decor as well, most notably the office in William Wyler's *Counsellor-at-Law* (1933) and the factory in Chaplin's *Modern Times* (1936), it is Ulmer who deserves the lion's share of the responsibility for the design of the villa of *The Black Cat*'s mad architect, Dr. Kjalmar Poelzig. (The name, in fact, was Ulmer's homage to the German architect Hans Poelzig.) Ulmer's unexpected use of modern design for a horror film is just the sort of idiosyncratic, almost surreal touch that distinguishes the work of this remarkable director. Born in Vienna in 1904, Ulmer came from a background in the theater, having designed for the Berlin impresario Max Reinhardt while still in his teens. It was during his tenure as a designer at UFA in the 1920s, though, that he developed a facility for modern architecture. This experience provided the inspiration for *The Black Cat*'s designs, as Ulmer revealed in an interview with Peter Bogdanovich, when he characterized the film as "very, very much out of my Bauhaus period."[20]

The very high level of conceptual detail in the decor of *The Black Cat,* remarkable in so ephemeral a construction as a film set, would be noteworthy in the context of an actual building. Each of the set's individual rooms exhibits an impressive formal and spatial complexity. The bedrooms, for example, are vertically divided by cantilevered projections supported along one wall by freestanding, wedge-shaped piers. Every room is sparsely furnished with chrome tubular chairs polished to a high sheen. Luminous walls and ceilings, light fixtures, sliding doors, and digital clocks are among the electrically driven devices that serve the inhabitants of this elegant Corbusian *machine à habiter.*

Artificial illumination also serves as a visual leitmotif throughout the film, suggesting the shifting mood of scenes on a much more subtle and poetic level than the film's insistent pop-classic musical score. The viewer's first glimpse of Poelzig—played with chilling detachment by Boris Karloff—is especially ominous as the architect slowly rises from his bed to an upright position, silhouetted against a luminous, gauzy backdrop. Backlit walls form, in fact, a major component in the decor and are often devised with great inventiveness. The luminous two-story wall in the central hall, for example, is actually an illusion: Although its surface appears to be formed of a square egg-crate grid of thin fins infilled with frosted glass, the wall is actually a flat assemblage of panels painted with trompe l'oeil fins and shadows (Illus. 100).

This wall plays a central role in the film's introduction of the house, when four stranded people, including an American newlywed couple, seek refuge after an accident on a rainy night. The scene opens with the sound of a doorbell and the sight of the villa's completely dark living room being slowly illuminated. Almost immediately, the camera of cinematographer John Mescall begins its passage toward the main door, gliding from the living room across the central hall to the entrance vestibule. The sequence is structured as a series of cadences: Traveling transversely across the screen, the camera records not only the changing height of each space, but also each subsequent area's gradual illumination as it enters in view: the living room via its hidden diffused lighting, the two-story wall of glass in the central hall via its interior lighting, the vestibule via its luminous ceiling. In this scene, artificial illumination, open planning, and mobile cinematography combine to transform the stranded couple–haunted house cliché into one of the most memorable sequences in the history of the cinema.

No examination of Hollywood modernist design would be complete without a discussion of Lyle Wheeler and Anton Grot. Wheeler is an architect, illustrator, and industrial designer. His work for David O. Selznick in the late 1930s established his reputation in film, particularly his designs for William Wellman's *A Star Is Born* (1937), Selznick's third feature as an independent producer and still one of the outstanding films Hollywood has made about itself. Wheeler's decor for movie producer Oliver Niles's studio commissary borrows its imagery from an ocean liner. Walls of freestanding round columns glazed with long, horizontal panes in red mullions divide the main room from dining "promenades." Horizontal blinds diffuse the light that enters through overscaled portholes. Pendant light fixtures made of silver disks complete the ensemble. In other of the forty-two sets Wheeler prepared for the film, light shining from recessed fixtures and through glass bricks brings life to the warm tones of wood and stone walls. Wheeler's design is important in marking the first time that these materials were used for a contemporary set in a color film (*A Star Is Born* was one of the first feature-length Technicolor films in the improved three-strip process).

The following year, Wheeler's nightclub for *The Young in Heart* (1938; Illus. 101), Selznick's screwball comedy about a family of con artists, showed how much richness film set designers were able to achieve within the confines of a monochromatic palette by using a variety of reflective surfaces. Symmetrical piers of backlit glass bricks

provide a sharp contrast to a pair of highly polished jet-black antelopes. Although the room's only visible source of illumination is the glass-brick piers and a single recessed fixture in the canopy, the decor fosters an effect of abundant light, which glows brightly in the metal frames of the chairs. A wall mural divided into square panels continues the space's theme of rigorous geometric clarity at the same time that its chiaroscuro rendering of lush jungle motifs serves as a tempering foil to the club's otherwise ultramodern vocabulary.

A background that included studies in art, illustration, and interior design before he emigrated from Europe to the United States in 1909 only partially accounts for Anton Grot's virtuosity. As with so many of his colleagues, designing for film itself seems to have tapped a latent architectural sensibility. As a top designer at Warner Bros. from 1927 until his retirement in 1948, Grot created superb designs for the studio's genre specialties: gangster films such as Mervyn Le Roy's *Little Caesar* (1930), Busby Berkeley musicals (see page 152 for a discussion of *Gold Diggers of 1935*), and swashbuckler epics like Michael Curtiz's *Private Lives of Elizabeth and Essex* (1939). For Warners' historical films of the 1930s, the studio's style, largely the brilliant creation of Grot himself, leaned toward a highly stylized Expressionism with dazzling foreshortened perspective and chiaroscuro; sometimes Grot used painted shadows for an effect even more artificial and shocking. But since Warners set many of its films of the 1930s in a contemporary working-class milieu, modern decor, perhaps perceived as having unsuitable conno-

100. (OPPOSITE TOP) Bela Lugosi in *The Black Cat* (1934, Edgar G. Ulmer). Art Director: Charles D. Hall.
101. (OPPOSITE BOTTOM) *The Young in Heart* (1938, Richard Wallace). Art Director: Lyle Wheeler.

tations of chic sophistication, was passed over in favor of more ordinary, realistic architecture. Grot's extensive sketch collection, however, clearly indicates what he could have achieved had he been given the opportunities of a designer at a studio like Paramount or MGM, and his drawings of nightclubs and residences for a number of unidentified films, most probably of a 1930s vintage, reveal a gift for the spatial dynamics of modern architecture.

One cafeteria sketch (Illus. 102) of Grot's is an excellent realization of De Stijl aesthetics, especially as defined by painter-sculptor-architect Theo van Doesburg, whose program for the modern house called for it to give "the impression of being suspended in space, of being opposed to natural gravity."[21] Grot exaggerates the illusion of his design's floating planes swooping over the viewer's head like the wings of low-flying aircraft by the manipulation of ground-level vantage points and foreshortened perspective lines.

A second Grot sketch, for a residence (Illus. 103) rendered in champagne, lemon, and white, transforms the rectilinear geometry of his cafeteria design into a curvilinear one, with no loss of spatial richness or vitality. Sheer draperies follow the line of a soffit and frame a curving, double-height living room. Space flows horizontally through broad openings and balconies, unimpeded by the room's sparse but elegant low-slung furnishings.

While the art departments at Paramount, RKO, and MGM were producing a large body of modern set decor, highly individual designers at studios that never developed a distinct modern idiom were inspired to create exceptional work—even, in some cases, sketches for sets that might never be realized. Cinematic anomalies like *The Black Cat,* and the isolated examples of Wheeler and Grot, attest to the compelling attraction of modernism in the 1930s, even outside the

fertile collaborative centers of modern film decor in Hollywood.

By the opening of the 1939 New York World's Fair and on the eve of World War II, modern film decor had virtually disappeared from the repertoire of film set designers around the world. One explanation for the decline is probably nothing more complicated than the vagaries of fashion: Modernism, having become popular among film designers because it was novel, would fall victim to the same impetus to change that had sparked it. Equally important was the turn toward greater realism, a conservative direction taken by many of the arts after the accentuation of abstraction during the 1920s. The attempt to record reality refuted the premium that film designers had placed on originality, artifice, and stylization, all necessary conditions for the adaptation of a style as new as modernism. And finally, the fragmentation of the modern movement itself had its effect. When it presented moviemakers with an easily defined and recognizable style, modernism could be readily adapted; as it became less focused, it became less discernible to set designers, who relied almost solely upon the examples they saw in magazines and books.

In France, the scene of much pioneering film decor produced in the 1920s, filmmakers no longer pursued original modern design for their work. Marcel L'Herbier's sound films, such as *Le Parfum de la Dame en Noir* (1931) and *Le Bonheur* (1935), lack the visual excitement of many of their silent predecessors and suffer from the blandest decor, mainly a mediocre Art Deco. One reason innovation declined is perhaps the economic and technical restraints imposed on L'Herbier during the French cinema's difficult transition to sound, for which it was ill-prepared. L'Herbier's *Le Vertige* (1926) had featured what proved to be the last modern set of Mallet-Stevens, whose in-

102. Drawing of a cafeteria for an unidentified film. Delineator: Anton Grot.

103. Drawing of a living room for an unidentified film. Delineator: Anton Grot.

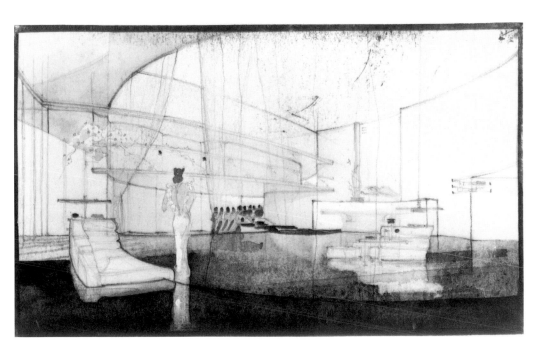

terest in film did not resurface until the 1937 International Exposition in Paris, where nighttime film projections illuminated the enormous curving facade of his Electricity Pavilion. In this, his last important building, Mallet-Stevens strikingly reaffirmed his commitment to the cinema and reminded his countrymen of his responsibility for its heady successes of the 1920s.

After Meerson's sets for *A Nous la Liberté,* his best in the modern idiom, the quality of his modern decor also waned. His "poetic realist" style, already evident in films of the early '30s like Clair's *Sous les Toits de Paris,* dominated his efforts of the middle of the decade. In *Le Grand Jeu* (1934) and *La Kermesse héroïque* (1935), both for Feyder, Meerson carefully chose realistic details that evoked specific locales, eras, and characters, and wove these random elements together into brilliant abstract compositions, displaying the rigorous sense of form that was the modernist legacy to his later films.

In Germany, the decline of modern film decor coincided with the rise of the Nazis. On its coming to power in January of 1933, the Nazi government and the state-sanctioned architects who would rise to prominence during its twelve-year reign dismissed the modern movement, in part as a result of its socialist leanings, but also because its internationalist ideology rankled their strong Germanic nationalism. In April 1933, the Nazis forced the closing of the Bauhaus, which was then located in Berlin under the directorship of Mies. Throughout the decade, most of Germany's best modernists would emigrate, many eventually settling in the United States: Erich Mendelsohn in 1933, Gropius in 1934, Mies in 1938. With modernism absent from the German architectural scene (except in the designs of industrial buildings), a native cottage style achieved new prominence for residential construction, while government buildings adopted an elephantine neo-classicism.

The Nazis' anti-Semitism, right-wing politics, and anti-intellectualism also drove out many of Germany's best film directors, of whom Fritz Lang was among the most prominent. Although the Third Reich's propaganda minister, Goebbels, met with Lang to offer him the highest position in the German film industry (largely because of Hitler's great admiration for the grandiosity of *Metropolis*), the director left Germany within hours of their meeting. He first fled to France, but shortly afterward moved to Hollywood, where he made a number of films over the next twenty years, though none in the modernist vein. Lang's designers —Hasler, Kettelhut, and Hunte—produced little notable work in the 1930s. Although Hasler's decor for *Winternachtstraum* (1935) was a continuation of the functionalist modern he had employed in his films for Lang, it no longer contained Lang's brilliant abstract compositions that had enlivened the earlier sets. The only outstanding exception to the inferior output of this group was Hunte's fabulous atomic reactor for the science fiction epic *Gold* (1934), though even this design was impressive more as a representative of technological gadgetry than of modern architecture.

In Italy, the increasing popularity of neo-classical decor in the cinema of the late 1930s paralleled the direction Italian architecture had been taking in the course of the decade. Consider the specific case of two large-scale projects by the architects Luigi Figini and Gino Pollini. The Palazzo Littorio Competition (1933), which was designed by them in collaboration with Luigi Danusso and the architectural firm BBPR, was a fine example of modernist design; in contrast, their competition entry for the Square of the Fighting Services and Its Edifices (1938) for the 1942 Universal Exposition in Rome was all neo-classical bombast, a veritable movie set of grand stairways, heroic statuary, and theatrically rendered skies.

The career of Guido Fiorini repeats this pattern in the context of film design. Fiorini's "Tensistruttura," a construction system for multistory buildings with floors suspended by cables from a central core, so fascinated Le Corbusier and Pierre Jeanneret that they experimented with it for their own large-scale proposals for Algiers in the early 1930s. From 1933, however, Fiorini devoted himself largely to the cinema as a professor at Rome's famous film school, Centro Sperimentale di Cinematografia, and as a set designer, most notably for grand historical spectacles. By the late 1930s, even sets that would have called for modern decor only a few years earlier were given by Fiorini a historical flavor: His neo-classical department store interior for *I Grandi Magazzini* (1939; Illus. 104), for example, features classical columns and entablatures.

Finally, in the United States, Hollywood's film designers, likewise responding to the trend toward realism, began to choose less and less adventurous plans for film decor. Cedric Gibbons's work for MGM during this period was typical of the style other Hollywood studios were producing. By the mid-1930s, Gibbons had diluted his modern film designs with mannered reworkings of classical elements. In the bedroom of *Manproof* (1938; Illus. 105), wide, flat pilasters frame an entrance door crowned with a broken pediment and decorated with bold triangular facets. A lone keystone floats below a hemispherical niche. Overscaled panels travel along the lower portion of the walls, while thin strips carry around the top. *Manproof*'s sets signaled a reversion to established and familiar devices: More symmetrical planning schemes returned; space was shaped by the enclosure of walls rather than by the interpenetration of transparent and opaque planes; and sleek, machine-made materials and glass walls gave way to wood, stone, textured wallpapers, and wall-to-wall carpeting. Upholstered chairs and sofas in

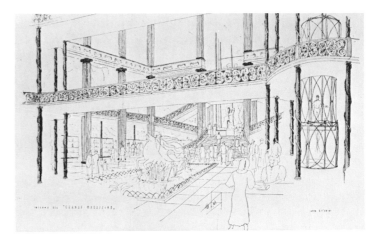

104. (TOP) Drawing of a department store for *I Grandi Magazzini* (1939, Mario Camerini). Delineator: Guido Fiorini.
105. (BOTTOM) *Manproof* (1938, Richard Thorpe). Supervisory Art Director: Cedric Gibbons.

traditional fabrics took the place of tubular furniture, now banished to the kitchen. Even at Paramount, the studio most influenced by Bauhaus modernism, Dreier and Robert Usher designed a Paris apartment for a wealthy American, played by Gary Cooper, in Lubitsch's *Bluebeard's Eighth Wife* (1938) that merged a modern vocabulary with a stripped classicism of columns and moldings. (For a discussion of a similar development at RKO, see page 152.)

Two design trends moved Hollywood in this direction. The reemergence of Frank Lloyd Wright shifted interest to traditional building materials that created a warmer, more natural look. Second was the resurgence of colonial revival architecture, which had appeared in the 1920s but was more widely popularized after 1932 and the reconstruction of Williamsburg, Virginia. Nurtured throughout the decade by Depression-era America's yearning to return to an agrarian past, the colonial revival also expressed the country's growing awareness of and confidence in its architectural heritage.

Until his retirement in the 1950s, Gibbons would continue to select decor that remained safely between the two modes of colonial revivalism and "warm" modernism. Gibbons's updated colonial designs suited MGM's view of itself as a bastion of traditional American values, a view that had emerged during the mid-1930s. These new sets received prominent coverage in interior decoration magazines, in contrast to Hollywood's previous—and ironically better—designs, which the magazines now criticized as too fanciful and extravagant.

In retrospect, the history of modern architectural decor in Hollywood, and especially at MGM, can be regarded as having followed a path similar to that of the history of modern architecture in America, if lagging a few years behind it. A brilliant period of experimentation in the early 1930s capped a period of discovery in the 1920s. After the comfortable successes of the mid-1930s, however, modernism virtually disappeared from the American screen, and Hollywood's decade of high style, and the period of its greatest achievements in set decor, came to a close.

Although the decline of modern architectural film decor in the late 1930s may have been the result of changing fashion, the shift toward greater realism, and the fragmentation of the modern movement, another reason may be suggested. During the late 1920s and the 1930s, moviemakers had ascribed connotations to modern architecture that were both positive and negative, alluring and frightening. As the 1930s drew to a close, the more negative connotations came to the fore, and modernism was largely discredited in the eyes of moviegoers. The mystique that modern architecture found at the movies, then lost at the end of the 1930s, is the subject of the following chapters.

CHAPTER 5
The Modern Mystique

As with so many radically new visions in the arts, modern architecture was initially received by the public rather less than enthusiastically. The stark, severe lines of the modern building impressed many as being sterile and discomforting, and too close a fulfillment of the functional efficiency foreseen by Aldous Huxley's *Brave New World* to be a welcome development. An article in a 1938 issue of *California Arts and Architecture* magazine, for example, summarized public sentiments succinctly when it described Cedric Gibbons as "an architect of advanced Functional persuasion"[1]—as if he had reached an unfortunate stage in an illness or allied himself with a political party of suspect leanings.

What was objectionable at the center of one's city, however, often carried a different connotation within the context of the cinema. As many examples of films discussed thus far have suggested, when modern architecture appeared in the movies it acquired connotations that, whether positive or negative, were usually far removed from what its creators intended. If modern pioneers hoped that their architecture would be viewed in social terms, as a humanist discipline and as a vanguard force in the struggle for an egalitarian society, filmmakers were understandably more inclined to focus on its external aspects, its aesthetic value in set design. While the political content of modernism's leanings had been largely ignored during its adaptation to European films in the 1920s, the sea change the movement underwent in its emigration to Hollywood circa 1930 redefined it even more dramatically.

Although the films of the late 1920s and the '30s generally used modern architectural decor to imply progressive or at least forward-looking values in the characters or themes of the film in which it appeared, the connotations attached to modernism were contradictory. On one hand, modern design was the province of newly acquired affluence, the inevitable setting—in penthouses, executive offices, or nightclubs—for well-to-do characters, or characters in disguise aspiring to that state. For these fortunate few, modern design and technology were a boon, the means by which they were freed to pursue wordly pleasures, whether on board a luxurious ocean liner, in a private airplane, or in a brilliantly lit interior atop a skyscraper. On the other hand, many films of the period responded to the public's uneasiness with modernism by making it a metaphor for new, and thus possibly threatening, currents in contemporary life. These ranged from the boudoirs of the emasculating "new woman," to the chilling regimentation of the assembly-line factory, to finally the dystopia of the underground city of Lang's *Metropolis,* where human beings have become indistinguishable from robots, the victims of industrialized society.

This chapter will examine the "modern mystique" by offering subjective readings of the different aspects of modern architecture that have thus far been discussed objectively. Whether used in the design of small-scale residential rooms—the kitchen, boudoir, and bathroom—or large-scale public architecture—the office, nightclub, hotel, and ocean liner interior—or the *sine qua non* of modern structures, the skyscraper and the city itself, modern decor had a powerful and long-lasting resonance in the cinema of this period, and how we have come to regard modernism even today has been conditioned, to some degree, by our encounters with it on the screen.

Modernism in the Home

"The problem of the house," Le Corbusier wrote in *Vers une Architecture,* "is a problem of the epoch. The equilibrium of society today depends upon it."[2] During the 1920s, modern European architects concentrated their efforts on the construction and planning of the modern dwelling. But their goal of making the house efficient had, in fact, already been the subject of much investigation. By the middle of the nineteenth century, American women reformers had

undertaken their own efficiency studies to ease the domestic workload of a country without a large servant class. In 1869, for example, Catherine Beecher proposed her American Woman's Home, based on the concept of placing the house's habitable rooms around a central core of stairs, bathrooms, and chimney.[3] (As the historian Reyner Banham has noted, Beecher anticipated the plan of R. Buckminster Fuller's Dymaxion House by almost sixty years.[4]) In the early part of the twentieth century, the rational planning of specific rooms would be addressed through diagrams: In her 1915 book, *Scientific Management in the Home,* Christine Frederick offered her readers a plan for the efficient layout of the kitchen and its appliances.[5]

The modernists' own solution to the problem was through the medium of technology. In *Vers une Architecture,* Le Corbusier followed his proclamation about the problem of the house with a series of residential prototypes, from his 1921 scheme for a multilevel "Citrohan" house, named after the automobile and, as its architect notes, "conceived and carried out like an omnibus or a ship's cabin,"[6] to his 1922 proposal for a housing complex containing one hundred living units. Throughout these designs, the five points of architecture he would codify in 1926 produced rich variations on the modern house, which could be economically mass-produced, were spatially efficient, and imitated products of technology in their sleek and simplified appearance. Through these qualities the modern house would become, in Le Corbusier's famous dictum, "a machine for living."[7]

While modern architects sought to reform the design of the house and progressive reformers worked to make women's lives easier with more efficient and humane settings for their labors, the cinema's response to domestic issues was a highly conservative one, reflecting popular anxieties about the status of women. In part as a result of the sexual freedom of the Flapper Era and the new economic realities of the Depression, when men felt that they had the right to scarce jobs, it was urgent that women be returned to their "proper" domestic roles. That home had to be, as it had always been, the seat of tradition—not an arena of progressive ideas, as modernists and reformers had proposed.

The inappropriateness of modernism in the middle-class home was a subject that found support from filmmakers, even in their writings. In the same 1938 article that described Gibbons's "advanced Functional persuasion," Paramount's Hans Dreier stated that modern architecture has "its place in the world of today, particularly in America. For skyscrapers, broadcasting stations, steamships, factories, warehouses and other structures of an industrial and impersonal nature, having few ties with the past, Contemporary design and materials are indicated. The more functional the better. But in the home, the emotions as well as the intelligence have their place. As an institution it is ageless, and its design should express the many ties and facets of its essentially intimate role in our lives."[8]

The public's sexual conservatism and its distrust of modernism thus joined together in Depression-era films with extremely interesting results. Modern design came to be associated with forces that were threatening domestic security: The technologically advanced kitchen which might free women to pursue activities outside the home was lampooned, while the bedroom and the bathroom became natural backdrops for loose-living women who had turned their backs on homemaking and indulged themselves in a life of pleasure. A look at how these three residential rooms were depicted in the films of the period will therefore reveal how popular culture assimilated a radical architectural vision after it had collided with a conservative social ideology.

KITCHENS In one of the many startling text-and-illustration juxtapositions included in Le Corbusier's *Vers une Architecture*, a chapter on airplanes, illustrated with prominent examples, contains a section entitled "The Manual of the Dwelling," which exhorts the reader to demand hygienic, efficient living quarters. Le Corbusier explains that a discussion of the home is included in a chapter on aircraft because the "lesson of the airplane lies in the logic which governed the statement of the problem and its realization":[9] This same process of analysis should therefore be applied to the design of a home as well. Furthermore, as a "machine for living," the twentieth-century home should take as an ideal model for its appearance the polished look of airplanes, automobiles, and ocean liners.

As the setting for most of the new mechanization of the home, the kitchen gained considerable attention from modern architects, who saw the laboratory as its perfect analogue. In the Frankfurter Küche (Illus. 106) designed by Grette Schütte-Lihotzky, the kitchen is conceived as the control center for the modern house and the housewife as its master technician, prepared to control the family functions of food preparation, cooking, and household cleaning with ease.

In contrast to modern architects' attempts to style the kitchen in the sleek machine imagery that they considered an expression of the room's technological functions, moviemakers often turned the kitchen-as-laboratory into a source of comedy or parody. In director Preston Sturges's *Sullivan's Travels* (1941), the streamlined kitchen of the house trailer is the scene for slapstick disaster. In the mid-1930s, one of the most beautifully designed examples of a modern kitchen appeared in *Sailing Along* (1938), a British musical comedy starring Jessie Matthews, with decor by German-born émigré Alfred Junge. Tradition-respecting Britons had already taken particular pleasure in satirizing

106. (LEFT) Frankfurter Küche, Frankfurt (1926, Grette Schütte-Lihotzky).
107. (RIGHT) Drawing of a dining room from the book *How to Live in a Flat* (1936). Delineator:
W. Heath Robinson.

the idiosyncrasies of modern design, such as in W. Heath Robinson's clever drawings for the 1936 book *How to Live in a Flat,* which revealed the oddity that many contemporary observers had come to ascribe to the new architecture (Illus. 107). K. R. G. Browne's text for the book had a similar point of view, and in a typically wry passage stated that "the ultra-modern living room resembles a cross between an operating-theatre, a dipsomaniac's nightmare, and a new kind of knitting."[10] In *Sailing Along,* Matthews portrays a talented performer who is the protégée of a wealthy, rather eccentric soup manufacturer. A collector of "geniuses," the magnate has also acquired the services of the "crazy" abstract artist Sylvester, whose designs include a streamlined house trailer, the ultramodern half of a living room suite divided by a wall from a Victorian half, and a kitchen (Illus. 108). In its

enormous size alone, Junge's kitchen setting suggests the engine room of an ocean liner —and, in fact, may have been directly inspired by RKO's chrome-and-white ship's boiler room in which Fred Astaire had cavorted in *Shall We Dance* the previous year (see page 147). The room's curving forms, executed in highly polished finishes decorated with mechanical gadgets and control panels, convey all too well the "operating-theatre" iconography ridiculed by Browne.

Provocative modern kitchen decor, even satirically treated, appeared infrequently in films of the period, and a moviegoer was far more likely to encounter the standardly appointed hearth of the traditional family, particularly in the popular features about the domestic life of the lower and middle classes. Around the kitchen table the family ate its meals, managed its finances, did its

108. Drawing of a kitchen for *Sailing Along* (1938, Sonnie Hale). Delineator: Alfred Junge.

schoolwork, and discussed its problems. Whatever concessions that films were willing to make in allowing women the convenience of technology required "taming" the new machines by placing them within a familiar context. The kitchen in Howard Hawks's *Bringing Up Baby* (1938; Illus. 109) represented one solution to the problem by combining twentieth-century devices with nineteenth-century trappings. The room is a collage of disparate elements: a modern range set into thick stone walls, a streamlined electric mixer placed next to the butter churner and "aged" pewter ware, and an electric bulb set in a petroleum lantern. Here, tradition won out, as it would con-

109. *Bringing Up Baby* (1938, Howard Hawks). Supervisory Art Director: Van Nest Polglase; Unit Art Director: Perry Ferguson.

tinue to do for the next thirty years, the kitchen proving one of the settings most resistant to the advances of modernism.

BEDROOMS AND BATHROOMS At the same time that films were glorifying the traditional image of woman as wife, mother, and housekeeper, they attempted to condemn—or at least chastise—the "new woman," who might be either the sexually liberated descendant of the flapper, living only for fleshly pursuits, or the professional woman who abandoned her home and went to work. Just how far these characters had strayed from their appropriate roles was made clear when the movies placed them

back in the kitchen, where their ineptitude at domestic chores was the occasion of high comedy. Katharine Hepburn in *Woman of the Year* (1942), directed by George Stevens, played a sophisticated professional woman whose attempts to make her husband breakfast were mocked and thwarted by her inability to work the simplest kitchen appliances. In contrast to the working woman (who will be discussed in the following section), the sexually liberated woman had left the kitchen behind and installed herself in the bedroom/boudoir, the typical setting for nineteenth-century stage and opera heroines, and the bath, which had appeared relatively recently as a new convenience in the home. Film decor for these rooms was consequently glamorous, never practical; only the family-oriented woman was likely to regard bathing as a purely sanitary duty, or the bedroom as a chamber that contained twin beds which were primarily used for sleeping.

For the decor of the movie bedroom the set designer was presented with a curious challenge. While the kitchen involved the active functions of cooking and cleaning, both of which were acceptable to the film censor, the sleeping and sexual functions of the bedroom were either static or taboo. The designer was therefore forced to transform the typical functions of the bedroom to allow a heroine to be engaged in an acceptable activity while at the same time expressing her liberated sexuality obliquely. One way of accomplishing the former was to raise the double bed itself on a platform or to position it within a curtained niche. This tactic acknowledged the necessary presence of this piece of furniture in the boudoir, but prevented it from being approached onscreen in the company of men. Another stratagem was to exaggerate both the scale and the position of dressing and makeup tables, stressing the grooming function of the room.

Portraying the eroticism of the "new woman" was less a problem. A heroine's sexual allure could be subtly suggested by placing her on a daybed—a popular item of decor of the period—chaise longue, or sofa, furniture that allowed her to assume a reclining position for reading, telephoning, smoking, or just lounging in elegant pajamas like the world-weary Garbo in *The Single Standard* (1929; Illus. 110) or Jean Harlow, swathed in white, in George Cukor's *Dinner at Eight* (1933; Illus. 111). Designers

111. (BOTTOM) Wallace Beery and Jean Harlow in *Dinner at Eight* (1933, George Cukor). Supervisory Art Director: Cedric Gibbons; Unit Art Director: Hobe Erwin.

110. (TOP) Greta Garbo in *The Single Standard* (1929, John S. Robertson). Supervisory Art Director: Cedric Gibbons.

112. Bebe Daniels in *The Affairs of Anatol* (1921, Cecil B. De Mille). Art Director: Paul Iribe.

were also able to fall back on tried-and-true signifiers of sexual danger. Lampstands decorated with cobras, octopus-shaped clocks, and mirrors framed with bat wings hint at the lethal and entrapping sexuality of Satan Synne (Illus. 112), the seductive "vamp" in *The Affairs of Anatol,* created by Paul Iribe for De Mille.

A more unusual "erotic decor" strategy involved the use of open planning, which permitted bedrooms to open directly off liv-

ing rooms. In its 1920s Art Deco updating of Alexandre Dumas's nineteenth-century romance of a dying Parisian courtesan, Natacha Rambova's design for *Camille* was an early example of the cinema's recurring association of modernist decor with the demimondaine. In a memorable scene (Illus. 113), a reclining Camille (Alla Nazimova) gazes seductively at a supplicant Armand (Rudolph Valentino), while her bed beckons in the background, visible through a pair of open glass doors; easy access, it seemed, suggested easy virtue. In *The Easiest Way* (Illus. 114), a 1931 MGM movie about a poor fashion model who becomes the mistress of a worldly advertising executive, the design for the heroine's penthouse consists of a glass-enclosed breakfast terrace raised on a black platform that links bedroom and living room. The easy flow of space in the apartment is emphasized by a dropped beam and the pronounced horizontality of the glass wall. The interior's cubic forms echo the jagged skyline of Manhattan, which is seen outside the windows, and help establish the restlessness of the characters' lives.

However risqué the bedroom designs that appeared regularly in the movies, no film interior was as potentially expressive of the new woman's liberated sexuality as her bathroom. Unlike bedrooms, which remained unaffected by twentieth-century science, bathrooms were, like kitchens, sites of significant technological innovation. Although the bathroom had moved indoors at the end of the nineteenth century, it only became a regular feature of new residential construction during the building boom of

113. Alla Nazimova and Rudolph Valentino in *Camille* (1921, Ray C. Smallwood). Art Director: Natacha Rambova.

114. *The Easiest Way* (1931, Jack Conway). Supervisory Art Director: Cedric Gibbons.

the 1920s. The most significant advances in bathroom design in America during that decade were not actually in styling but in the standardization of the five-by-seven-foot, three-fixture facility. By 1929, the Crane Company's "Corwith" design illustrated the state of the art, and the Thanksgiving editorial that year in *The American Home* could be confident of addressing the majority of the magazine's readers when it mused: "I sometimes wonder if we are quite thankful enough for these two magic common blessings, bath tubs and plenty of water!" [11]

Worldwide sanitary improvement was hardly of interest to moviemakers, who transformed bathrooms into sybaritic temples of Roman sumptuousness, on one hand, or parodic gymnasiums dedicated to the rigorous hygiene that was the foundation of what was nearly a religious cult to modern architects. Lazare Meerson's bathroom (Illus. 115) for Jacques Feyder's *Gribiche* (1925) fulfilled the principles that Le

Corbusier had extolled in *Vers une Architecture* two years earlier. "Demand a bathroom," the architect urged, ". . . one of the largest rooms in the house or flat, the old drawing room for instance," and instructed that the room be equipped with "the most up-to-date fittings with a shower-bath and gymnastic appliances."[12] The master bath at Le Corbusier's Villa Savoye—albeit without the gymnastic appliances—was a theatrical realization of his formula. Almost equal in size to the bedroom, the bath is a series of compartments separating bathing, washing, and toilet functions, while the shower-bath is divided from the bed by a built-in, blue-tiled chaise longue. In Meerson's beautiful design, luminous suspended ceilings highlight an enormous tub recessed in a niche and an open shower stall raised on a black plinth. Despite its progressive aesthetic, *Gribiche,* like the Meerson-designed *A Nous la Liberté,* lampooned the modernist mania for physical culture. After the lovable pauper Gribiche is adopted by wealthy Madame Maranet, he is subjected to a scientific regime of modern child-rearing which orders

115. *Gribiche* (1925, Jacques Feyder). Art Director: Lazare Meerson.

his every waking hour. An early bath is followed by a boxing lesson, itself followed by a cold shower; private lessons and homework complete the day. Only after returning to his real mother does a normal existence resume for Gribiche.

The more typical cinematic bathroom was the scene of recreation that was more amorous than athletic, the lair of temptresses, whose only occupation was to be erotic. De Mille's risqué films of the teens and '20s set a Hollywood precedent for the use of exotic bathrooms to heighten a scenario's sexual titillation. In the same way that he used his supposedly morally uplifting religious epics as the pretext for some of the cinema's lewdest Roman orgies,

De Mille often exploited bathrooms as a means of slipping in a little racy sex. In *Male and Female* (1919; Illus. 116), designed by Wilfred Buckland, Gloria Swanson scandalized the American public by stepping into a sunken tub nearly nude.

De Mille introduced movie audiences to such novel bathroom luxuries that they reportedly provided the models for everything from the latest designs by plumbing corporations around the United States to the settings for starlets in soap advertisements. "He made of the bathroom," his brother William boasted, "a delightful resort . . . a mystic shrine dedicated to Venus, or sometimes to Apollo, and the art of bathing was shown as a lovely ceremony rather than a

116. *Male and Female* (1919, Cecil B. De Mille). Art Director: Wilfred Buckland.

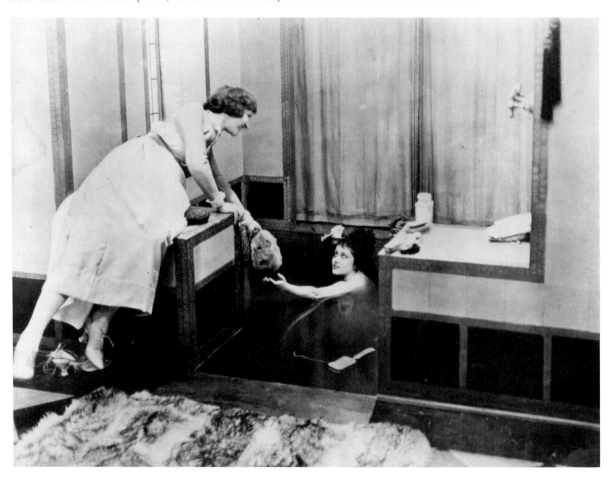

117. *Dynamite* (1929, Cecil B. De Mille). Supervisory Art Director: Cedric Gibbons; Unit Art Directors: Mitchell Leisen and Eddie Imazu.

merely sanitary duty.''[13] When confronted with his penchant for bathrooms in his films, however, De Mille himself would defend their use as being socially beneficial:

I do not shy away at all from the fact that bathtubs and bathrooms have appeared in many of my pictures; and if the modern American bathroom is a clean and comfortable part of the modern American home, my pictures may

have had something to do with that wholesome development. . . . When I had the opportunity to show on the screen that this room could be bright and clean and comfortable, I took it.[14]

Perhaps the epitome of the bright, clean, and comfortable De Mille bathroom was MGM's glamorous creation for the wealthy socialite in *Dynamite* (1929; Illus. 117). The gilt-lined tub replicates the languid curves

118. *The Magnificent Flirt* (1928, Harry d'Abbadie d'Arrast). Art Director: Van Nest Polglase.

and motifs of the chaise longue, swags and all. As an added fillip for the audience, the front of the bath is made out of glass. A black marble platform and symmetrical gilded pilasters make the tub the focal point of the room's decor; even the faucets harmonize with the monumental symmetry of the design. Textured towels and rugs in black and white geometric patterns complete the ensemble.

After De Mille's baroque extravagances had set the pattern for Hollywood, films of the period outdid themselves to include ever lusher bathroom decor. A remarkable example was Van Nest Polglase's design for *The Magnificent Flirt* (Illus. 118), Paramount's 1928 comedy, directed by Harry d'Abbadie d'Arrast. D'Arrast, whose flair for directing sophisticated fare set in jeweled Art Deco cases enlivened *Laughter* (1930)

and *Topaze* (1933), here excelled with one of the '20s' most deluxe film designs. Surrounded by marble walls and raised on an altar-like dais, the film's heroine serenely contemplates her reflection in an enormous round mirror before bathing in a sunken tub. Both tub and dressing table stand in niches of inverted scallop shells, perhaps a reference to Botticelli's *Birth of Venus*.

Although modern architects themselves created a number of spectacular bathrooms, they tended to work almost exclusively within the language of modernism and rejected the moviemakers' use of neo-classic touches as being ill-suited to the twentieth century. A few movie designs of the '30s did, however, parallel the work of more eclectic Art Deco designers, such as the Briton Oliver Hill. Hill's bathroom (Illus. 119) at London's North House, completed in 1932

119. North House, London (1932, Oliver Hill).

for Robert Hudson, features classical fluting around a marble tub inset with gold mosaics and surrounded by thin facets of mirror. Two sylphic nudes complete the photographer's conception of the luxurious decor.

At North House, Hill used mirrors to achieve quicksilver, space-expanding effects, which were also much in favor with movie designers. In MGM's *Sadie McKee* (1934), directed by Clarence Brown and starring Joan Crawford as an impoverished working girl who marries an alcoholic millionaire, mirrors in conjunction with glass walls visually unite Sadie's bath, dressing, and sitting rooms into one composite decor. Although largely obscured by fringe, chandeliers, and swags, the design nonetheless reveals what to many Depression moviegoers were the architectural wages of sin for a woman who traded in romantic love for

material rewards. As a star persona who exuded a tough and glamorous sexiness, Crawford often played characters who found the exotic bathroom a natural habitat. The dressing area of her flapper character in Harry Beaumont's *Our Dancing Daughters* (1928) was an emporium of cosmetics displayed in glass shelves, while at the end of the 1930s, in her role as the home wrecker in the all-female cast of George Cukor's *The Women* (1939), Crawford seemed to live in a bathtub elaborately fitted with makeup shelf and telephone.

With filmmakers eager to provide heroines with well-appointed decor, the standard bathroom, which was an increasingly familiar sight in the home, rarely appeared in the movies. The consensus among modern architects and the general public alike that the sanitary bathroom constituted a necessity of modern life in the twentieth century was not one shared by the cinema, in which so functional a setting could carry only the most pedestrian of connotations.

Offices

Once characters in a film of the 1920s and '30s left their modern homes, they were likely to have jobs in offices designed in an equally up-to-date style. The modern office, when developed in conjunction with the century's newly emergent managerial class, was a product of both real and symbolic forces. The white-collar environment was shaped as much by the actual requirements of handling more complex business tasks, technologies, and types of communication as it was by the perceived need to give the office a mystique of rational control and efficiency. This progressive public image, which was valuable for both inspiring confidence in the marketplace and establishing the corporation as a leader in its field, was perhaps best characterized in Mies van der Rohe's 1923 description of the office building as "a house of work, of organization, of clarity, of economy." [15]

The majority of offices seen in film interiors of the 1920s and '30s pertained to the prosperous industries of fashion, finance, and especially the media. Radio facilities were particularly popular, and NBC's move early in the '30s into what was to become New York's Rockefeller Center inspired a wave of modern movie radio stations. Few were more striking than those created for Paramount's series of *Big Broadcast* musicals, especially the "National Network Broadcasting Company" designed by Dreier and Usher for Mitchell Leisen's *The Big Broadcast of 1937*. The quality of modern details— glass walls, marquees with translucent soffits, tubular furniture—is remarkable throughout the company's suites of svelte offices and public reception areas. Leading to the recording studio, for example, is an enormous sliding wall decorated with an abstract design of clear and translucent glass set in chrome mullions.

Offices for the advertising profession, which the movies often portrayed as a promising area for get-rich-quick schemes, were another preferred setting. Through their stylish hallways passed low-paid clerks dreaming of coming up with one winning ad jingle, and young women waiting for the break that would allow them to pursue careers in modeling. *It Pays to Advertise* (1931), with its Art Deco sets, satirized the profession in a comedy about a scam to sell a nonexistent product. Publishing and finance were two businesses that were frequently the subjects of the designs created by the Paramount Famous Lasky studios in New York. William Saulter designed many of these sets as showcases for the extravagant commercial architecture rising across the river in Manhattan: Not only did shards of New York skyscrapers continually appear in the background of his decor, but sconces reminiscent of the winged radiator caps pro-

truding from the corners of the Chrysler Building are brought into an interior to decorate Saulter's boardroom for the bank conglomerate in *The Laughing Lady* (1929). Similarly, his office for *Gentlemen of the Press* (1929; Illus. 120) combines the characteristic faceted vertical piers, setback profiles, and chevron motifs of the new style of skyscrapers. Even the supports of a desk use the zigzag profiles Art Deco designers favored.

A large percentage of the office staffs in these films consisted of women. World War I, which had made it necessary for them to replace fighting men in the office, had been a powerful impetus to the emancipation of women, and throughout the 1920s female fashions would reflect their new status. Simpler, looser-fitting clothes, shorter skirts, and less complicated hairstyles allowed them to move more freely, and women driving automobiles or playing golf became recurring images in fashion magazines. By the end of the 1920s, as the Depression began to make its impact felt on movie heroines, actresses who had played wealthy flappers now were cast as characters who went to work: In *Our Dancing Daughters* (1928) and *Our Modern Maidens* (1929), the characters played by Joan Crawford were wild and reckless; in the next and last film of the series, Harry Beaumont's *Our Blushing Brides* (1930), released nine months after the crash of the stock market, Crawford was cast as a hard-working department store employee.

If the movies had come to recognize that women had become a vital part of the American work force, they nonetheless soon found it necessary to remind them that their proper place was, finally, at home. As the Depression continued and the job market constricted, the few jobs that were available were expected to go to men. Consequently, during the early 1930s, a new genre appeared in which innocent secretaries found employment, only to be subjected to

120. *Gentlemen of the Press* (1929, Millard Webb). Art Director: William Saulter.

a series of frightening trials and tribulations. In its review of *Big Business Girl* (1931; Illus. 121), a comedy about a young woman whose rises from humble stenographer to high-salaried advertising writer, one American newspaper described the environment of these films as one "where sex rears its head and peeks from behind office doors and lurks tantalizingly on the typewriter keyboard between the letters and the spacer."[16] But as in a fairy tale, these tribulations did not often go unrewarded. In 1931 alone, four international versions of a modern-day Cinderella scenario appeared, in which a secretary, first pursued by a lecherous manager, eventually marries the boss after comic complications have been ironed out. Germany's *Die Privatsekretärin,* starring Renate Müller, was set in architect Emil Fahrenkamp's recently completed Shell Building in Berlin. Müller repeated her role for the British version of the same film, *Sunshine Susie.* France saw *Dactylo,* and Italy produced *La Segretaria privata,* with sets by Futurist Vinicio Paladini.

An alternate version of the woman-in-business theme—and a striking variation on the Hollywood theme of the "New Woman"—cast the heroine herself as an executive. In Michael Curtiz's *Female* (1933), Alison Drake, heir to and director of the Drake Motor Company, pursues men as ardently as they pursue women, manages her company forcefully, and remains independent—until the last reel, that is, when "typical" female instincts lead her to marry and concede her business to her husband. Modernity surrounds her at both the office (Illus. 122) and at home (Illus. 123), where designer Jack Okey reproduced the cubic massing and the knit-block facades of the Los Angeles–area residences designed by

121. *Big Business Girl* (1931, William A. Seiter). Art Director: Jack Okey.

Frank Lloyd Wright in the 1920s. (The opening shot of the heroine's house was, in fact, filmed on location at Wright's Ennis House (1924), in the hills above Hollywood.)

The interior of Alison Drake's office features a series of horizontal lines that run across the room's large window, a geometric pattern that for the modern architect often symbolized the notion of the rational control that technology could exert on modern life. Moviemakers likewise would include in their office designs some form of grid, which served variously as a convenient and flexible metaphor for the honeycomb of the beehive, with each worker performing his assigned, regimented task; for the chessboard predetermining and limiting the possible moves that a player might make; or for the graph paper that establishes order across

the accountant's ledger sheet. While *Metropolis* is the best-known example of the use of rigid geometric design to suggest the anonymity and regimentation of work, grids were used equally effectively in the decor of King Vidor's *The Crowd* (1928), designed by Arnold Gillespie and Cedric Gibbons for MGM. The film follows the career of a small-town boy who comes to New York seeking success and the distinction of being "somebody." He works as one of a hundred clerks in an insurance company (Illus. 124), gets married, has a family. Dissatisfied with his career, he quits his job and tries others, but still success eludes him, and he descends into poverty. He finally manages to pull himself up and, in the film's final sequence, goes with his wife to the movies, where they are submerged in a crowd of anonymous faces. For the exterior of the insurance

122. (ABOVE) Ruth Chatterton in *Female* (1933, Michael Curtiz and William Dieterle). Art Director: Jack Okey.

123. (BELOW) *Female* (1933).

company where the hero is employed, Gillespie and Gibbons designed a field of monotonous windows, which Vidor in a memorable sequence dissolved into an equally ominous sea of clerks' desks.

The most frequent use of the orthogonal grid, however, was as the foundation for the design of large glass walls. Since in a movie set a window's grids of mullions were required only to register the positions of planes of glass, set designers were able to disregard such practical considerations as ventilation and waterproofing. The spider-web-thin mullions and wide expanses of glass that became a commonplace of modern architecture only as the result of the introduction of modular glass-and-metal building skins after World War II were a commonplace in films of the 1920s and '30s. The enormous glass window of *Metropolis* (Illus. 125), for example, affords a spectacular view of the film's city of the future, its grid functioning not only as a visual device to exaggerate the depth of the background but also as a potent sign for the order and control that the executive maintained over his or her domain. For offices connected to industrial plants, designers often preferred horizontal fenestration patterns. Long windowpanes and virtually uninterrupted horizontal mullions—a design scheme that mirrored the assembly lines within—feature prominently in the phonograph factory in *A Nous la Liberté,* the machine works in *Sprengbagger 1010* (1929), and the automobile factory in *Female.*

In designer Richard Day's office for the automobile manufacturer in *Dodsworth*

(1936; Illus. 126), the two-dimensional grid is expanded into a three-dimensional framework that carries the square window pattern across the walls and the partial ceiling. The one-point perspective of this space, heightened by the depth implied by Day's backcloth of the factory, focuses the viewer's attention on the all-powerful industrialist who stands at the center of a vast empire. The following year, Day reworked Dodsworth's office and, with only slight modifications—the addition of horizontal window blinds and wall-to-wall carpeting; a skyscraper view instead of the factory one—created the office of inventor and real estate developer B. J. Nolan for *Woman Chases Man,* a screwball comedy about an unemployed female architect.

Dressed in an average business suit, the modern executive lacked the visible insignia of power that distinguished his aristocratic counterpart. To indicate his authority, filmmakers turned to technology, and often gave the executive a huge, mechanized desk that placed him or her at the center of a powerful communications network. *Metropolis*'s Joh Fredersen, the archetypal industrialist of the 1920s, controls his vast empire not by physical force but with the latest mechanical devices. Giant chevrons suggestive of machinery parts decorate his office walls, while his huge semicircular desk is equipped with a ticker-tape machine, clocks, telephones, and a variety of switchboard control panels. Fredersen communicates with his subordinates via a wall television. In *Female,* Jack Okey repeated the horizontal emphasis he had given to the executive's glass wall in his design for an exaggeratedly long auditor's desk, which matched in length the incremental wall graphs posted behind it. The executive office Gordon Wiles designed for McGloin Enterprises in *Rackety Rax* (1932; Illus. 127) is a vast, palatial space dominated by an altar-like executive desk. Raised on a plat-

124. (OPPOSITE TOP) *The Crowd* (1928, King Vidor). Supervisory Art Director: Cedric Gibbons; Unit Art Director: Arnold Gillespie.
125. (OPPOSITE BOTTOM) Alfred Abel and Gustave Fröhlich in *Metropolis* (1927, Fritz Lang). Art Directors: Otto Hunte, Erich Kettelhut, and Karl Vollbrecht.

126. Walter Huston in *Dodsworth* (1936, William Wyler). Art Director: Richard Day.

form and decorated with a pair of candelabras, the desk stands in front of a master control panel and a wall-size map of the McGloin empire. Often such desks were designed merely to suggest executive authority, and made no pretense of being functional work spaces. Douglas Fairbanks's desk in *Reaching for the Moon* (1931), for example, has sixteen telephones (Illus. 128).

The cinema's executive offices rarely did

reflect the true working environments of the captains of industry and financial magnates whose "behind closed doors" machinations typical movie plots purported to reveal. Even the actual offices designed for the moguls of the movie industry—a group not uninterested in supporting its own claims of architectural trend-setting—pale by comparison with their cinematic counterparts. The differences between real and reel Hol-

127. (ABOVE) *Rackety Rax* (1932, Alfred Werker). Art Director: Gordon Wiles.
128. (BELOW) Douglas Fairbanks (right) in *Reaching for the Moon* (1930, Edmund Goulding). Art Director: William Cameron Menzies.

129. David O. Selznick in his office, Los Angeles, 1936.

lywood are tellingly illustrated in a comparison of all the grandiose executive suites pictured in this section with the quaint office of David O. Selznick himself (Illus. 129).

The grand scale, commanding views, and technological armory of the movie office were ultimately less an accurate re-creation of reality than an amplification of the executive role itself. In this respect they also lent support to the popular cinema's equally simplified notions about the conflict between labor and management, fulfilling the fearful fantasies of the moviegoing audience that placed The Boss in a context of enviably absolute power and themselves at his mercy.

Nightclubs

Along with the lavish residence and the executive office, nightclubs were the most frequent subjects for modern architectural decor. As the peerless recreational activity of the well-to-do, nightclub-hopping was for movie audiences the prerogative of a leisured life-style, a fulfillment of the ideal dream of life as a mad whirl of debonair,

tuxedoed roués, wealthy debutantes, cocktails, and dancing until dawn.

During the 1920s, the films of Fritz Lang ascribed wicked, albeit alluring, connotations to the nightclub. Lang often took as his subject German society as it had evolved after the war, a period he described as one of "hysteria, despair and unbridled vice, full of the excesses of an inflation-ridden country."[17] Nightclubs, the perfect setting for his scenarios, "were in full swing, supported by the easily earned money of uncaring war —and inflation. . . . In these places the up and coming classes of the new rich could gamble and the sky was the limit."[18] The most spectacular of the clubs in Lang's work appeared in *Metropolis,* a film set in the future but clearly reminiscent of the frenzy of contemporary Berlin in its portrait of a decadent society. *Metropolis*'s Voshiwara club (Illus. 130) plays a pivotal role in the film's action: It is here that the scientist Rotwang unveils his evil robot, Maria, before a wild, lascivious mob; together they cavort while the enslaved workers destroy the city before their eyes.

Far more mundane connotations were ascribed to Hollywood movie nightclubs of the 1920s. These were usually little more than urban saloons where small-time gangsters involved in bootlegging made their devious plans and took advantage of innocent young girls from the country. By the late 1920s and the coming of sound, however, these dens of petty iniquity had not only begun to attract a less criminal clientele but had also grown to elephantine proportions, perfect settings for new lavish musicals. An extraordinary example was the Paradise Club designed by Charles D. Hall for *Broadway* (1929; Illus. 131), one of many movies that took advantage of the nightclub setting for a scenario mixing backstage drama with onstage extravaganzas. Cinematographer Hal Mohr described the genesis of the design for the club in an interview with Leon-

130. *Metropolis* (1927, Fritz Lang). Art Directors: Otto Hunte, Erich Kettelhut, and Karl Vollbrecht.

ard Maltin in the early 1970s. The original plot for *Broadway* concerned a small-time entertainer performing in a low-life cabaret from which he dreams of escaping to play the Palace. The film's director, Paul Fejos, decided that a more spectacular setting was needed to highlight the film's musical numbers, and the result was decor that would have engulfed "the Palace, the Winter Garden, and the Hippodrome all in one."[19] So huge were the film's sets, however, that they could not be photographed with regular equipment, and a special set-up had to be built: the Broadway camera crane, which cost $50,000 and had an arm extending forty feet. From the opening shots, in which the viewer travels along the canyons of Times Square and glides into the Paradise Club, Mohr's mobile camera is the perfect guide to explore Hall's vertiginous, Art Deco space filled with merrymakers perched on balconies.

Ironically, the "nightclub decade" on the screen was only just dawning as the deepening Depression forced more and more clubs to close, tempering the recklessness of the 1920s. Although the repeal of Prohibition in America in 1933 did legitimize nightclubs, they continued to be popular movie locations, appealing now as a palliative to the economic hardships that most filmgoers were enduring. Glamorous environments perched at the top of skyscrapers far above the breadlines and tenements of a struggling city, urban nightclubs were, metaphorically as well as literally, raised above economic and political problems, where nothing could impede the pursuit of fun. Even plot was "streamlined" to a minimum: Nightclubs often provided a sufficient raison d'être for films that typically used short scenes involving a thin story to link elaborate production numbers.

No aesthetic feature evoked the nightclub's glamour as effectively as artificial illumination. While, as a visual device, large quantities of lighting added to the beauty of film sets, they also suggested the abundance and the luxurious sheen of the high life. Light heightened virtually every element of decor in movie nightclubs, making objects highly reflective, and stressing smooth sur-

131. *Broadway* (1929, Paul Fejos). Art Director: Charles D. Hall.

face over texture and mass. Light also turned night into day within the club and allowed the idle rich to play while workers rested. Although many movie nightclubs used light to a limited degree for clever decorative applications—as a glittering fringe to surround the stage in the nightclub of the Soviet film *Moscow Laughs (Vesolye Rebyata)* (1934), for example, or as the translucent glass sign of the Casa d'Oro club in *Der Tanzstudent* (1928)—the nightclub designed for MGM's *Broadway Melody of 1936* (Illus. 132) is a space conceived with light as its main component. Light emanates from iridescent globes, passes through curving walls of glass bricks, and is reflected off gleaming metallic furniture. Tall columns of backlit cloth pass through chrome rings from which cantilevered arms support billowing sails. These sails seem to draw the interior decor outward and toward the ubiquitous cinematic city of skyscrapers, where

132. *Broadway Melody of 1936* (1935, Roy Del Ruth). Supervisory Art Director: Cedric Gibbons.

every illuminated window promises more revelers enjoying themselves far into the night.

With their audiences in place, huge floor spaces, and theatrical lighting, nightclubs were the logical settings for many musicals of the decade, epitomized by the Astaire and Rogers series. The promise of an escape from economic hardship had its clearest expression in the Silver Sandal decor designed at RKO for Astaire and Rogers's

sixth and perhaps best film, *Swing Time* (1936), directed by George Stevens. While other film nightclubs were located within the pinnacles of Manhattan's skyline, the Silver Sandal Club (Illus. 133) floated in the stratosphere *above* the skyscrapers. This feat was revealed in the first view the audience had of the club: As the camera seems to rise through a field of painted skyscrapers, it suddenly passes through an opening in the club's floor at the foot of the cantilevered

133. *Swing Time* (1936, George Stevens). Supervisory Art Director: Van Nest Polglase; Unit Art Director: Carroll Clark.

orchestra stand, and finally ascends in front of the curving double staircase. Further enhancing the expansive stellar setting are the nightclub's "walls," which are actually metallic frames; the stars' glow visible between them minimizes the sense of enclosure. Sparkling light twinkles in the highly pol-

ished black-and-white floors, chrome accessories, and furniture wrapped in crinkled cellophane or white satin.

The following year, a companion piece to the Silver Sandal Club appeared in the Moonbeam Room in *Top of the Town* (1937; Illus. 134). Designed for Universal by John

134. Mischa Auer in *Top of the Town* (1937, Ralph Murphy). Art Director: John Harkrider.

Harkrider, who had become the studio's supervisory art director shortly before, the Moonbeam Room, in its reported size—one acre—and cost—$100,000—provoked the same publicity hoopla that the same studio's Paradise Club had eight years earlier.[20]

Harkrider's reputation for extravagance had been established the previous decade when he served as artistic director, costumist, and sometimes associate producer on nineteen lavish Ziegfeld productions, many in collaboration with Joseph Urban. Although he had worked for Hollywood during the early 1930s, Harkrider achieved his first West Coast success in 1936 through his involvement in *The Great Ziegfeld* (1936), MGM's biography of his mentor. According to one published source, that film's decor caused such envy at rival studios that RKO halted production of *Swing Time* so that Harkrider could concoct a nightclub for Astaire and Rogers that would outdo his efforts at MGM.[21] Although RKO credited Harkrider with designing the entire Silver Sandal Club, he himself admitted to creating only the part of it that formed the backdrop for Astaire's "Bojangles of Harlem" number.

In any event, Harkrider brought many of the best ideas of the Silver Sandal set with him to Universal, where he used them to great effect on the Moonbeam Room. Most notable is the field of stars that illuminates *Top of the Town*'s three-story club, which was situated at the top of New York's tallest skyscraper, 102 stories in the air. One unusually expressive element of the decor is the deck-like balcony that extends between a pair of upturned ship's hulls—an explicit reference to the nightclub's role as a place of escape. As in the Silver Sandal, Harkrider defined the room's design with light, which models the curves of brushed-metal spandrels and stairs, and shines from cellophane tablecloths and along smoothly contoured moldings. Even the shrubbery seems to be made of glistening black coral.

With their gargantuan size and hyperbolic decor, nightclubs were the most elaborate of the dreams offered to movie audiences of the Depression, a fact heightened by their very inaccessibility. They remained unquestionably the domain of the wealthy; the only entry possible for the majority of the public was as a performer, a waiter, a hatcheck girl, or a golddigger on the arm of a rich suitor. Because nightclubs were finally outside the normal experiences of most moviegoers, they became a powerful subject for film fantasy; in the hands of moviemakers,

nightclubs were transformed into urban paradises, imperturbable and confident in the heights above the city.

Hotels

If most moviegoers could enjoy nightclubs only vicariously, as observers, other public spaces represented in films of the 1920s and '30s not only were more accessible, but also functioned as social elevators. Hotels, particularly, were portrayed in the cinema as places where the classes could intermingle and intermarry. That social mobility *was* possible seemed to be the message of these films; it required only a measure of ambition and craftiness on the part of the average person to take advantage of the opportunities such settings offered.

The popularity of hotels in the movies during these years reflected the increase of travel between the wars and, in particular, the rush of hotel construction around 1930. London witnessed the building of the Dorchester, Grosvenor House, the Mayfair, the Park Lane, and the Strand Palace between 1927 and 1932, while during the comparable period in New York arose the Barbizon Plaza, the Hotel Carlyle, and the new Waldorf-Astoria (the original Waldorf had been torn down to make way for the Empire State Building).

In the public lobbies of the movie versions of these large urban hotels moved a broad spectrum of society. Random collisions between characters of different social and economic backgrounds were the basis of innumerable plots of this period, whether they involved shopgirls and secretaries pursuing or being pursued by lecherous tycoons; heiresses falling in love with poor bellhops against the protestations of their dowager mothers; or young girls squandering their meager savings to spend the weekend at an expensive hotel, where they masqueraded as socialites in order to hook wealthy husbands.

As the crossroads where guests encountered one another and confronted their fates, the hotel lobby predictably contained architectural elements that visually conveyed movement. Although stairs and elevators appeared in many modern settings, they were used most expressively in the cinema's hotel lobbies of the 1920s and '30s. The lobby of director F. W. Murnau's *The Last Laugh (Der letzte Mann;* 1924) is introduced via one of the movies' most famous examples of mobile cinematography. To shoot the scene, cameraman Karl Freund, who later co-photographed *Metropolis,* placed the camera inside the hotel's elevator from which it could gradually reveal the lobby as the cab descended. The flurry of movement around the lobby is implied by a revolving door at the entry, its endless spinning captured in the changing patterns of light reflecting from its glass leaves. Movement is also at the heart of the film's plot, a story that follows the changing fortunes of the hotel's proud and boastful doorman (played by one of Germany's leading actors, Emil Jannings), who is replaced by a younger and stronger man. Stripped of his imposing uniform, the former doorman is reduced to serving as the washroom attendant until, as if by magic, he inherits a fortune from one of the hotel's previous visitors and returns triumphant, now as one of the hotel's most pampered patrons.

Since filming the confined space of an elevator proved too difficult for most moviemakers, they usually resorted to building elaborate stairways to accommodate the comings and goings of a hotel's guests. Robert Neppach's design for a crisscrossing stairway dominates the lobby of the hotel in *Das grüne Monokel* (1929; Illus. 135), while the multileveled lobby in *Die tolle Komtesse* (1928) provides the perfect setting for the film's romantic antics, which involve the mingling of the upper crust (in the persons of the crazy countess of the title and an equally wealthy woman, who are staying at the hotel) and the working class (the woman's maid and her boyfriend, who works there).

The fantasy of easily accomplished matches with rich hotel patrons, another myth reinforced by the severity of the Depression, found no greater vehicle than MGM's *Grand Hotel* (1932). As the most expensive accommodations in Berlin, frequented by the best people, the Grand Hotel features snappy bellhops carrying luggage from chauffeured limousines to luxuriously appointed suites, awestruck newlyweds wandering through richly appointed decor, and high-finance conferences. Rapidly intercut scenes of telephone conversations begin the film and succinctly introduce its interconnected scenarios of characters spending, losing, and seeking money. John Barrymore, playing an impoverished baron, is reduced to scheming to steal the pearls of a world-weary Russian ballerina (Greta Garbo)—until he falls in love with her. Changing his plan, he attempts to rob an industrialist (Wallace Beery) who faces financial ruin unless he clinches an important merger. His ex-employee (Lionel Barrymore), an incurably ill bookkeeper, spends his meager life savings on one last, extravagant fling. An ambitious stenographer (Joan Crawford) is pursued by Beery but won by Lionel Barrymore, and goes off with him to the Grand Hotel in Paris. A cynical doctor (Lewis Stone) acts as the detached narrator of these brief episodes in the life of the Grand Hotel and its ever-changing cast of characters.

Circles are prominent in every aspect of the Grand Hotel's design (Illus. 136)—an appropriate image for the spinning-wheel-of-fortune scenario. The circular motif appears in the hotel's round, multilevel atrium with open balconies, in the continually re-

135. *Das grüne Monokel* (1929, Rudolf Meinert). Art Director: Robert Neppach.

volving doors, and in ornaments on balcony railings. It also appears in the round reception desk, which acts as a pivot for the curving shots that follow the movement of the film's characters, who travel across the black-and-white floor like pawns in a chess game. Movie plot and architecture have seldom been so closely harmonized.

The grand urban hotels of the 1930s movies were relatively short-lived, victims, ironically, of the very process of social elevation they suggested was possible. Traveling, once the prerogative of the wealthy, began by the late 1930s to become affordable

to a broader range of society, and as its clientele became more heterogeneous, the hotel lost much of its allure as an arena of social maneuvers. Replacing the urban hotels of the movies were small-scale rustic retreats, anticipations of one of the standard formats of the postwar motel. Designed as groupings of private bungalows, these new hotels substituted courtyards of a South American flavor for public lobbies and in the process greatly diminished the role of public meeting places. One explanation for this architectural trend was the fashion that arose in Hollywood at the end of the '30s for films set in warmer, southern climates. The war had closed much of Hollywood's European market, and the studios consequently intensified efforts to increase their South American audience. The importing of Brazilian bombshell Carmen Miranda was Hollywood's most spectacular effort in that direction, but a barrage of "south of the border" decorative influences infiltrated Hollywood design as well. Wicker and rattan furniture, straw matting, and sun-shielding screens were seen more and more often in cinematic decor, and palm tree motifs appeared everywhere.

136. *Grand Hotel* (1932, Edmund Goulding). Supervisory Art Director: Cedric Gibbons; Unit Art Director: Alexander Toluboff.

137. *Moon Over Miami* (1941, Walter Lang). Supervisory Art Director: Richard Day; Unit Art Director: Wiard Ihnen.

Twentieth Century–Fox's Technicolor musical *Moon Over Miami* (1941; Illus. 137) is a particularly telling example of the change in decor—and sensibilities—of the hotel film. For the Flamingo Hotel, the smart resort where two young women stay hoping to catch wealthy men, designers Richard Day and Wiard Ihnen designed small private cabins that present closed facades onto a barren plaza, the setting for lavish dance routines. Postwar American motels would fill the plaza with parked cars —a remarkable shift from public to private

functions. The art of seeing and being seen while one circulated through the lobby of the Grand Hotel would be reduced to the practice of spying from one bungalow to the next, and the boulevardier would be forced to become the voyeur.

Ocean Liners

In many respects, there existed no more perfect movie setting than the ocean liner. It not only fulfilled most unequivocally the audience's dreams of escape, carrying its fortu-

138. Drawing of the dining room on the *Normandie* (1935). Delineator: uncredited.

nate cargo off to exotic foreign parts, but as a self-contained entity far removed from the social strictures of the mainland, it also promised a respite from everyday existence, in a shipboard life that was more socially and romantically adventurous. (Trains in the movies acquired connotations similar to those of ocean liners. They are not explored here, however, because movie art directors relied heavily on stock footage for a train's exterior, while they usually treated its confined interior less architecturally than in a purely utilitarian fashion.)

Like the skyscraper, to which it was often compared in scale, the ocean liner was a source of endless fascination to the public. A trip to New York City during the '20s and '30s would certainly have included a visit to one of the many ships docked along the Hudson River. The grandest of all, the liner *Normandie,* which had its maiden voyage in 1935, had been funded by the French government as a floating goodwill ambassador displaying the glories of French design on an enormous scale. The *Normandie*'s main dining room, for example, measured 305 feet in length, 46 feet in width, and 25 feet in height, and accommodated seven hundred passengers for dinner each evening (Illus. 138). Thirty-eight luminous wall panels, two chandeliers, and twelve set-back light columns, all designed by René Lalique, created for the *Normandie* an ambience as dazzling as that of any movie set. Advertising for the liner promoted its *haute monde* glamour, as did innumerable movie fan magazines filled with the transatlantic comings and goings of Marlene Dietrich, Josephine Baker, and Noël Coward. The *Normandie* itself would appear as the setting of at least two French films: *Les Perles de la Couronne* (1937), directed by Christian-Jaque and Sacha Guitry, and *Paris–New York* (1940), a shipboard murder mystery that ends in the French Pavilion at the 1939 New York World's Fair.

As well as being a popular attraction, the ocean liner was proposed by modernists as a formal model to be emulated by the new architecture. In *Vers une Architecture,* Le Corbusier wrote that if he and his fellow architects could "forget for a moment that a steamship is a machine for transport and look with a fresh eye, we shall feel that we are facing an important manifestation of temerity, of discipline, of harmony, of a beauty that is calm, vital and strong."[22] Throughout the 1920s, the designs of Le Corbusier, Mallet-Stevens, and the Bauhaus architects used subtle references to ship motifs—white surfaces with horizontal windows, open promenades and terraces, powerful sculptural forms, and thin railings —to impart their connotations of innovation and speed to buildings. During the 1930s and the heyday of streamlining, Art Deco designers turned to more overt references to the maritime style, especially in the form of teardrop contours. Robert Darrah decorated the "hull" of his streamlined Coca-Cola Bottling Company Plant in Los Angeles (1936–7) with deck-like catwalks

and portholes; the building is capped by a giant mast, which doubles as a sign.

French filmmakers of the late 1920s featured ocean liners with the sleek styling promoted by Le Corbusier in a number of beautiful ship settings, including André Barsacq's in *Maldone* (Illus. 139) and Robert-Jules Garnier's in *Le Diable au Coeur* (see page 57). French design itself influenced the ship interiors created by Paul Nelson for *What a Widow!* (Illus. 140): His stairway, with its undulating walls, virtually copies Maurice Dufrene's design of the store interior for the Compagnie des Arts Français. Nelson's design would, however, have little influence on Hollywood ship architecture, which relied most often on streamlining for its inspiration. Astaire's "Slap That Bass" dance number in the gleaming ship's boiler room of RKO's *Shall We Dance* is Léger's *Ballet mécanique* gone pop (Illus. 141). But although every other studio launched its own streamlined ships during the mid-1930s, the most extravagant were those that sailed the miniature water tanks and sound-stages of Paramount. The S.S. *Americana,* designed by Hans Dreier and Ernst Fegté, was the setting for *Anything Goes* (1936) when the studio filmed Cole Porter's Broadway success. Since most of the scenes take place inside the ship's staterooms, nightclubs, or corridors, and so do not provide many opportunities to view its sleek hull and decks, the typical maritime motifs were applied to smaller, architectural elements. The shape of columns and even tables, for example, replicates the extremely oblong configuration of the ship itself. Dark-gray horizontal strips running across the walls are standard streamlining decor, as are the teardrop shapes of the portholes. Traditional round "portholes" are used to puncture ceilings. In *Big Broadcast of 1938,* Paramount pitted the *Gigantic,* a replica of the ocean liner Norman Bel Geddes proposed in 1932, against the *Colossal* in

139. Drawing of an ocean liner bar for *Maldone* (1928, Jean Gremillon). Delineator: André Barsacq.

a transatlantic race sponsored by a radio station. To heighten the suggestion of the ship's speed, the studio attached an enormous airplane propeller to Bel Geddes's streamlined design, an overt and functionally useless addition that transformed the original into a cartoon.

Whether adapted from modern or streamlined sources, movie liners' imagery of movement and speed reinforced the narrative's message that escape, both literal and figurative, was possible on ships. In the movie *What A Widow!,* for example, the heroine, Tamarind Brooks, decides to experience the carefree life she had missed by being married at an early age, boards the *Île de France* for Europe, and, as the film's publicity claimed: ". . . found men . . . all kinds . . . and all kinds of love . . . She met a dancer . . . and decided to take dancing lessons! Met a Spanish baritone . . . and wanted to sing! Met a Russian virtuoso . . . and took violin lessons!"[23]

The lure of the unusual also attracts the main characters of *Dodsworth* to sea travel (Illus. 142). After the film's hero, Sam Dodsworth (Walter Huston), retires as the head of an American automobile company, his wife, Fran (Ruth Chatterton), convinces him that living in Europe will help them shed their provincialism. Ironically, Fran's newfound worldliness turns her bitter and

140. *What a Widow!* (1930, Allan Dwan). Art Director: Paul Nelson.

cold, while Sam is renewed by meeting a warm and sophisticated expatriate (Mary Astor), with whom he falls in love.

Ocean liners, like hotels, combined many public settings which offered opportunities to meet people outside one's own social level. The gold digger in *Bachelor's Affairs* (1932), for example, successfully snares a millionaire during an ocean cruise, while the shipboard convergence of a wealthy American heiress, a stowaway, a nightclub singer, and a gangster produces the plot's complications in *Anything Goes*. Occasionally, though, because the ocean liner was strictly segregated into classes, social friction, and not social mobility, formed a film's subtext. In Mario Camerini's Italian film *Il Signor Max* (1937), a Roman newspaper vendor receives a first-class ticket for a Mediterranean cruise from a wealthy friend; on board ship, he only partially succeeds in impressing his wealthy friends by being disguised as "Max," a rich gentleman from Genoa, and eventually he tires of his new acquaintances' snobbery. He ends up marrying one of their maids.

Ocean travel also freed characters from the moral constraints of land, and provided a liberating setting for romance. Jean Arthur and Charles Boyer carry on an illicit shipboard affair away from her evil husband's machinations in *History Is Made at Night* (1937), until the husband, who happens to own the liner, attempts to end their relationship by sinking the ship. Two years later, in *Love Affair* (1939), Boyer, playing a painter, and Irene Dunne, a successful singer, begin their romance while on the *Napoli,* traveling from Europe to New York.

By the time of the Second World War, however, ocean liners had already seen their best days. Air travel had established itself as both a quicker and a cheaper means of transportation. The *Normandie,* which was commandeered by the United States in the early

141. Fred Astaire in *Shall We Dance* (1937, Mark Sandrich). Supervisory Art Director: Van Nest Polglase; Unit Art Director: Carroll Clark.

142. Walter Huston and Ruth Chatterton (right of center) in *Dodsworth* (1936, William Wyler). Art Director: Richard Day.

years of the war, caught fire and sank in New York harbor in 1942 while being converted into a warship. In the cinema, the ship that was designed for Paramount's *The Lady Eve* (1941), directed by Preston Sturges, would make only passing reference to the glamorous liner imagery of the 1930s, with porthole-like openings cut into the dining room's walls. Although ocean liners in film went much the way of immense nightclubs, in the decade that they lent their grandeur to the cinema they were the source of some of its most unusually evocative designs. In realizing two of the era's most compelling ideas, speed and streamlining, these ships were among popular culture's most vivid expressions of the swiftness and ease with which escape could be made.

Skyscrapers

At the close of the 1920s, a decade of optimism about the human potential of cities and one that saw a great deal of fevered construction, the skyscraper was the quintessential expression of modern American architecture. As the combined product of advances in structural engineering, mechanical technology, urban planning, and corporate finance, it was progress incarnate. In New York City alone, many of the world's finest examples appeared, among them Walker and Gillette's Fuller Building (1929), Sloan and Robertson's Chanin Building (1930), William Van Alen's Chrysler Building (1930), and the greatest of all, Shreve, Lamb & Harmon's Empire State Building (1931). Public interest in skyscrapers was so great that a project such as Rockefeller Center (1931–40), conceived in the 1920s and the only complex of skyscrapers constructed in the 1930s, was publicized even before the ground was broken. As popular as the buildings themselves, skyscraper motifs like setback profiles influenced the design imagery of furniture, advertising, fashion, and, of course, the movies—in forms ranging from the extravagant futurist decor of science fiction epics to the credit and title design of low-budget silent features.

As skyscraper mania was reaching its strongest pitch, the stock market crashed, and within a few years the Depression almost completely halted new building activity. But although little actual construction occurred during the 1930s, the decade was the peak of the movies' infatuation with the skyscraper, its continuing appeal evident in the abundance of fantastic rooftop nightclubs, penthouses, and executive offices in the period's films. In the absence of new buildings, the cinema was thus for a number of years the most powerful purveyor of skyscraper mythology available to the public,

and as such kept the flame lit until real construction could resume after the double hiatus of depression and war.

Throughout the 1930s, especially in the American cinema, skyscrapers were an essential element of urban films. They could embody an aspiring engineer's dream project, built against nearly impossible odds in *Skyline* (1931); be the rendezvous of hopeful lovers in *Love Affair* (1939); or serve as the unexpected means of good fortune in a film like *Easy Living* (1937), in which a sable coat falls from a Fifth Avenue high-rise onto an underpaid secretary. Suddenly, her life is transformed: Everyone assumes that she is as wealthy as she looks, she leaves her humble apartment for a regal suite at the Hotel Louis, finds herself in a riot at the Automat and in a sea of mistaken identities.

Skycrapers also were in demand in films for the rich imagery they provided. The decade's musicals, often fairy-tale scenarios of the search for romance, fame, and fortune in Manhattan, were particularly imaginative in their use of skyscraper decor. Chorus members dressed as skyscrapers—simply fenestrated "torsos," setback "shoulders," and elaborately crowned "heads"—joust with Ruby Keeler and Dick Powell in Lloyd Bacon's *42nd Street* (1933; Illus. 143), Warner Bros.'s gritty backstage musical. Busby Berkeley's choreography for this sequence matches the extravagance of the design, as Ethan Mordden describes vividly in *The Hollywood Musical:*

> Keeler launches it, tapping on what is revealed to be a limousine taxicab; the dancers take over as the set expands to beyond theatre proportions, and Powell surveys the scene from a second-floor window, bootleg hootch in hand. Now occurs the strongest indication so far of what was to come from Berkeley, as files of dancers line up on a broad stairway carrying dark . . . patterns,

143. Ruby Keeler in *42nd Street* (1933, Lloyd Bacon). Art Director: Jack Okey.

cardboard cutouts of the New York skyline. A center aisle between them dissolves into the projection of a sky-scraper, and Berkeley flies up to its summit, where Powell and Keeler grin delightedly.[24]

MGM's *Broadway Melody of 1938* (1937), directed by Roy del Ruth, showed the influence of Berkeley's best pieces of architectural choreography. Receding rows of dancers are arranged to repeat the grouping of floodlit, faceted towers. In keeping with the towers' monochromatic color scheme, all the dancers are dressed in white tie and

tails, de rigueur urban garb in the mythical metropolises of movie musicals.

Moviemakers predictably opted for a romantic and fanciful aesthetic in their designs for skyscraper exteriors, rather than the simpler, less decorative style of the few modern-movement designs executed in the 1930s, such as Philadelphia's PSFS. While modern architects expressed skyscrapers functionally as flat-topped stacks of horizontal floors, movie skyscrapers took their cues from the innumerable Art Deco skyscrapers of the 1920s. Like the Chrysler Building, they resembled nothing so much as modern-day Gothic cathedrals, tall arrows aspiring to the sky. Vertical black and silver stripes, a standard Art Deco motif, emphasize the height of the miniature skyscrapers that decorate the Paradise Club of *Broadway,* while those rendered in the club's backcloth replicate the optical illusion of converging verticals familiar from the skyscraper photographs of Berenice Abbott and Edward Steichen. With their heavenly halos and nimbuses, these skyscrapers literally "scrape the sky." To emphasize their height, the designer of *Child of Manhattan* (1933, Illus. 144) used foreshortening to distort the original source of the film's skyscraper designs, Hugh Ferriss's visionary 1929 book, *The Metropolis of Tomorrow.* Although a renderer by profession, Ferriss prepared an astonishing series of drawings in which he proposed a future city of crystalline towers, ethereal in a misty light.

Moviemakers' use of graphic distortions to exaggerate the skyscraper's verticality was an implicit recognition that height was the source of the building's mystique. With their cinematography, however, they probed further and suggested that the fundamental appeal of tall buildings rested in their ability to elevate people above the noise, congestion, and filth of the city. The outstanding example of this is of course *Swing Time*'s Silver Sandal Club, which "floats" serenely in the peaks of skyscrapers, splendidly detached from urban problems. A lesser-known but equally fine design is Kem Weber's nightclub for Paramount's musical *The Big Broadcast* (1932), which nestles in a setting that animates Ferriss's vision of a cityscape of terraced skyscrapers. For Ferriss, the terrace was the inevitable but welcome by-product of the setback skyscraper profiles dictated by New York's 1916 zoning code. In *The Big Broadcast,* Weber's nightclub is introduced by a camera that appears to descend among the city's towers until it stops to focus the viewer's attention on one of the many lofty, elegant

144. John Boles and Nancy Carroll in *Child of Manhattan* (1933, Edward Buzzell). Art Director: uncredited.

terraces. A lap dissolve—an editing technique in which one scene fades out while another fades in—then effects a transition from this cityscape to the studio-built nightclub, creating the illusion that the moviegoer is actually visiting the club's elite caste of cliff dwellers high above the city.

145. (TOP) *King Kong* (1933, Merian C. Cooper and Ernest B. Schoedsack). Art Directors: Carroll Clark and Al Herman.
146. (BOTTOM) Ginger Rogers and Fred Astaire in *Carefree* (1938, Mark Sandrich). Supervisory Art Director: Van Nest Polglase; Unit Art Director: Carroll Clark.

The unprecedented size of skyscrapers, however, could take them outside the range of human control, making them potentially dangerous structures. In Busby Berkeley's

Gold Diggers of 1935, a rooftop nightclub designed by Anton Grot is atypically the scene of a violent and unexpected death. A crowd of performers pressures a playgirl to dance with them. Although she refuses, they continue to insist until, fleeing the club, the girl seeks refuge on a tiny terrace. The persistent crowd forces its way through doors no longer able to restrain them, and accidentally pushes the girl to her death. And when, in one of the most resonant images in the history of the cinema, the great ape climbs the Empire State Building at the end of *King Kong* (1933; Illus. 145), the skyscraper paradoxically becomes both the stage for a great urban spectacle and the instrument of the city's potential destruction. Goaded into a rampage by the greed of promoters who abducted him from his natural jungle habitat, King Kong unleashes his rage from the pinnacles of one of the most familiar symbols of urban capitalism.

Ironically, it was the very factors that made the heights of Hollywood skyscrapers so attractive an escape that were responsible for their declining popularity as movie subjects late in the 1930s. By mid-decade, the nightclubs, penthouses, and executive offices set on top of Manhattan skyscrapers had already begun to seem less celebrations of urban life than expressions of disenchantment with it. Tracing the history of urban nightclubs in films of the period, for example, we begin in 1929 at the base of modernistic skyscrapers with Charles D. Hall's Paradise Club for *Broadway,* and conclude in the hovering spaceships that float above the towers: 1936's Silver Sandal Club in Astaire and Rogers's *Swing Time* and the Moonbeam Room in *Top of the Town,* the following year. Both were perched for takeoff, and take off they ultimately did. In *Carefree* (1938), the penultimate Astaire and Rogers musical for RKO, the rooftop nightclub returned to earth, where it was transformed into the country club (Illus. 146). Having left the city behind for the peaceful security of the suburbs, the nightclub also abandoned its sophisticated luster for a neo-colonial style of wood beams and stone walls. In this film we encounter a remarkable anticipation not only of postwar suburban architecture, but also of the widespread flight of city dwellers from the increasingly inhospitable urban setting.

Cities of the Future

This discussion of the modern mystique properly concludes with a subject that in many ways represented the most challenging undertaking of film design. Futurist cities, whether utopias or dystopias, appeared infrequently in movies—and only in the context of the fantasy genre—but when they did, set designers not only had to prepare the usual interior and exterior decors, but had also to develop a complete urban environment, including plans for streets, large-scale buildings, and public transportation systems. Most important, the design had to reflect the ideology of the future society that was the film's subject, whether that of a peaceful, rational civilization or of a cruel, mechanized autocracy. Although the futurist movies of the 1920s and '30s more often than not ended with a reconciliation between society and science, their drama almost invariably arose as a result of the conflict between characters' opposing views of technology and progress. Whether conservative or progressive, their alternatives represented, in essence, popular culture's own hopes for and fears of the technological present: How the city (and consequently humankind) would evolve would depend on how carefully its growth —and the growth of technology itself— could be controlled.

Prior to the mid-nineteenth century, urban planning was primarily an aesthetic discipline, concerned with the layout of for-mal avenues linking public monuments and the design of landscape schemes. With the enormous social changes wrought by the Industrial Revolution, however, a shift from *art urbain* to the science of urbanism occurred throughout Europe and the United States. Urbanists considered not only the formal appearance of the city but also the complex interrelationship between aesthetics, circulation, sanitation, and social welfare. Their most innovative plan of the mid-nineteenth century called for multilevel streets to separate pedestrians, rail, service, and, later, automobile traffic as a means of alleviating the city's congestion. In 1865, Henri-Jules Borie proposed a city of eleven-story buildings ("aerodromes"), which would house public institutions on their roofs and be linked by aerial pedestrian walkways. The most famous of the new urbanists was Eugène Hénard. Best known for his recommendation that Paris's traffic problems could be solved by means of split-level intersections, Hénard also envisioned schemes for future cities that proved to be highly prophetic. Among his designs was a proposal that flat roofs be used not only for roof gardens, a concept that became one of Le Corbusier's five points of architecture, but also for aircraft landing platforms, an idea that would be forwarded in the realm of science fiction by H. G. Wells in his 1908 book, *The War in the Air*.

Throughout the first decade of the twentieth century, New York City seemed to be developing in a manner that fulfilled many urbanists' prophecies. A series of visionary illustrations of Beaux-Arts skyscrapers connected by tenuous bridges, Moses King's *King's Dream of New York* (Illus. 147), had established in the popular imagination Manhattan's potential to become a complex urban center. On its completion in 1910, Grand Central Terminal became one of the first realizations of the multilevel urban structure, containing overlapping yet dis-

147. Drawing of New York City in the future from *King's Dream of New York* (1908–9). Delineator: Harry M. Pettit.

crete paths of five modes of circulation. Both designs would anticipate the urban strategies of the Futurist Antonio Sant' Elia in his drawings of the *Città Futurista* (1913–14), as well as Le Corbusier's Plan Voisin (1925).

New York—in both its real and its imaginary aspects—provided the model for the cinema's first city of the future in the German science fiction epic *Metropolis*. Fritz Lang conceived the idea for a film about a great future city while entering New York harbor in 1924. The Manhattan Lang saw, a jumble of masonry spires (which *Metropolis*'s designers would compress into a com-

position of overlapping facets reminiscent of a cubist collage), may have stirred in him the same sentiments the photographer Alfred Stieglitz expressed a decade earlier: "It is fascinating. It is like some giant machine, soulless, and without a trace of heart. . . . Still I doubt whether there is anything more truly wonderful than New York in the world just at present." [25]

Lang would share Stieglitz's ambivalence in the plot of his film, the script for which was written by his wife, Thea von Harbou, as both nightmare *and* dream. Freder Fredersen (Gustav Fröhlich), the son of Metropolis's master, learns of the horrible netherworld existence of the slaves through the innocent Maria (Brigitte Helm), spiritual nurse of the oppressed. Freder (dressed in white silk) first encounters Maria (surrounded by urchins in tattered rags) in a rooftop pleasure garden, a pastoral Eden of trees and fountains that isolates the elite from the commotion of the technological city (Illus. 148). It is finally this shocking contrast between the two existences that jolts Freder and convinces him to investigate the subterranean city he has never seen. Freder confronts his father with the suffering he has witnessed and tells him of Maria's efforts to alleviate it. But the corrupt elder Fredersen decides instead to subvert the revolutionary stirrings of the slaves by discrediting Maria. He convinces the mad scientist Rotwang (Rudolf Klein-Rogge) to create an evil, "false" Maria from a robot. The plan backfires, however, when the mechanized double incites the slaves to riot and to demolish the machines that fuel the upper city. The film ends as the "false" Maria is destroyed and the real Maria effects a reconciliation between master and worker.

Like many films of the genre, *Metropolis* was ambivalent in its treatment of modern industrial society. While it upheld the posi-

148. *Metropolis* (1927, Fritz Lang). Art Directors: Otto Hunte, Erich Kettelhut, and Karl Vollbrecht.

tivist belief in technology that underlay the nineteenth-century utopias of science fiction writers Jules Verne and H. G. Wells, it at the same time shared the desperate fear of technology's inhumanity that had been expressed as early as Mary Shelley's *Frankenstein* (1818) and Samuel Butler's dystopian novel *Erewhon* (1872). *Metropolis*'s most powerful illustration of the latter view was its underground city of slaves. "Moloch" (Illus. 149), the foul, smoke-belching machine that in Freder's nightmare feeds on human sacrifices, recalled the style of Aztec pyramids, which had in fact been proposed by urban visionaries as models for New York's setback skyscrapers. Futurism, as previously noted, was the source of Kettelhut's design for the *"Herzmaschine,"* the underground city's power center, which required constant human tending. But once again, what had originated as a positive visual expression of technology—a basic tenet of the Futurists—was negated in the film. The *"Herzmaschine"* controlled human action, not vice versa, and Freder's attempts to service the device forced his movements into mechanical, staccato rhythms, his outstretched arms forming the image of a man "crucified" by machinery.

This dark, Dickensian vision of industrialization so flagrantly challenged the pro-technological beliefs of the architects of the modern movement that *Die Form,* the magazine of the Deutscher Werkbund, found it necessary to rebut *Metropolis*'s representation of "Moloch" with that of a clean, efficient power station requiring the custodianship of only one skilled technician. *Die Form*'s contributors might have found less fault with other aspects of the film, especially in the designs for the upper city, which revel in the potential of technology. No element of architectural decor was so innovatively explored in these sets as artificial illumination. For both architects and film designers, light was energy made manifest, and the ability to harness its power was a distinctly modern achievement. Nocturnal lighting fascinated skyscraper architects of the 1920s, whether as a means of satisfying their clients' desire for commercial publicity or to satisfy their own yearning to turn the nighttime city into an aesthetic event. The Expressionist lighting plans of the architect

Bruno Taut and the theatrical illumination schemes of Adolphe Appia, Gordon Craig, and Max Reinhardt were carried out on an urban scale in many New York skyscrapers, whose crowns were lit brilliantly at night. In the cinema, the persistence of the use of light as a visual motif throughout the silent and the sound eras testified to the strength of its symbolic resonance. In the laboratory of *L'Inhumaine,* for example, luminous zigzags quiver on the walls, illuminated signs flash warnings—*Alerte!* and *Danger de Mort* —and the movie frame itself pulsates with lightning as the scientist Einar Noorsen defies death to infuse life into Claire Lescot's corpse. In *Metropolis,* rays of light announce the technological "birth" of the robot Maria, while not only is the upper city defined largely by illuminated signs and searchlights, but its destruction is signaled by its lights being extinguished. One of the movie's most spectacular effects, that of floodlights crossing the faces of the city's skyscrapers, is thought to have been achieved through the use of stop-motion animation. Kettelhut painted a shifting series of white cones simulating light onto a rendering of the towers, and each step in their passage was filmed separately. Here, with minimal effort, the cinema realized one of the aims of modern architecture, which was rarely accomplished, let alone so dramatically, in actual construction (Illus. 150).

Steady refinements in the area of special effects encouraged studios to undertake further projects in the science fiction genre, and among *Metropolis*'s many imitators was Britain's *High Treason* (1929), with its imagined model of a 1940 New York. Although in the mid-1920s, Hollywood's Famous Players–Lasky Corporation had started a film about a futurist city, with designs by Jock Peters, the studio canceled it after the release of *Metropolis.* Another studio, Fox, produced a movie that both featured the first futurist city of the 1930s and was the first science fiction musical comedy, *Just Imagine* (1930). *Just Imagine* is set in 1980, when American society is divided by the freedom won by technological advances and the regimentation that assigns everyone an identifying number, establishes "new laws for love,"[26] and packages preordained marriages as easily as it mechanically dispenses food in the form of pills.

Designed by Stephen Goosson, *Just Imagine*'s New York was an elaborate miniature (Illus. 151), large enough, according to its designer, to fill an entire balloon hangar four hundred feet long by two hundred feet wide.[27] Although Goosson cited Le Corbusier as an inspiration for the film's design,[28] it replicated the architect's Voisin Plan only in its similar multilevel construction; Le Corbusier's cool and machine-honed urban imagery was too austere for the movies. More likely sources were architect Harvey Wiley Corbett's prediction that New York in 1975 would resemble a "very modernized Venice,"[29] and the version of the city presented in Hugh Ferriss's *The Metropolis of Tomorrow*.

Ferriss's collection of urban designs quickly became the single most important architectural text to influence Hollywood's interpretations of future cities (as well as skyscrapers; see page 151) in the 1930s. A notion of progress underlies the Ferriss book's organization. An urban scenario in three acts, *The Metropolis of Tomorrow* proceeds from the present ("Cities of Today") to the foreseeable future ("Projected Trends") to a futurist dream ("An Imaginary Metropolis"). Designers were seduced equally by the book's evanescent, evocative rendering style and its poetic language. The opening passage of "An Imaginary Metropolis," for example, used an almost cinematic imagery:

Let us return to the parapet which provided us with our original bird's-eye

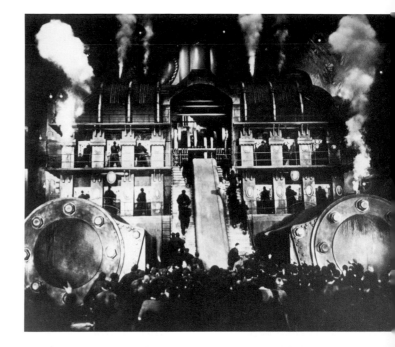

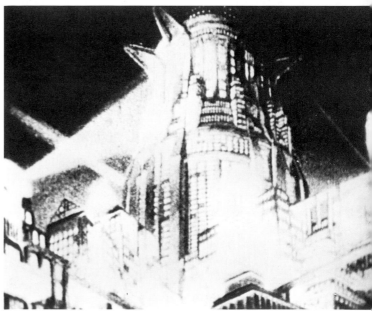

149. (TOP) *Metropolis* (1927).
150. (BOTTOM) *Metropolis* (1927).

view of the existing city. It is again dawn, with an early mist completely enveloping the scene. Again, there lies beneath us, curtained by the mist, a

Metropolis—and the curtain, again, is about to rise but, in this case, let us have it rise, not on the existing city, but on a city of the imagination.[30]

The Business Center of Ferriss's "city of the imagination" (Illus. 152) provided the most direct inspiration for Goosson's futurist New York. Broad superhighways establish a geometric ground plan that extends upward through overlapping levels of bridges, terraced walkways, and streets. The grid of circulation systems is pierced by enormously high freestanding skyscrapers surrounded by lower setback buildings. Having created this design as an analogy to the natural world of "towering mountain peaks . . . surrounded by foothills"[31] (a comparison that held true for Goosson's design as well), Ferriss explained that, while appreciation of individual towers was impossible when the towers were closely spaced,

> in the city, now before us, each great mass is surrounded by a great spaciousness; here, we may assume, the citizen's habitual prospects are ample vistas. Without altering his upright posture, his glance may serenly [*sic*] traverse the vista and find at its end a dominating and upright pinnacle.[32]

Ferriss and Goosson differed in the stylistic "clothing" of their towers. Although both designers accentuated verticality by employing pronounced corner pylons bracketing facades of pilasters and windows, Ferriss opted to cast them in the simplified mode, familiar from New York's Panhellenic Hotel (1927–28) by John Mead Howells, while Goosson chose the neo-Gothic

151. *Just Imagine* (1930, David Butler). Art Director: Stephen Goosson; Miniature Supervisor: Ralph Hammeras.

152. Drawing of a business center of the future, published in *The Metropolis of Tomorrow* (1929). Delineator: Hugh Ferriss.

mode of arches and finials, prominent in the Chicago Tribune Building (1922–24) by Raymond Hood and Howells.

Films like *Just Imagine* delighted their audiences by displaying a wide range of technologically advanced consumer goods, especially televisions—a movie staple since at least 1924—picture phones, and the private aircraft, the ultimate vehicle for individual mobility. Air travel among the pinnacles of skyscrapers was a notion common to film designers like Goosson as well as to urban planners and architects. However impractical such schemes were, low-flying airplanes crowded the skies in the visionary cities of Moses King, in the drawings of Sant' Elia, and in the cities proposed by Le Corbusier and *Metropolis.* Urban panoramas seen *from* airplanes were another popular theme. Viewers of *Città Futurista,* for example, could via Sant' Elia's illustrations imagine themselves preparing to land amid the future city's multilevel terraces and spires.

The affinity of architecture for air travel was not just the dream of ideologues. In 1930, Francis Keally proposed building an airfield on New York's Pennsylvania Station. Initial plans for the Empire State Building included using its pinnacle for a dirigible mast. That this suicidal scheme of using the tops of buildings as landing platforms for aircraft never materialized would have come as no surprise to moviegoers who had seen De Mille's *Madame Satan* (1930). The ultimate in "Jazz Age" movies, the film follows Angela Brooks's attempts to regain her husband's affections, which include masquerading as *femme fatale* Madame Satan. During a lavish society ball aboard a dirigible that is flying over Manhattan, Ted Kosloff dances the part of "Electricity" in the "Ballet Mechanique," foreshadowing the airship's imminent destruction in a lightning storm. Most of the passengers are saved by parachuting into Central Park's lake, an event staged to appear to be part of the fun.

Impending disaster notwithstanding, the association of cities with airplanes would remain a recurring motif throughout the movies of the 1930s. Batteries of attacking airplanes brought down King Kong in 1933. Ernö Metzner's designs for *The Tunnel* (1935; Illus. 153), a pro-technology British science fiction film, most noted for its streamlined New York–to–London tunnel, its trains, and its automobiles, include an airborne device that closely approximated

Eugène Hénard's formula for the type of aircraft suited for urban travel: "a light aeroplane, equipped with horizontal helices in addition to the vertical propeller, and capable of remaining stationary in the air, hovering over a given point."[33] This concept was the foundation for the helicopter, which Hénard himself credited to science fiction writer H. G. Wells's 1908 book, *The War in the Air.*

As a pioneering writer in the field of science fiction, Wells had already formulated a number of predictions about life in the future that anticipated the cinema's own treatment of the subject. For example, when the hero in Wells's novel *When the Sleeper Wakes* (1899) awakens, in the manner of Rip Van Winkle, two centuries in the future, he finds a city whose features resemble those of *Metropolis,* with its "Titanic buildings, curving spaciously in either direction," "mighty cantilevers," "gossamer suspension bridge[s] dotted with foot passengers flung across the chasm," and enormous facades "broken by great archings, circular perforations, balconies, buttresses, turret projections, myriad of vast windows, and an intricate scheme of architectural relief."[34] Wells himself, however, would have been at pains to disclaim any influence he might have had: "The other day I saw the most foolish film," he wrote in his 1927 review of *Metropolis.* "I cannot believe it would be possible to make a more foolish one."[35]

A decade later, Wells took steps to guarantee that *Things to Come* (1936), a film version of his 1933 novel, *The Shape of Things to Come,* would be a more acceptable piece of moviemaking. Wells's book was an attack against the laissez-faire economy of the 1920s and the rise of nationalism throughout Europe, which the novelist saw as destructive forces that would eventually lead to the collapse of Western civilization. Only an elite corps of progressive men and women, free of all anti-technological sentiment,

153. *The Tunnel* (1935, Maurice Elvey). Art Director: Ernö Metzner.

could avert disaster. Wells's optimism about scientific progress thus provided the ideological foundation for one of the period's few unequivocally pro-technological films —as well as its last.

Things to Come opens at Christmastime 1936. Amid preparations for the holidays, the citizens of Everytown (the film's recreation of London) ignore the ominous portents of war, which are heeded only by the clearsighted John Cabal. After decades of subsequent conflict, mankind reverts to a medieval, feudal society ruled by barbarous chieftains. Wells's elite rises out of the destruction and, headed by John Cabal, begins the reorganization of society along progressive, technocratic lines. Everytown, 2036: The persistent conflict of traditionalists and progressivists, the latter led by Cabal's grandson, erupts over a proposed scheme for space exploration. The progressivists are victorious, however, and the film ends with a moon shot and a paean to Wells's technological creed.

Although *Things to Come* opened to excellent reviews, it went on to become a popular failure. Many found Wells's ideology coldly totalitarian, and insightful moviegoers perceived how closely Wells's technological utopia echoed the chilling dystopia predicted by Aldous Huxley four years earlier in his novel *Brave New World*. As a response to the film, *The Architectural Review* reprinted without comment a passage from novelist Evelyn Waugh's *Decline and Fall*. Written almost a decade earlier, Waugh's novel rejected what was *Things to Come*'s most forbidding implication: that the individual human being was little more than a channel for the distribution of mechanical forces. In addition, *Decline and Fall*'s Professor Silenus was a prescient parody of two of the major individuals involved in *Things to Come,* producer Alexander Korda and designer László Moholy-Nagy. Professor Silenus's only completed work—other than "a rejected chewing gum factory whose design was reproduced in a progressive Hungarian quarterly" (both Korda and Moholy-Nagy were Hungarians)—was the "*décor* for a cinema-film of great length and complexity of plot—a complexity rendered the more inextricable by the producer's austere elimination of all human characters, a fact that had proved fatal to its commercial success."[36]

Things to Come was produced by Alexander Korda's London Films at its Denham studios, outside London. Directed by William Cameron Menzies, the project was from its inception a big-budget picture, and it ended up costing £350,000 (about $1,720,000). Korda, who rivaled Hollywood's producers in his insistence on high production values, first asked Le Corbusier and Fernand Léger, a member of the team that had designed *L'Inhumaine,* to design the film's futurist sequences. When both declined, he turned to the former Bauhaus professor László Moholy-Nagy, whose abstract films brought

him to Korda's attention after the artist moved to London in 1935. The emigration of Continental designers like Moholy-Nagy, Marcel Breuer, and Walter Gropius greatly furthered the development of modern architecture in England, just as the arrival of Continental film designers like Lazare Meerson and Alfred Junge (see page 112) rejuvenated British film design. Although Moholy-Nagy was not an architect, his mastery of virtually every field in the visual arts—he had designed stage sets for Erwin Piscator's avant-garde theater in Berlin and experimented with photography, painting, and typography—more than qualified him for Korda's commission.

Moholy-Nagy's plan for *Things to Come* involved a utopia in which fantastic technology would "eliminate solid form. Houses were no longer obstacles to, but receptacles of, man's natural life force, light. There were no walls, but skeletons of steel, screened with glass and plastic sheets. The accent was on perforation and contour, an indication of a new reality rather than reality itself"[37] (Illus. 154). Such abstract architecture was inspired by avant-garde Russian Constructivist designs of the 1920s. Compare it, for example, with a 1927 proposal for the Lenin Institute (Illus. 155) by Ivan Leonidov, a student of the Vesnin brothers at the Soviet Vkhutemas design school. In both designs, pure geometric forms—cones in Moholy-Nagy's scheme, a sphere in Leonidov's—appear to defy gravity but are actually supported by taut, virtually imperceptible wires. Both plans also include some form of tall building, Moholy-Nagy anticipating, as had Mies van der Rohe in his glass skyscraper projects of 1922, the "skin-and-bones" skyscraper style that would emerge after World War II.

Regrettably, Moholy-Nagy's designs were not used—they were, perhaps, too abstract for a popular movie—and the cinema forfeited a great opportunity to use modern architectural decor. The artist did, however, contribute ninety seconds of abstract footage to a section of *Things to Come* that used flash-forward editing to compress time and depict years of progress in a five-and-one-half-minute sequence. Before our very eyes, Everytown is transformed from twentieth-century postwar rubble to twenty-first-century gleaming metropolis.

The metropolis that finally did appear in the film was the work of Vincent Korda, the brother of the producer and a well-known set designer in his own right. Korda's decor was in keeping with a directive Wells had written in one of the countless memoranda he issued during filming. As opposed to the noisy and chaotic world of *Metropolis,* the decor of the final scenes of *Things to Come* was to convey

> a higher phase of civilization than the present, where there is greater wealth, finer order, higher efficiency. Human affairs in that more organized world will not always be hurried, they will not be crowded, there will be more leisure, more dignity. The rush and jumble and strain of contemporary life due to the uncontrolled effects of mechanism are not to be raised to the nth power. On the contrary, they are to be eliminated. Things, structures, in general, will be great, yes, but they will not be monstrous.[38]

After months of searching through magazines and ransacking libraries for suitable modern designs, Korda unveiled his "avant-garde" city of the future (Illus. 156), which is little more than a cartoon of streamlining,

154. (TOP) Model of a city of the future for *Things to Come* (1936, William Cameron Menzies). Designer: László Moholy-Nagy.
155. (BOTTOM) Model of a proposed Lenin Institute (1927, Ivan Leonidov).

then at the height of its commercial success. Streamlining is also the influence for the shape of the costumes, whose broad-shouldered silhouette—the fashion in 1936—concealed all the personal technological gadgetry beneath a smooth contour. However disappointing in their actual design, Korda's curving balconies, pedestrian walkways, monorail, and glass elevator are built on so large a scale that they do suggest a utopian grandeur, one reminiscent of that achieved by an eighteenth-century French "revolutionary" designer like Étienne-Louis Boullée. Like Boullée's proposal for a cenotaph for Newton, Korda's is a space so vast that its upper reaches are perceived only in a diffused haze of blazing light.

While the atrium of MGM's Grand Hotel is a hub of intense activity that replicated the vitality of the exterior urban scene, Korda's town center is beneath the ground and, with its smooth, plain contours, executed completely in white, is a conscious rejection of the frenetic pace associated with the Futurist-inspired cities of earlier films like *Metropolis* and *Just Imagine*. A similar sense of comfort and protection was evoked by Normal Bel Geddes's version of the future Manhattan at the 1939 New York World's Fair, where his Futurama exhibit shared the vision of Wells as well as of Thomas Adams in *The Regional Plan of New York and Its Environs*. The latter predicted that after a city of raised walkways and arcades became a reality, "Walking would become a pastime. . . . Shopping would be a joy. The overwrought nerves of the present New Yorker would be restored to normalcy and the city would become a model for all the world."[39] While neither Bel Geddes's nor Korda's schemes have proven viable urban models, the architectural vocabulary of *Things to Come* was an uncanny foreshadowing of the style of the hotels designed by architect and developer John Portman three decades later. Designed as antidotes to the congestion,

crime, pollution, and noise that Wells's ideal city would have abolished, Portman's hotels turned the author's utopian prototype into one of the most commercially successful and most often imitated real estate models of the last few decades.

As Europe and Asia moved toward war in the late 1930s, threatening the security of much of the world, the appeal of rigid social planning and technological progress became more equivocal. The success of totalitarian governments abroad and the development of unimaginably destructive weapons showed up the deficiencies of both these ideals, and the attractiveness of flight took a more idyllic, pastoral form in Frank Capra's *Lost Horizon* (1937; Illus. 157). Capra's Shangri-La, a closed community cut off from civilization by virtually impassable mountains, rejects the modern technological world *in toto,* in favor of a more serene, more contemplative existence. Ironically, this utopia was created under the direction of none other than Stephen Goosson, who a half decade earlier had designed the frenzied metropolis of *Just Imagine*. Like Korda, Goosson predicated his design on the ideas of enclosure and protection: Shangri-La's lamasery is a landscaped courtyard surrounded by white, floodlit buildings with broad flights of stairways, terraces, and colonnaded pavilions. Wide, flat eaves, which reinforce the sense of sanctuary within the courtyard, are a sharp contrast to the apparently unending rows of skyscraper spires in *Just Imagine*.

Lost Horizon and *Things to Come* are representative of the general shift in the cinema of the later 1930s away from the exciting urban schemes of *Just Imagine* and *Metropolis* and toward a calmer, quieter environment. After 1936, the popularity of science fiction films themselves fell dramatically, and the

156. *Things to Come* (1936, William Cameron Menzies). Art Director: Vincent Korda.

157. Ronald Colman in *Lost Horizon*
(1937, Frank Capra). Supervisory Art Director:
Stephen Goosson.

future cities visited by such late-'30s inter-
galactic heroes as Flash Gordon and Buck

Rogers were only pale imitations of earlier
designs. While *Lost Horizon* took the conservative position of repudiating modern technology, *Things to Come,* more than any
other film of the period, rode the same wave
of utopian fervor that bore many modern
architects. These visionaries zealously strove
to achieve a union of art and technology that
they hoped would, in some future time,
provide solutions to such urban problems as
congestion and overcrowding. Although
this dream underlay some of the most striking architecture and cinema decor of the
1930s, it had actually begun to sour for architects early in the decade, when the
Depression and increasing social unrest suggested that they had perhaps aimed too
high, placed too much credibility in a ther-
apeutic mission for art. By the decade's end,
both architects and filmmakers would be affected by the approaching war, which
would reveal the terribly destructive potential of technology. After the war, the best
examples of modern architecture, executed
in an elegant and sophisticated style, lacked
the foundation of the utopian hope for a harmonized society which infused, for example, the Bauhaus around 1930. While the
cinema likewise continued to produce provocative science fiction films, the positive
effects of technology would be largely overlooked, the legacy of the Bomb leading us
instead to explore its darkest ramifications.

Epilogue

As films cited in the previous chapters have shown, the second half of the 1930s saw a decline in the quality of modern cinema decor, as such settings became more and more often diluted pastiches of modern and traditional elements. During the 1940s, as postwar modern architecture became a vernacular style more often than not associated with anonymous office buildings and housing complexes, modern decor virtually disappeared from the movies. *Film noir,* a predominantly American type of thriller, often set in nighttime urban milieus populated by *femmes fatales* and alienated antiheroes, was an unsuitable vehicle for the modernist aesthetic of the previous decade. The *film noir*'s favorite theme of entrapment within a closed society ran counter to modernism's connotations of spatial openness, social mobility, and escape, while its cinematography explored dark and menacing shadows, reversing the modernist's manipulations of brilliant light. Other developments in cinematography allowed filmmakers to render spatial depth by means of the camera. Gregg Toland's cinematography and Perry Ferguson's set designs for Orson Welles's *Citizen Kane* (1941), the most brilliant example of deep-focus photography in the cinema, defined with equal clarity objects and characters in the background and in the foreground. The 1940s also saw a marked increase in films dealing with serious, problematic themes: In Hollywood, in *Lost Weekend* (1945), director Billy Wilder treated the subject of alcoholism; in *The Best Years of Our Lives* (1946), William Wyler portrayed the readjustment of war veterans; and in *Crossfire* (1947), Edward Dmytryk examined anti-Semitism; while in Italy, neo-realist directors dealt frankly with war and its aftermath. Within these realistic contexts, the studio-bound artifice that had fostered modernism would have provided an inappropriate mise-en-scène, and more and more films were shot on location. Roberto Rossellini's *Roma, Città aperta* (1945) was filmed in Rome itself at the end of the war, Billy Wilder's *A Foreign Affair* (1948) in Berlin, and as Hollywood found it more economical than shooting on a soundstage or a backlot, location shooting soon became the norm.

Modernism did have one last, extravagant gasp at the movies, however, in a vehicle that, ironically, remains for many filmgoers the most memorable use of modern architecture as set design. *The Fountainhead,* directed by King Vidor, was released by Warner Bros. in the summer of 1949, six years after the publication of Ayn Rand's mammoth best-selling novel, a popular culture phenomenon that announced modern architecture's new status as an establishment style. Through almost seven hundred pages of elaborate plot, stilted speeches, and overwrought emotions, Rand's ideological cartoon of a book (she also wrote the screenplay) pits the individual, whose undaunted ego is the fountainhead of all praiseworthy human activity, against the common man, Rand's rabble, who, fearing the individual, attempts to destroy or reduce him to its own base level. To translate her philosophy into fiction, the author cast her hero as an architect, a profession she had researched by conducting interviews and even, at one point, working briefly as a typist for Ely Jacques Kahn, one of New York's doyens of the Art Deco skyscraper. *The Fountainhead* is the story of Howard Roark (Gary Cooper), a lone champion of modernism who must struggle to have his designs built against the machinations of critics and clients, the public, and even the vast, stupid majority of his own profession. Roark's campaign is aided by two individualists-in-training: Dominique Francon (Patricia Neal), the cerebral daughter of the fashionable—thus reprehensible—elder architect Guy Francon; and her husband, Gail Wynand (Raymond Massey), a Hearst-like yellow journalist who ultimately sees the value in Roark's individualist position. Wynand uses the full weight of his populist tabloid to defend Roark in print during the architect's

trial for blowing up the Courtland Homes, a housing complex he secretly designed but which was not built to his exacting plans. Eventually, though, Wynand succumbs to his plebeian readership's demands that Roark be convicted for the deed, and he writes an editorial that condemns the architect. Yet Roark is acquitted, largely through the convincing force of his summation speech, and Wynand, realizing that he has not made the grade as a stalwart individual, sees no other option but to commit suicide. The act conveniently frees Dominique to marry Roark, whom, of course, she has loved all along—it was she who, at Roark's instigation, had actually planted the Courtland Homes bombs. In the closing scene of the film (the cinema's most unapologetic attempt to present the skyscraper as a phallic symbol), Dominique visits Roark at the Manhattan construction site of the Wynand Building (Illus. 158), the world's tallest tower, which had been financed by the publisher before his death, as his legacy to individualism. She ascends the side of the building in an open construction elevator, traveling ever higher and higher, eventually rising above the Empire State Building, which is seen in the distance. The final shot of the film is taken from Dominique's viewpoint as she nears the top of the structure and sees Roark, standing arms akimbo on a steel beam, alone and invincible.

In her novel's descriptions of the buildings Roark designs, Rand leaves little doubt that she found much of the real-life inspiration for her architect hero in Frank Lloyd Wright. The cliffside house by the sea that Roark designs for his client Austen Heller, for example, bears more than a little resemblance to Fallingwater: "It was as if the cliff had grown and completed itself and proclaimed the purpose for which it had been waiting. The house was broken into many levels, following the ledges of the rock, rising as it rose, in gradual masses, in planes

158. Architectural design for the Wynand Building for *The Fountainhead* (1949, King Vidor). Delineator: Cheseley Bonestell.

flowing together up into one consummate harmony."[1] Even Roark's personal life was analogous in many details to Wright's: Wright's apprenticeship to Louis Sullivan, a major modern architectural force at the turn of the century but largely forgotten at the end of his life, is echoed in Roark's relationship to Henry Cameron. And, like Roark's, Wright's life was a series of personal battles against conventions, whether of building styles or social mores.

When work began on *The Fountainhead*, the search for a set designer who could translate Roark's buildings onto the screen led the film's producer to approach Wright himself. The architect's astronomical fee— $250,000—made employing him out of the

question, and Warner Bros. turned instead to the young film designer Edward Carrere. Ironically, responsibility for Hollywood's last grandiose display of modern decor had fallen to a designer who was making his first solo effort in what would be a twenty-year film career.

Carrere's designs for *The Fountainhead* reflected the divergent paths that modern architectural imagery had taken after the war: the comfortable, "warm" modernism influenced by Wright and Scandinavian designers like Alvar Aalto running concurrently with the "cool," machined look of skyscrapers like New York's Lever House (1952), among the first buildings to use the spare style favored by corporate America.

159. *The Fountainhead* (1949). Art Director: Edward Carrere.

Carrere's design for Roark's first commission, the Enright House (Illus. 159), located at the southeast edge of New York's Central Park, takes as its model the new form of the postwar skyscraper. Yet unlike these buildings, which wrapped their simple rectangular volumes in skins of metal and glass, the Enright House is a series of thin floor slabs virtually floating in space and connected only by a small, glass-enclosed core. The theme of gravity-defying planes is repeated in the interior (Illus. 160), where a stairway

is formed of cantilevered treads, and even the tabletops are hovering sheets of glass.

The most controversial and unsuccessful of the film's designs were those that made clear references to Wright's style. Carrere's houses for *The Fountainhead* are an amalgam of Wright's work of the late 1930s and '40s, which had been published in two sumptuous issues of *Architectural Forum* in January 1938 and January 1948.[2] Roark's sketch for a small house nestled in the California hills recalls Wright's Pausen House of 1940, with its battered windowless masses balanced by cantilevered balconies. The house for Gail Wynand and one for the Atlantic shore both repeat Fallingwater's concept of floating trays visually moored by a vertical stone chimney block (Illus. 161). In the former, Carrere exaggerates Wright's subtle allusion to ocean liners by transforming the house's floors into ship's decks. The latter is Carrere's most extravagant design (Illus. 162), with the upward sweep and outward thrust of its many pergolas and balconies heightened by rendering the building from a low vantage point, a favorite practice of Wright's.

The reaction to *The Fountainhead*'s designs on the part of the architectural community was astonished outrage. Never before or since has the professional press been so vociferous in its condemnation of a film's decor. How dared the Hollywood philistines attempt to interpret the great master himself? *The Journal of the American Institute of Architects* supported its attack on Carrere by gleefully reprinting negative reviews of the film from the popular press.[3] The fiercest onslaught came from architect and designer George Nelson, in *Interiors* magazine. Not even deigning to mention Carrere by name, Nelson accused "Hollywood" of creating "the silliest travesty of modern architecture that has yet hit the films" and "a total perversion of formal and structural elements."[4] The house on the Atlantic was cited as a major offender on both structural and functional grounds: "We observe that the balcony itself could only support itself if its structure continued through the room

160. *The Fountainhead* (1949).

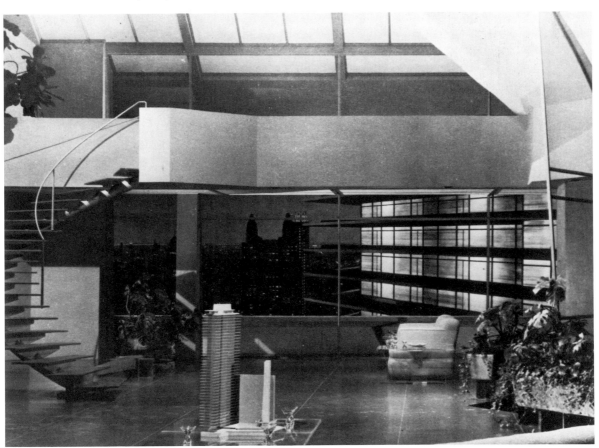

161. (TOP) Drawing of the Wynand residence in *The Fountainhead* (1949).
162. (BOTTOM) Drawing of a residence in *The Fountainhead* (1949).

163. *The Fountainhead* (1949).

behind, making it useless. And at this point we note an entirely new architectural invention—a cantilevered balcony holding up a cantilevered roof or trellis below it."[5]

Although Nelson's argument rested on the contention that Carrere mimicked only the superficial aspects of Wright's work while ignoring its underlying moorings, the opposite was actually the case. Carrere caricatured Wright's work, and, as all caricaturists do, exaggerated *only* the essentials: the dynamic outward thrust of interior space achieved through dramatic cantilevers. Nelson's scorn was also directed toward the living room of the Wynand residence (Illus. 163). A complete misunderstanding of the principle of the Wrightian module as a gen-

erator of form and space, Carrere's interior is an uneasy collision of orthogonal and hexagonal grids. Wright himself had certainly used both grids throughout the later years of his career, but never in a manner so jarring. In the Wynand living room, Carrere begins with an orthogonal module established in the floor paving, which he reinforces by the generally orthogonal shape of the room and by a rectangular area rug woven with a pattern of squares. This system is then contradicted by the polygonal shape of the fireplace hood, the diagonal placement of the sofa, and the sculptured mass behind the sofa. The room's pentagonal end table ambiguously responds to both modules, though why its irregular shape deserved such scorn from Nelson while Wright's equally forced hexagonal ottoman of the similarly planned Hanna House (1937) escaped ridicule is unclear.

If *The Fountainhead*'s designs have been judged harshly here, it is due to their having taken shape more as a response to the film's plot requirements than as the natural expression of an architectural sensibility, whether on the part of Carrere specifically or Hollywood in general. As the film was *about* architects, its sets were *about* design, which it made an accessible concept to audiences by caricature; had Howard Roark been a member of any other profession, the sets would not have been modern. While the filmmakers of the 1920s and '30s had been able to use modern architecture with the confidence that its mystique would carry powerful connotations to movie audiences about glamour, affluence, or escape, by 1949 that mystique had vanished. Modernism had less resonance, and modern decor in *The Fountainhead* was only feasible within the pragmatic confines of narrative necessity.

However equivocal its use of modern architecture, *The Fountainhead* remains a distinctive monument to the achievements of Hollywood set design of the Depression era. A mainstream feature that had as its protagonist an architect must certainly have seemed a risky venture to producers, even taking into account the impressive sales record of Ayn Rand's best-selling novel. That the film was ever made is a credit not only to the box-office drawing power of its stars and the talents of its director, but also to movie audiences' willingness to accept a career of designing modern buildings as a heroic endeavor, and the buildings themselves as dramatic, revolutionary works of art. If *The Fountainhead* was accessible (in a way that a popular film about a modernist painter, sculptor, composer, or writer could never have been), it was in large measure due

to the public's familiarity with modern building styles—a legacy, as this book has argued, of the film decor of the 1920s and '30s, a period when both movie sets and architecture were on the cutting edge of modern design.

While film and architecture had many aesthetic affinities—most notably in their shared interest in spatial inventiveness, artificial illumination, and movement—moviemakers contributed to modernism a sense of fantasy, whimsy, and drama, qualities that modern buildings, so often intimidatingly serious and sober, lacked. And even if modern architects had placed a higher premium on theatricality, which of them could have created environments as alluring as the ones through which Gloria Swanson and Greta Garbo flickered? Furthermore, the movies were able to execute modern designs on a grandness of scale that modernism's own outstanding achievements—which tended to be in the form of private houses, temporary exhibition pavilions, and unbuilt proposals—never attained. The Versailles of the modern movement is the nightclub of the Hollywood musical; its Gothic cathedral is the skyscraper of the futurist epic.

If the cinema finally ascribed to modernism a cluster of connotations of affluence, glamour and escape that were far removed from what its creators intended, it left a heritage of an enduring body of design, one that was seen and appreciated by an audience far vaster than architects could ever have hoped to reach. Modern architecture itself may have left the public cold, but modern architecture in the movies caught its imagination by embodying in forms both tangible and beautiful their fears, hopes, and aspirations. Today the efforts of modern film architects stand not only as a model of creative confluence of the artistic disciplines, but as a challenge waiting to be taken on by their successors, the future generations of designers of dreams.

Notes

Introduction

1. Paul Scheerbart, "Glass Architecture," in *Glass Architecture/Alpine Architecture,* ed. Dennis Sharp (London: November Books, 1972), p. 41.
2. These attendance figures are from Lloyd Lewis, "The Deluxe Picture Palace," *The New Republic,* March 27, 1929, p. 175; Margaret Farrand Thorp, *America at the Movies* (London: Faber and Faber, 1946), captions to illustrations between pp. 16 and 17; and Joseph M. Valerio and Daniel Friedman, *Movie Palaces: Renaissance and Reuse* (New York: Educational Facilities Laboratories Division, Academy for Educational Development, 1982), p. 35.
3. Interview, Anne Kandelman, Fréjus, France, April 28, 1981.
4. The model of the Maison Suspendue is in the collection of the Department of Architecture and Design at The Museum of Modern Art.
5. The Barcelona Pavilion has recently been rebuilt in that city.

Chapter 1: Projecting the New Architecture

1. "Introduction à l'Exposition," *Art et Décoration,* May 1925, p. 171.
2. Sheldon Cheney, *The New World Architecture* (London, New York and Toronto: Longmans, Green and Co., 1930), p. 272.
3. Henry-Russell Hitchcock, *Architecture: Nineteenth and Twentieth Centuries* (Harmondsworth: Penguin Books, 1977). p. 504.

4. "A Century of Progress Exposition . . . Chicago, 1933," *Architectural Record,* July 1933, p. 72.
5. Alfred H. Barr, Jr., quoted by Philip L. Goodwin, "Preface," in *Built in USA 1932–1944,* ed. Elizabeth Mock (New York: The Museum of Modern Art, 1944), p. 8.
6. David Gebhard and Harriette von Breton, *Kem Weber—The Moderne in Southern California, 1920 Through 1941* (Santa Barbara: The Art Galleries, University of California, 1969), pp. 31–2.

Chapter 2: Building the Seventh Art

1. Georges Méliès, "Les Vues Cinématographique," *La Revue du Cinéma,* October 15, 1929, p. 24.
2. [D.], "Feature Films of the Week: 'CABIRIA' The Best Yet," in *Spellbound in Darkness: A History of the Silent Film,* ed. George C. Pratt (Greenwich, Conn.: New York Graphic Society 1973), p. 124.
3. Ibid., p. 126.
4. Vachel Lindsay, *The Art of the Moving Picture* (New York: Macmillan, 1915), p. 245.
5. Kenneth MacGowan, "Enter—The Artist," *Photoplay,* January 1921, pp. 73–5.
6. Jesse L. Lasky, *I Blow My Own Horn* (Garden City, N.Y.: Doubleday, 1957), pp. 103–4.

Chapter 3: Europe at the Forefront

1. Virgilio Marchi, "Problemi tecnici, storici ed estetici della scenografia in Italia," in *La Scenografia Cinematografica in Italia,* ed. Guido Cincotti (Rome: Bianco e Nero, 1955), p. 13.

2. Elaine Mancini, "The Free Years of the Italian Film Industry 1930–1935" (Doctoral dissertation, New York University, 1981), p. 39.

3. Jean Tedesco as quoted by Standish D. Lawder, *The Cubist Cinema* (New York: New York University Press, 1975), n. 55 on p. 103.

4. Publicity release for *Enchantment,* undated, unpaginated.

5. Robert Mallet-Stevens, *Le Décor Moderne au Cinema* (Paris: Charles Massin, 1928), Preface.

6. Michel Louis, "Mallet-Stevens and the Cinema, 1919–1929," in *Rob Mallet-Stevens: Architecte,* ed. Hubert Jeanneau and Dominique Deshoulières (Brussels: Archives d'Architecture Moderne, 1980), p. 153.

7. Ibid., p. 154.

8. Program printed for the American premiere of *L'Inhumaine* [English title: *The New Enchantment*] at the Klaw Theater, New York City, March 14, 1926.

9. Marcel L'Herbier quoted by Michel Louis, p. 152.

10. Sonia Delaunay quoted by Sherry A. Buckberrough, *Sonia Delaunay: A Retrospective* (Buffalo, N.Y.: Albright-Knox Art Gallery, 1980), p. 79.

11. Léon Barsacq, *Caligari's Cabinet and Other Grand Illusions: A History of Film Design* (Boston: New York Graphic Society, 1976), p. 78.

12. Lazare Meerson quoted by Georges Sadoul in *Le Cinéma Français (1890–1962)* (Paris: Flammarion, 1962), p. 205.

13. Ludwig Mies van der Rohe quoted by Philip Johnson, *Mies van der Rohe* (New York: The Museum of Modern Art, 1978), p. 140.

14. Le Corbusier, *Towards a New Architecture* [*Vers une Architecture,* originally published in London, 1927] (New York: Praeger Publishers, 1970), p. 41.

15. "L'Arredamento Moderno nel Cinema," *La Casa Bella* 11, November 1932, pp. 32–41.

16. [Leader], "Arredamento di un Film," *La Casa Bella* 9, October 1931, pp. 22–36.

17. Giuseppe Capponi quoted by Marcello Piacentini, "Giuseppe Capponi, Architetto," *Architettura* 18 (1939), p. 271.

18. Andrew Burov quoted by V. Khazanova, "A. Burov 1900–1957," *Architectural Design,* February 1970, p. 102.

19. Alfred H. Barr, Jr., "Notes on Russian Architecture," *The Arts,* February 1929, p. 105.

Chapter 4: Hollywood Unlimited

1. John J. Floherty, *Moviemakers* (New York: Doubleday, Doran, 1935), Preface.

2. F. Scott Fitzgerald, *The Last Tycoon* (New York: Charles Scribner's Sons, 1970), p. 25.

3. Robert Sklar, *Movie-Made America: A Cultural History of American Movies* (New York: Random House, 1975), p. 41.

4. Thorp, p. 87.

5. Interviews with Mrs. Jan deSwart, Eagle Rock, Calif., December 1980, and with Mrs. Peter Edwards, Santa Barbara, Calif., December 1980.

6. Lewis Jacobs, *The Rise of the American Film: A Critical History* (New York: Teachers College Press, 1968), p. 445.

7. Martin Battersby, *The Decorative Thirties,* (London: Studio Vista, 1971), p. 78.

8. Richard Neutra, "Homes and Housing," in *Los Angeles: Preface to a Master Plan,* ed. George W. Robbins and L. Deming Tilton (Los Angeles: Pacific Southwest Academy, 1941), p. 196.

9. Arlene Croce, *The Fred Astaire and Ginger Rogers Book* (New York: Galahad Books, 1972), p. 56.

10. Paul T. Frankl, *Form and Re-Form* (New York: Harper & Brothers, 1930), p. 163.

11. "Streamline Ladies," *Silver Screen,* September 1931, p. 23.

12. Ibid.

13. Telephone conversation with Maurice Zuberano, Los Angeles, Calif., September 24, 1985.

14. Croce, p. 25.

15. Erté, *Things I Remember* (New York: Quadrangle, New York Times Book Company, 1975), p. 80.

16. Ibid., p. 81.

17. *Encyclopaedia Britannica,* 14th ed. (1929–36), s.v. "Motion Picture Sets," by Cedric Gibbons.

18. Patrick Downing and John Hambley, *The Art of Hollywood* (London: The Victoria and Albert Museum, 1979), p. 68.

19. *Baltimore Post,* September 11, 1928.

20. Edgar G. Ulmer quoted by Peter Bogdanovich, "Edgar G. Ulmer," in *Kings of the Bs: Working Within the Hollywood System,* ed. Todd McCarthy and Charles Flynn (New York: E. P. Dutton, 1975), p. 389.

21. Theo van Doesburg quoted by Dominique Deshoulières and Hubert Jeanneau, "The Demands of Architecture," in *Rob Mallet-Stevens: Architecte,* p. 45.

Chapter 5: The Modern Mystique

1. Anson Bailey Cutts, "Homes of Tomorrow in the Movies of Today," *California Arts and Architecture* 54 (November 1938), p. 18.

2. Le Corbusier, p. 210.

3. Reyner Banham, *The Architecture of the Well-*

Tempered Environment (London: Architectural Press; Chicago: University of Chicago Press, · 1969), p. 96.

4. Ibid.

5. *Scientific Management in the Home,* illustrated by Adrian Forty in "Unit 20: The Electric Home," *British Design* (Milton Keynes: The Open University Press, 1975), p. 46.

6. Le Corbusier, p. 222.

7. Ibid., p. 10.

8. Hans Dreier quoted by Cutts, p. 17.

9. Le Corbusier, p. 10.

10. K. R. G. Browne and W. Heath Robinson, *How to Live in a Flat* (London: Hutchinson, 1936), p. 30.

11. "Thanksgiving 1929," in *The American Home,* November 1929, p. 129.

12. Le Corbusier, p. 114.

13. William De Mille quoted by Kenneth MacGowan in *Behind the Screen* (New York: Delacorte Press, 1965), p. 262.

14. Cecil B. De Mille, *The Autobiography of Cecil B. De Mille* (Englewood Cliffs, N.J.: Prentice-Hall), p. 210.

15. Ludwig Mies van der Rohe, "1923: The Office Building," reprinted by Philip Johnson in *Mies van der Rohe* (New York: The Museum of Modern Art, 1978), p. 188.

16. [Unidentified newspaper clipping] June 12, 1931.

17. Fritz Lang quoted by Lotte Eisner, *Fritz Lang* (New York: Oxford University Press, 1977), p. 95.

18. Ibid.

19. Hal Mohr as quoted by Leonard Maltin in *The Art of the Cinematographer* (New York: Dover Publications, 1978), p. 86.

20. Publicity book for the film *Top of the Town,* dated November 23, 1936.

21. *The New York Times,* June 28, 1936.

22. Le Corbusier, pp. 96–7.

23. Publicity material for the film *What a Widow!*

24. Ethan Mordden, *The Hollywood Musical* (New York: St. Martin's Press, 1981), p. 47.

25. Alfred Stieglitz quoted by Dorothy Norman, *Alfred Stieglitz: An American Seer* (New York: Random House, 1973), p. 80.

26. Advertisement for *Just Imagine, Photoplay,* January 1931, p. 9.

27. Stephen Goosson, personal letter to Dr. Robert Knutson, University of Southern California, July 18, 1972.

28. Ibid.

29. ·Harvey Wiley Corbett quoted by Thomas Adams, *The Regional Plan of New York and Its Environs,* vol. 2 (New York: Regional Plan of New York and Its Environs, 1931), p. 309.

30. Hugh Ferriss, *The Metropolis of Tomorrow* (New York: Ives Washburn, 1929), p. 109.

31. Ibid., pp. 109–10.

32. Ibid., p. 110.

33. Eugène Hénard quoted by Peter M. Wolf, "Eugène Hénard and the City Planning of Paris 1910–1914" (Doctoral dissertation, New York University, 1968), p. 101.

34. H. G. Wells quoted by James Gunn, *Alternate Worlds: The Illustrated History of Science Fiction* (Englewood Cliffs, N.J.: Prentice-Hall, 1975), p. 95.

35. H. G. Wells quoted by Eisner, p. 84.

36. Evelyn Waugh, *Decline and Fall* (Boston: Little, Brown, 1977), p. 159.

37. Sibyl Moholy-Nagy, *Experiment in Totality* (Cambridge, Mass.: M.I.T. Press, 1969), p. 129.

38. H. G. Wells, "Rules of Thumb for Things to Come," *The New York Times,* April 12, 1936.

39. Harvey Wiley Corbett quoted by Thomas Adams, p. 309.

Epilogue

1. Ayn Rand, *The Fountainhead* (New York: Bobbs-Merrill, 1971), p. 125.

2. The January 1938 and January 1948 issues of *Architectural Forum* were devoted to the work of Frank Lloyd Wright.

3. "The Fountainhead," *Journal of the American Institute of Architects,* July 1949, p. 27.

4. George Nelson, "Mr. Roark goes to Hollywood," *Interiors,* April 1949, pp. 110–11.

5. Ibid., p. 108.

Filmography

Donald Albrecht and Ronald S. Magliozzi

This filmography lists all the films that appear in the text, as well as select films produced during the period under study that contain Art Deco or modern architectural sets. Documentaries and abstract films, which are not mentioned in the text, are not included.

The films are listed by date of release in the country of production.

Key to Abbreviations:
Dir.—Director
Art Dir.—Art Director
★Films distributed by The Museum of Modern Art Department of Film

1895

★ARRIVAL OF A TRAIN (L'ARRIVÉE D'UN TRAIN EN GARE À LA CIOTAT). Société Lumière. Dir. Louis Lumière.

1902

★A TRIP TO THE MOON (LE VOYAGE DANS LA LUNE). Star Film. Dir./Art Dir. Georges Méliès. With Bluette Bernon, Georges Méliès.

1904

THE IMPOSSIBLE VOYAGE (LE VOYAGE À TRAVERS L'IMPOSSIBLE). Star Film. Dir./Art Dir. Georges Méliès. With Georges Méliès.

1906

LA VIE DU CHRIST. Gaumont. Dir. Alice Guy-Blaché and Victorin Jasset. Art Dir. uncredited.

1914

★CABIRIA. Italia Film, Turin. Dir. Giovanni Pastrone. Art Dir. uncredited. With Letizia Quaranta, Dante Testa.

1915

UNA VITA FUTURISTA. Producer uncredited. Dir. Arnaldo Ginna, in collaboration with Filippo Marinetti, Giacomo Balla, Bruno Corra, Lucio Venna, Emilio Settimelli, Mario Carli, Neri Nannetti.

1916

★INTOLERANCE. Wark Producing Co. Dir. D. W. Griffith. Art Dir. Walter L. Hall. With Lillian Gish, Mae Marsh.

IL PERFIDO INCANTO. Novissima. Dir. Anton Giulio Bragaglia. Art Dir. Enrico Prampolini, Anton Giulio Bragaglia. With Thais Galitzky, Renée April.

1919

FUMÉE NOIRE. Parisia Films. Dir. Louis Delluc and René Coiffard. Art Dir. Francis Jourdain, Van Dongen. With Eve Francis, Jean Hervé.

★MALE AND FEMALE. Paramount-Artcraft. Dir. Cecil B. De Mille. Art Dir. Wilfred Buckland. With Gloria Swanson, Thomas Meighan.

DIE PEST IN FLORENE. Decla–Bioscop AG, Berlin. Dir. Otto Rippert. Art Dir. Franz Jaffé, Hermann Warm, Walter Reimann, Walter Röhrig. With Otto Mennstaedt, Anders Wikman.

1920

★THE CABINET OF DR. CALIGARI (DAS KABINETT DES DR. CALIGARI). Decla–Bioscop AG, Berlin. Dir. Robert Wiene. Art Dir. Hermann Warm, Walter Röhrig, Walter Reimann. With Werner Krauss, Conrad Veidt.

LE CARNAVAL DES VÉRITÉS. Gaumont-Série Pax. Dir. Marcel L'Herbier. Art Dir. Claude Autant-Lara, Michel Dufet. With Suzanne Déprés, Paul Capellani.

GENUINE. Decla-Bioscop AG, Berlin. Dir. Robert Wiene. Art Dir. César Klein, Bernhard Klein, Kurt Hermann Rosenberg. With Fern Andra, Ernst Gronau.

★DER GOLEM, WIR ER IN DIE WELT KAM. Projektions-AG "Union," Berlin. Dir. Paul Wegener and Carl Boese. Art Dir. Hans Poelzig. With Paul Wegener, Lyda Salmonova.

LE SECRET DE ROSETTE LAMBERT. Adolphe Osso Entreprises Cinématographiques. Dir. Raymond Bernard. Art Dir. Robert Mallet-Stevens. With Lois Meredith, Henri Debain.

1921

THE AFFAIRS OF ANATOL. Famous Players–Lasky. Dir. Cecil B. De Mille. Art Dir. Paul Iribe. With Gloria Swanson, Wallace Reid.

BUNTY PULLS THE STRINGS. Goldwyn. Dir. Reginald Barker. Art Dir. Cedric Gibbons. With Leatrice Joy, Raymond Hatton.

CAMILLE. Nazimova Productions. Dir. Ray C. Smallwood. Art Dir. Natacha Rambova. With Alla Nazimova, Rudolph Valentino.

L'EMPEREUR DES PAUVRES. Pathé-Consortium-Cinéma. Dir. René Leprince. Art Dir. uncredited. With Gina Relly, Léon Mathot.

ENCHANTMENT. Cosmopolitan Productions. Dir. Robert G. Vignola. Art Dir. Joseph Urban. With Marion Davies, Forrest Stanley.

JETTATURA. Société des Films Artistiques. Dir. Gilles Veber. Art Dir. A. Fabre, Robert Mallet-Stevens. With Elena Sagrary, Jean Dehelly.

LE JOCKEY DISPARU. L'Art Muet. Dir. Jacques Riven. Art Dir. Robert Mallet-Stevens. With François Angely, Constant Rémy.

PAYING THE PIPER. Famous Players–Lasky. Dir. George Fitzmaurice. Art Dir. Paul Iribe. With Dorothy Dickson, Rod LaRocque.

VILLA DESTIN. Gaumont–Série Pax. Dir. Marcel L'Herbier. Art Dir. Georges Lepape, Robert-Jules Garnier, Claude Autant-Lara. With Alice Field, Saint-Granier.

THE WILD GOOSE. Cosmopolitan Productions. Dir. Albert Capellani. Art Dir. Joseph Urban. With Mary MacLaren, Holmes E. Herbert.

1922

★DR. MABUSE, DER SPIELER. UCO-Film, Berlin. Dir. Fritz Lang. Art Dir. Otto Hunte, Stahl-Urach, Erich Kettelhut, Karl Vollbrecht. With Rudolf Klein-Rogge, Bernhard Goetzke.

ROBIN HOOD. United Artists. Dir. Allan Dwan. Art Dir. Wilfred Buckland. With Douglas Fairbanks, Wallace Beery.

SALOME. Nazimova Production. Dir. Charles Bryant. Art Dir. Natacha Rambova. With Alla Nazimova, Rose Dione.

THE YOUNG DIANA. Cosmopolitan Productions. Dir. Albert Capellani and Robert G. Vignola. Art Dir. Joseph Urban. With Marion Davies, Maclyn Arbuckle.

1923

ADAM AND EVA. Cosmopolitan Productions. Dir. Robert G. Vignola. Art Dir. Joseph Urban. With Marion Davies, T. Roy Barnes.

DON JUAN ET FAUST. Gaumont. Dir. Marcel L'Herbier. Art Dir. Robert-Jules Garnier. With Marcelle Pradot, Jaque Catelain.

THE ENEMIES OF WOMEN. Cosmopolitan Productions. Dir. Alan Crosland. Art Dir. Joseph Urban. With Alma Rubens, Lionel Barrymore.

RASKOLNIKOW. Lionardi-Film der Neumann Produktions GmbH. Dir. Robert Wiene. Art Dir. Andrei Andrejew. With Gregori Chmara, Pawal Pawloff.

1924

AELITA. Mezhrabpom-Russ. Dir. Yakov Protazanov. Art Dir. Sergei Kozlovsky, Isaac Rabinovich, Victor Simov, Alexandra Exter. With Valentina Kuinzhi, Nikolai Tsereteli.

★BALLET MÉCANIQUE. Fernand Léger. Dir. Fernand Léger.

LE FANTÔME DU MOULIN ROUGE. Film René Fernand. Dir. René Clair. Art Dir. Robert Gys. With Sandra Milowanoff, Georges Vaultier.

★FEU MATHIAS PASCAL. Cinégraphic-Albatros. Dir. Marcel L'Herbier. Art Dir. Alberto Cavalcanti, Lazare Meerson. With Marcelle Pradot, Ivan Mosjoukine.

L'INHUMAINE. Cinégraphic. Dir. Marcel L'Herbier. Art Dir. Robert Mallet-Stevens, Fernand Léger, Alberto Cavalcanti, Claude Autant-Lara. With Georgette Leblanc, Jaque Catelain.

JOCASTE. Films de France. Dir. Gaston Ravel. Art Dir. Tony LeKain. With Sandra Milowanoff, Gabriel Signoret.

★THE LAST LAUGH (DER LETZE MANN). UFA. Dir. F. W. Murnau. Art Dir. Robert Herlth, Walter Röhrig. With Emil Jannings, Hermann Vallentin.

★DIE NIBELUNGEN (TEIL I: SIEGFRIEDS TOD/TEIL II: KRIEMHILDS RACHE). Decla-Bioscop AG, Berlin. Dir. Fritz Lang. Art Dir. Otto Hunte, Erich Kettelhut, Karl Vollbrecht. With Paul Richter, Margarete Schön.

A SAINTED DEVIL. Famous Players–Lasky. Dir. Joseph Henabery. Art Dir. Lawrence Hitt. With Nita Naldi, Rudolph Valentino.

1925

LE DOUBLE AMOUR. Films Albatros. Dir. Jean Epstein. Art Dir. Pierre Kefer. With Nathalie Lissenko, Jean Angelo.

GRIBICHE. Films Albatros. Dir. Jacques Feyder. Art Dir. Lazare Meerson. With Françoise Rosay, Jean Forest.

THE RAT. Gainsborough. Dir. Graham Cutts. Art Dir. Charles W. Arnold. With Mae Marsh, Ivor Novello.

1926

ANTOINETTE SABRIER. Sté des Cinéromans. Dir. Germaine Dulac. Art Dir. Louis Nalpas, Silvagni. With Eve Francis, Gabriel Gabrio.

BELPHEGOR. Sté des Cinéromans. Dir. Henri Desfontaines. Art Dir. Louis Nalpas, Jean Perrier. With Elmire Vautier, Rene Navarre.

DANCING MOTHERS. Famous Players–Lasky. Dir. Herbert Brenon. Art Dir. Julian Boone Fleming. With Alice Joyce, Clara Bow.

THE LITTLE PEOPLE. Welsh-Pearson. Dir. George Pearson. Art Dir. Alberto Cavalcanti. With Mona Maris, Frank Stanmore.

LA PROIE DU VENT. Films Albatros. Dir. René Clair. Art Dir. Lazare Meerson, Bruni. With Sandra Milowanoff, Charles Vanel.

LE P'TIT PARIGOT. Luminor. Dir. René Le Somptier. Art Dir. Robert and Sonia Delaunay. With Marquisette Bosky, Georges Biscot.

LE VERTIGE. Cinégraphic. Dir. Marcel L'Herbier. Art Dir. Robert Mallet-Stevens, Lucien Aguettand, André Lurçat, Robert and Sonia Delaunay. With Emmy Lynn, Jaque Catelain.

1927

★METROPOLIS. UFA. Dir. Fritz Lang. Art Dir. Otto Hunte, Erich Kettelhut, Karl Vollbrecht. With Brigitte Helm, Alfred Abel.

NAPOLÉON. Société du Film Napoléon/Société Générale de Films. Dir. Abel Gance. Art Dir. Alexandre Benois, Jacouty, Ivan Lochakoff, Eugène Lourié, Meinhardt and Pierre Schildknecht. With Annabella, Albert Dieudonné.

L'OCCIDENT. Cinéromans–Films de France. Dir. Henri Fescourt. Art Dir. Robert Gys. With Claudia Victrix, Jaque Catelain.

★SUNRISE. Fox Film Corp. Dir. F. W. Murnau. Art Dir. Rochus Gliese, Edgar G. Ulmer, Alfred Metscher. With Janet Gaynor, George O'Brien.

LES TRANSATLANTIQUES. Films Diament. Dir. Pierre Colombier. Art Dir. Jacques Colombier. With Aimé Simon-Girard, Pepa Bonafé.

1928

ANGST. Orplid-Film GmbH., Berlin. Dir. Hans Steinhoff. Art Dir. Franz Schroedter. With Elga Brink, Henry Edwards.

L'ARGENT. Ciné-Mondial. Dir. Marcel L'Herbier. Art Dir. Lazare Meerson, André Barsacq. With Brigitte Helm, Pierre Alcover.

THE BATTLE OF THE SEXES. Art Cinema Corp. Dir. D. W. Griffith. Art Dir. William Cameron Menzies, Park French. With Jean Hersholt, Phyllis Haver.

THE CROWD. MGM. Dir. King Vidor. Art Dir. Arnold A. Gillespie, Cedric Gibbons. With Eleanor Boardman, James Murray.

LE DIABLE AU COEUR. Cinégraphic-Gaumont British. Dir. Marcel L'Herbier. Art Dir. Robert-Jules Garnier, Claude Autant-Lara, Louis Le Bertre. With Betty Balfour, Jaque Catelain.

DUEL. Société des Cinéromans–Films de France. Dir. Jacques de Baroncelli. Art Dir. Robert Gys. With Mady Christian, Gabriel Gabrio.

THE MAGNIFICENT FLIRT. Paramount Famous Lasky Corp. Dir. Harry d'Abbadie d'Arrast. Art Dir. Van Nest Polglase. With Florence Vidor, Albert Conti.

LA MADONE DES SLEEPINGS. Natan. Dir. Marco de Gastyne. Art Dir. Eugène Carré. With Claude France, Olaf Fjord.

MALDONE. Société des Films C. Dullin. Dir. Jean Grémillon. Art Dir. André Barsacq. With Genica Athanasiou, Charles Dullin.

LES NOUVEAUX MESSIEURS. Albatros–Sequana Films. Dir. Jacques Feyder. Art Dir. Lazare Meerson. With Gaby Morlay, Albert Préjean.

OUR DANCING DAUGHTERS. Cosmopolitan Productions/ MGM. Dir. Harry Beaumont. Art Dir. Cedric

Gibbons. With Joan Crawford, Johnny Mack
Brown.

PANAME N'EST PAS PARIS. A.C.E. Dir. Nikolai Malikoff.
Art Dir. V. Meinhardt, Boris Bilinsky. With Ruth
Weyer, Jaque Catelain.

SHOW FOLKS. Pathé Exchange. Dir. Paul L. Stein. Art
Dir. Mitchell Leisen. With Eddie Quillan, Lina
Basquette.

★SPIONE. UFA. Dir. Fritz Lang. Art Dir. Otto Hunte,
Karl Vollbrecht. With Lien Deyers, Lupu Pick.

DER TANZSTUDENT. UFA. Dir. Johannes Guter. Art
Dir. Jacques Rotmil. With Suzy Vernon, Willy
Fritsch.

TESHA. Burlington Films, Wardour. Dir. Victor
Saville. Art Dir. Hugh Gee. With Maria Corda,
Jameson Thomas.

DIE TOLLE KOMTESS. Richard Eichberg–Film GmbH,
Berlin. Dir. Richard Löwenbein. Art Dir. Max
Heilbronner. With Dina Gralla, Werner Fuetterer.

VIVRE. Phénix-Films AG–Studios Réunis. Dir. Robert
Boudrioz. Art Dir. Hays. With Elmire Vautier,
Bernhard Goetzke.

VOM TÄTER FEHLT JEDE SPUR. UFA. Dir. Constantin J.
David. Art Dir. Jacques Rotmil. With Hani Weisse,
Gritta Ley.

WEIB IN FLAMMEN. Tschechowa–Film GmbH, Berlin.
Dir. Max Reichmann. Art Dir. Alexander Ferenczy.
With Olga Tschechowa, Ferdinand Von Alten.

A WOMAN OF AFFAIRS. MGM. Dir. Clarence Brown.
Art Dir. Cedric Gibbons. With Greta Garbo, John
Gilbert.

1929

BROADWAY. Universal Pictures. Dir. Paul Fejos. Art
Dir. Charles D. Hall. With Glenn Tryon, Evelyn
Brent.

DYNAMITE. MGM. Dir. Cecil B. De Mille. Art Dir.
Mitchell Leisen. Cedric Gibbons. With Kay Johnson,
Conrad Nagel.

DIE FRAU IM MOND. UFA. Dir. Fritz Lang. Art. Dir.
Otto Hunte, Emil Hasler, Carl Vollbrecht. With
Gerda Maurus, Willy Fritsch.

GENTLEMEN OF THE PRESS. Paramount Famous Lasky
Corp. Dir. Millard Webb. Art Dir. William Saulter.
With Katherine Francis, Walter Huston.

GOLD DIGGERS OF BROADWAY. Warner Bros. Dir. Roy
Del Ruth. Art Dir. Max Parker, Lewis Geib. With
Nancy Welford, Conway Tearle.

DAS GRÜNE MONOKEL. Deutsches-Lichtspiel-Syndikat
AG, Berlin. Dir. Rudolph Meinert. Art Dir. Robert
Neppach. With Betty Bird, Ralph Cancy.

HIGH TREASON. Gaumont. Dir. Maurice Elvey. Art
Dir. Andrew L. Mazzei. With Benita Hume,
Jameson Thomas.

THE KISS. MGM. Dir. Jacques Feyder. Art Dir. Cedric
Gibbons. With Greta Garbo, Conrad Nagel.

THE LAUGHING LADY. Paramount Famous Lasky Corp.
Dir. Victor Schertzinger. Art Dir. William Saulter.
With Ruth Chatterton, Clive Brook.

★LES MYSTÈRES DU CHÂTEAU DU DÉ. Man Ray–Vicomte
de Noailles. Dir. Man Ray. With Man Ray, J. A.
Boiffard.

DIE NACHT GEHÖRT UNS. Froelich-Film GmbH. Dir.
Karl Froelich. Art Dir. Franz Schroedter. With Hans
Albers, Charlotte Ander.

OBLOMOK IMPERII. Sovkino, Leningrad. Dir. Friedrich
Ermler. Art Dir. Yevgeni Enei. With Ludmilla
Semyonova, Fyodor Nikitin.

OLD AND NEW (STAROYE I NOVOYE). Sovkino, Moscow.
Dir. Sergei Eisenstein and Grigori Alexandrov. Art
Dir. Andrew K. Burov, Vasili Kovrigin, Vasili
Rakhals. With Marfa Lapkina, Vasya Buzenkov.

OUR MODERN MAIDENS. MGM. Dir. Jack Conway. Art
Dir. Cedric Gibbons. With Joan Crawford, Rod La
Rocque.

SENSATION IM WINTERGARTEN. Lothar Stark–Film
GmbH, Berlin. Dir. Gennaro Righelli. Art Dir.
Hans Sohnle, Otto Erdmann. With Claire Rommer,
Paul Richter.

THE SINGLE STANDARD. MGM. Dir. John S. Robertson.
Art Dir. Cedric Gibbons. With Greta Garbo, Nils
Asther.

SOLE. Augustus Production. Dir. Alessandro Blasetti.
Art Dir. Gastone Medin. With Marcello Spada,
Vasco Creti.

SPRENGBAGGER 1010. Achaz-Duisberg, Berlin. Dir. Carl
Ludwig Achaz-Duisberg. Art Dir. Andrei
Andrejew. With Heinrich George, Viola Garden.

UNTAMED.MGM. Dir. Jack Conway. Art Dir. Cedric
Gibbons, Van Nest Polglase. With Joan Crawford,
Robert Montgomery.

THE WILD PARTY. Paramount Famous Lasky Corp. Dir.
Dorothy Arzner. Art Dir. uncredited. With Clara
Bow, Fredric March.

WONDER OF WOMEN. MGM. Dir. Clarence Brown. Art
Dir. Cedric Gibbons. With Lewis Stone, Leila
Hyams.

1930

ANIMAL CRACKERS. Paramount–Publix Corp. Dir.
Victor Heerman. Art Dir. William Saulter. With
Lillian Roth, the Marx Brothers.

THE CZAR OF BROADWAY. Universal Pictures. Dir.
William James Craft. Art Dir. uncredited. With John
Wray, Betty Compson.

DAVID GOLDER. Vandel et Delac. Dir. Julien Duvivier.
Art Dir. Lazare Meerson.With Jackie Monnier,
Harry Baur.

DELIKATESSEN. Deutsches Lichtspiel–Syndikat AG. Dir. Géza von Bolvary. Art Dir. Robert Neppach. With Georgia Lind, Harry Liedtke.

L'ÈTRANGÈRE. Jean de la Cour, Paris/Hegewald-Film. GmbH., Berlin. Dir. Gaston Ravel. Art Dir. Lazare Meerson. With Elvire Popesco, Cady Winter.

HAPPY DAYS. Fox Film Corp. Dir. Benjamin Stoloff. Art Dir. Jack Schulze. With Marjorie White, Charles E. Evans.

DER HERR AUF BESTELLUNG. Super-Film GmbH. Dir. Géza von Bolvary. Art Dir. Robert Neppach. With Willi Forst, Paul Hörbiger.

JUST IMAGINE. Fox Film Corp. Dir. David Butler. Art Dir. Stephen Goosson. With Maureen O'Sullivan, El Brendel.

DAS KABINETT DES DR. LARIFARI. Trio-Film GmbH. Dir. Robert Wohlmuth. Art Dir. Heinrich C. Richter. With Max Hansen, Paul Morgan.

LAUGHTER. Paramount–Publix Corp. Dir. Harry d'Abbadie d'Arrast. Art Dir. uncredited. With Nancy Carroll, Fredric March.

LILIES OF THE FIELD. First National Pictures. Dir. Alexander Korda. Art Dir. Anton Grot. With Corinne Griffith, Ralph Forbes.

MADAM SATAN. MGM. Dir. Cecil B. De Mille. Art Dir. Cedric Gibbons, Mitchell Leisen. With Lillian Roth, Kay Johnson.

ON YOUR BACK. Fox Film Corp. Dir. Guthrie McClintic. Art Dir. Jack Schulze. With Irene Rich, Raymond Hackett.

OUR BLUSHING BRIDES. MGM. Dir. Harry Beaumont. Art Dir. Cedric Gibbons. With Joan Crawford, Anita Page.

PAID. MGM. Dir. Sam Wood. Art Dir. Cedric Gibbons. With Joan Crawford, Robert Armstrong.

QUEEN HIGH. Paramount–Publix Corp. Dir. Fred Newmeyer. Art Dir. William Saulter. With Ginger Rogers, Stanley Smith.

SAFETY IN NUMBERS. Paramount–Publix Corp. Dir. Victor Schertzinger. Art Dir. uncredited. With Kathryn Crawford, Charles "Buddy" Rogers.

SEE AMERICA THIRST. Universal Pictures. Dir. William James Craft. Art Dir. Charles D. Hall. With Bessie Love, Harry Langdon.

SHOWGIRL IN HOLLYWOOD. First National Pictures. Dir. Mervyn LeRoy. Art Dir. Jack Okey. With Alice White, Jack Mulhall.

SOUS LES TOITS DE PARIS. Société des Films Sonores Tobis. Dir. René Clair. Art Dir. Lazare Meerson. With Pola Illery, Albert Préjean.

SUNNY. First National Pictures. Dir. William A. Seiter. Art Dir. uncredited. With Marilyn Miller, Lawrence Gray.

THOSE THREE FRENCH GIRLS. MGM. Dir. Harry Beaumont. Art Dir. Cedric Gibbons. With Fifi Dorsay, Reginald Denny.

WHAT A WIDOW! Gloria Productions/Joseph P. Kennedy. Dir. Allan Dwan. Art Dir. Paul Nelson. With Gloria Swanson, Owen Moore.

DIE ZÄRTLICHEN VERWANDTEN. Richard Oswald–Filmprod GmbH. Dir. Richard Oswald. Art Dir. Franz Schroedter. With Charlotte Ander, Harald Paulsen.

1931

★L'ARCHITECTURE D'AUJOURD'HUI. Producer uncredited. Dir. Pierre Chenal.

A NOUS LA LIBERTÉ. Société des Films Sonores Tobis. Dir. René Clair. Art Dir. Lazare Meerson. With Rolla France, Raymond Cordy.

ARROWSMITH. Samuel Goldwyn Production/United Artists. Dir. John Ford. Art Dir. Richard Day. With Helen Hayes, Ronald Colman.

BACHELOR APARTMENT. Radio Pictures. Dir. Lowell Sherman. Art Dir. Max Ree. With Irene Dunne, Lowell Sherman.

BIG BUSINESS GIRL. First National Pictures. Dir. William A. Seiter. Art Dir. Jack Okey. With Loretta Young, Frank Albertson.

DACTYLO. Pathé-Natan. Dir. Wilhelm Thiele. Art Dir. uncredited. With Marie Glory, Jean Murat.

DOCTORS' WIVES. Fox Film Corp. Dir. Frank Borzage. Art Dir. Joseph Urban, William Darling. With Joan Bennett, Warner Baxter.

DRACULA. Universal Pictures. Dir. Tod Browning. Art Dir. Charles D. Hall. With Bela Lugosi, Helen Chandler.

THE EASIEST WAY. MGM. Dir. Jack Conway. Art Dir. Cedric Gibbons. With Constance Bennett, Adolphe Menjou.

DIE FIRMA HEIRATET. Max Glass–Filmprod GmbH. Dir. Carl Wilhelm. Art Dir. Ernö Metzner. With Ralph Arthur Roberts, Charlotte Ander.

FIVE AND TEN. Cosmopolitan Productions/MGM. Dir. Robert Z. Leonard, Art Dir. uncredited. With Marion Davies, Leslie Howard.

FRANKENSTEIN. Universal Pictures. Dir. James Whale. Art Dir. Charles D. Hall, Herman Rosse. With Colin Clive, Mae Clarke.

DIE FREMDE. Jean de la Cour, Paris/Hegewald-Film GmbH., Berlin. Dir. Fred Sauer. Art Dir. Lazare Meerson. With Gerda Maurus, Peter Voss.

GENTLEMAN'S FATE. MGM. Dir. Mervyn LeRoy. Art Dir. Cedric Gibbons. With John Gilbert, Louis Wolheim.

HONOR AMONG LOVERS. Paramount Pictures. Dir. Dorothy Arzner. Art Dir. uncredited. With Claudette Colbert, Fredric March.

INDISCREET. United Artists. Dir. Leo McCarey. Art Dir. Richard Day. With Gloria Swanson, Ben Lyon.

IT PAYS TO ADVERTISE. Paramount Pictures. Dir. Frank Tuttle. Art Dir. uncredited. With Carole Lombard, Skeets Gallagher.

JUST A GIGOLO. MGM. Dir. Jack Conway. Art Dir. Cedric Gibbons. With Irene Purcell, William Haines.

LADIES' MAN. Paramount Pictures. Dir. Lothar Mendes. Art Dir. uncredited. With Kay Francis, William Powell.

LITTLE CAESAR. First National Pictures. Dir. Mervyn LeRoy. Art Dir. Anton Grot. With Douglas Fairbanks, Jr., Edward G. Robinson.

M. Nero–Film AG, Berlin. Dir. Fritz Lang. Art Dir. Karl Vollbrecht, Emil Hasler. With Ellen Widmann, Peter Lorre.

MEN CALL IT LOVE. MGM. Dir. Edgar Selwyn. Art Dir. Cedric Gibbons. With Leila Hyams, Adolphe Menjou.

PALMY DAYS. Samuel Goldwyn Production. Dir. Edward Sutherland. Art Dir. Richard Day, William Andrew Pogany. With Charlotte Greenwood, Eddie Cantor.

LE PARFUM DE LA DAME EN NOIR. Société des Films Osso. Dir. Marcel L'Herbier. Art Dir. Pierre Schildknecht. With Huguette, Vera Engels.

PATATRAC. Cines. Dir. Gennaro Righelli. Art Dir. Enrico Paulucci, Carlo Levi. With Armando Falconi, Arturo Falconi.

POSSESSED. MGM. Dir. Clarence Brown. Art Dir. Cedric Gibbons. With Joan Crawford, Clark Gable.

PRIVATE LIVES. MGM. Dir. Sidney Franklin. Art Dir. Cedric Gibbons. With Norma Shearer, Robert Montgomery.

DIE PRIVATSEKRETÄRIN. Greenbaum–Film GmbH. Dir. Wilhelm Thiele. Art Dir. Otto Hunte. With Renate Müller, Hermann Thimig.

REACHING FOR THE MOON. United Artists. Dir. Edmund Goulding. Art Dir. William Cameron Menzies. With Douglas Fairbanks, Bebe Daniels.

SCANDAL SHEET. Paramount Pictures. Dir. John Cromwell. Art Dir. uncredited. With Clive Brook, George Bancroft.

DER SCHLEMIHL. Mikrophon–Film GmbH. Dir. Max Nosseck. Art Dir. Heinrich C. Richter. With Curt Bois, La Jana.

LA SEGRETARIA PRIVATA. Cines. Dir. Goffredo Alessandrini. Art Dir. Vinicio Paladini. With Elsa Merlini, Nino Besozzi.

SKYLINE. Fox Film Corp. Dir. Sam Taylor. Art Dir. Duncan Cramer. With Thomas Meighan, Maureen O'Sullivan.

SUNSHINE SUZIE. Gainsborough. Dir. Victor Saville.

Art Dir. Alex Vetchinsky. With Renate Müller, Jack Hulbert.

SUSAN LENOX: HER FALL AND RISE. MGM. Dir. Robert Z. Leonard. Art Dir. Cedric Gibbons. With Greta Garbo, Clark Gable.

THIS MODERN AGE. MGM. Dir. Nicholas Grinde. Art Dir. Cedric Gibbons. With Joan Crawford, Pauline Frederick.

TRANSATLANTIC. Fox Film Corp. Dir. William K. Howard. Art Dir. uncredited. With Edmund Lowe, Lois Moran.

DER UNBEKANNTE GAST. Max Glass Film-Prod. GmbH. Dir. E. W. Emo. Art Dir. Ernö Metzner. With Szöke Szakall, Lucie Englisch.

1932

L'ARMATA AZZURRA. Cines. Dir. Gennaro Righelli. Art Dir. Gastone Medin. With Germana Paolieri, Leda Gloria.

BACHELOR'S AFFAIRS. Fox Film Corp. Dir. Alfred Werker. Art Dir. Max Parker. With Minna Gombell, Adolphe Menjou.

THE BIG BROADCAST. Paramount Pictures. Dir. Frank Tuttle. Art Dir. Hans Dreier. With Bing Crosby, Stuart Erwin.

EIN BISSCHEN LIEBE FÜR DICH. H. M.–Film GmbH. Dir. Max Neufeld. Art Dir. Ernö Metzner. With Magda Schneider, Lee Parry.

BLONDIE OF THE FOLLIES. MGM. Dir. Edmund Goulding. Art Dir. Cedric Gibbons. With Marion Davies, Robert Montgomery.

DIAMOND CUT DIAMOND. Cinema House–MGM. Dir. Fred Niblo and Maurice Elvey. Art Dir. Laurence Irving, R. Myerscough-Walker. With Benita Hume, Adolphe Menjou.

DUE CUORI FELICI. Cines. Dir. Baldassare Negroni. Art Dir. Gastone Medin. With Vittorio De Sica, Rina Franchetti.

ES WIRD SCHON WIEDER BESSER. UFA. Dir. Kurt Gerron. Art Dir. Julius von Borsody. With Dolly Haas, Heinz Rühmann.

FAITHLESS. MGM. Dir. Harry Beaumont. Art Dir. Cedric Gibbons. With Tallulah Bankhead, Robert Montgomery.

F.P.1. ANTWORTET NICHT. UFA. Dir. Karl Hartl. Art Dir. Erich Kettelhut. With Hans Albers, Sybille Schmitz.

GOLDBLONDES MÄDCHEN, ICH SCHENK' DIR MEIN HERZ. Elite–Tonfilmproduktion. GmbH. Dir. Rudolf Bernauer. Art Dir. Alfred Junge. With Charlotte Ander, Felix Bressart.

GRAND HOTEL. MGM. Dir. Edmund Goulding. Art Dir. Cedric Gibbons. With Greta Garbo, John Barrymore.

THE GREEKS HAD A WORD FOR THEM. Samuel Goldwyn Production. Dir. Lowell Sherman. Art Dir. Richard Day. With Madge Evans, Joan Blondell.

HASENKLEIN KANN NICHTS DAFÜR. Ben Fett–Filmproduktion. Dir. Max Neufeld. Art Dir. Heinrich C. Richter. With Jakob Tiedtke, Lien Deyers.

HOLZAPFEL WEISS ALLES. Elite–Tonfilmproduktion. GmbH. Dir. Viktor Janson. Art Dir. Jacques Rotmil. With Felix Bressart, Ivan Petrovich.

MÄDCHEN ZUM HEIRATEN. Fellner & Somlo-Film GmbH. Dir. Wilhelm Thiele. Art Dir. Hans Jacoby. With Renate Müller, Hermann Thimig.

NEW MORALS FOR OLD. MGM. Dir. Charles J. Brabin. Art Dir. Cedric Gibbons. With Margaret Perry, Robert Young.

ONE HOUR WITH YOU. Paramount Pictures. Dir. Ernst Lubitsch and George Cukor. Art Dir. Hans Dreier. With Jeanette MacDonald, Maurice Chevalier.

QUICK. UFA. Dir. Robert Siodmak. Art Dir. Erich Kettelhut. With Lillian Harvey, Jules Berry.

RACKETY RAX. Fox Film Corp. Dir. Alfred Werker. Art Dir. Gordon Wiles. With Greta Nissen, Victor McLaglen.

SINNERS IN THE SUN. Paramount Pictures. Dir. Alexander Hall. Art Dir. Hans Dreier. With Carole Lombard, Chester Morris.

SKYSCRAPER SOULS. MGM. Dir. Edgar Selwyn. Art Dir. Cedric Gibbons. With Maureen O'Sullivan, Warren William.

STRAFSACHE VAN GELDERN. Ellen Richter–Tonfilm GmbH. Dir. Willi Wolff. Art Dir. Hans Sohnle, Otto Erdmann. With Ellen Richter, Elga Brink.

LA TELEFONISTA. Cines. Dir. Nunzio Malasomma. Art Dir. Gastone Medin. With Isa Pola, Mimi Aymler.

THE TRIAL OF VIVIENNE WARE. Fox Film Corp. Dir. William K. Howard. Art Dir. Gordon Wiles. With Joan Bennett, Donald Cook.

TROUBLE IN PARADISE. Paramount Pictures. Dir. Ernst Lubitsch. Art Dir. Hans Dreier. With Miriam Hopkins, Herbert Marshall.

L'ULTIMA AVVENTURA. Cines. Dir. Mario Camerini. Art Dir. Gastone Medin. With Armando Falconi, Diomira Jacobini.

WENN DIE LIEBE MODE MACHT. UFA. Dir. Franz Wenzler. Art Dir. Julius von Borsody. With Renate Müller, Georg Alexander.

1933

BEAUTY FOR SALE. MGM. Dir. Richard Boleslawski. Art Dir. Cedric Gibbons, Alexander Toluboff. With Alice Brady, Madge Evans.

A BEDTIME STORY. Paramount Pictures. Dir. Norman Taurog. Art Dir. Hans Dreier, Roland Anderson. With Helen Twelvetrees, Maurice Chevalier.

BOMBSHELL. MGM. Dir. Victor Fleming. Art Dir. Cedric Gibbons, Merrill Pye. With Jean Harlow, Lee Tracy.

CHILD OF MANHATTAN. Columbia Pictures. Dir. Edward Buzzell. Art Dir. uncredited. With Nancy Carroll, John Boles.

CLEAR ALL WIRES. MGM. Dir. George Hill. Art Dir. Cedric Gibbons. With Benita Hume, Lee Tracy.

COUNSELLOR AT LAW. Universal Pictures. Dir. William Wyler. Art Dir. Charles D. Hall. With Bebe Daniels, John Barrymore.

DANCING LADY. MGM. Dir. Robert Z. Leonard. Art Dir. Cedric Gibbons, Merrill Pye. With Joan Crawford, Clark Gable.

DESIGN FOR LIVING. Paramount Pictures. Dir. Ernst Lubitsch. Art Dir. Hans Dreier. With Gary Cooper, Miriam Hopkins.

DINNER AT EIGHT. MGM. Dir. George Cukor. Art Dir. Cedric Gibbons, Hobe Erwin. With Jean Harlow, John Barrymore.

FEMALE. Warner Bros. Dir. Michael Curtiz. Art Dir. Jack Okey. With Ruth Chatterton, George Brent.

FLYING DOWN TO RIO. RKO. Dir. Thornton Freeland. Art Dir. Van Nest Polglase, Carroll Clark. With Fred Astaire, Ginger Rogers.

FORTY-SECOND STREET. Warner Bros. Dir. Lloyd Bacon. Art Dir. Jack Okey. With Bebe Daniels, Warner Baxter.

GOLD DIGGERS OF 1933. Warner Bros. Dir. Mervyn LeRoy. Art Dir. Anton Grot. With Joan Blondell, Warren Williams.

DAS HÄSSLICHE MÄDCHEN. Avanti–Tonfilm GmbH. Dir. Hermann Kosterlitz. Art Dir. Hans Richter. With Dolly Haas, Max Hansen.

IT'S GREAT TO BE ALIVE. Fox Film Corp. Dir. Alfred Werker. Art Dir. Duncan Cramer. With Gloria Stuart, Edna May Oliver.

KING KONG. RKO. Dir. Merian C. Cooper and Ernest B. Schoedsack. Art Dir. Carroll Clark, Al Herman. With Fay Wray, Robert Armstrong.

MADE ON BROADWAY. MGM. Dir. Harry Beaumont. Art Dir. Cedric Gibbons. With Sally Eilers, Robert Montgomery.

MÄDELS VON HEUTE. Matador–Film GmbH. Dir. Herbert Selpin. Art Dir. W. A. Hermann. With Lily Rodien, Leni Sponholz.

MEET THE BARON. MGM. Dir. Walter Lang. Art Dir. Cedric Gibbons. With Jack Pearl, Jimmy Durante.

MEN MUST FIGHT. MGM. Dir. Edgar Selwyn. Art Dir. Cedric Gibbons. With Diana Wynyard, Lewis Stone.

PENTHOUSE. Cosmopolitan Productions/MGM. Dir. W. S. Van Dyke. Art Dir. uncredited. With Myrna

Loy, Warner Baxter.

REUNION IN VIENNA. MGM. Dir. Sidney Franklin. Art
Dir. Cedric Gibbons. With Diana Wynyard, John
Barrymore.

SONNENSTRAHL. Serge Otzoup–Filmproduktion der
Tobis-Sascha, Wien. Dir. Paul Fejos. Art Dir. Heinz
Fenchel, Emil Stepanek. With Annabella, Gustav
Fröhlich.

T'AMERO SEMPRE. Cines. Dir. Mario Camerini. Art Dir.
Gastone Medin. With Elsa De Giorgi, Nino Besozzi.

DAS TANKMÄDEL. Aafa–Film AG. Dir. Hans Behrendt.
Art Dir. Ludwig Reiber, Max Knaake. With Fritz
Schulz, Werner Finck.

DAS TESTAMENT DES DR. MABUSE. Nero–Film AG. Dir.
Fritz Lang. Art Dir. Emil Hasler, Karl Vollbrecht.
With Rudolf Klein-Rogge, Rudolf Schündler.

TOPAZE. RKO. Dir. Harry d'Abbadie d'Arrast. Art
Dir. Van Nest Polglase, Hobe Erwin. With Myrna
Loy, John Barrymore.

TORCH SINGER. Paramount Pictures. Dir. Alexander
Hall and George Sommes. Art Dir. Hans Dreier.
With Claudette Colbert, Ricardo Cortez.

DER TUNNEL. Vandor–Film GmbH/Bavaria–Film AG,
München. Dir. Kurt Bernhardt. Art Dir. Max
Seefelder, Karl Vollbrecht. With Paul Hartmann,
Gustaf Gründgens.

TURN BACK THE CLOCK. MGM. Dir. Edgar Selwyn. Art
Dir. Cedric Gibbons. With Mae Clarke, Lee Tracy.

EIN UNSICHTBARER GEHT DURCH DIE STADT. Ariel–Film
GmbH. Dir. Harry Piel. Art Dir. Willi Herrmann.
With Lissy Arna, Harry Piel.

LA VOCE LONTANA. Cines. Dir. Guido Brignone. Art
Dir. Giuseppe Capponi. With Sandra Ravel,
Gianfranco Giachetti.

WEGE ZUR GUTEN EHE. Gnom–Tonfilm GmbH. Dir.
Adolph Trotz. Art Dir. Heinz Fenchel, Botho
Höfer. With Olga Tschechowa, Alfred Abel.

1934

THE BLACK CAT. Universal Pictures. Dir. Edgar G.
Ulmer. Art Dir. Charles D. Hall. With Boris
Karloff, Bela Lugosi.

L'ENFANT DU CARNAVAL. J. N. Ermolieff. Dir.
Alexandre Volkoff. Art Dir. Ivan Lochakoff. With
Tania Fédor, Ivan Mosjoukine.

EVERGREEN. Gaumont–British Prod. Dir. Victor
Saville. Art Dir. Alfred Junge. With Jessie
Matthews, Sonnie Hale.

FASHIONS OF 1934. First National Pictures. Dir. William
Dieterle. Art Dir. Jack Okey. With Bette Davis,
William Powell.

FRÄULEIN LISELOTT. Dr. V. Badal–Filmproduktion.
Dir. Johannes Guter. Art Dir. Erich Czerwonski.

With Magda Schneider, Albert Lieven.

GAY DIVORCEE. RKO. Dir. Mark Sandrich. Art Dir.
Van Nest Polglase, Carroll Clark. With Fred
Astaire, Ginger Rogers.

GEORGE WHITE'S SCANDALS. Fox Film Corp. Dir.
George White. Art Dir. William Darling. With Alice
Faye, James Dunn.

GOLD. UFA. Dir. Karl Hartl. Art Dir. Otto Hunte.
With Brigitte Helm, Hans Albers.

LE GRAND JEU. Films de France. Dir. Jacques Feyder.
Art Dir. Lazare Meerson. With Marie Bell, Pierre
Richard-Willm.

DER HERR DER WELT. Ariel–Film GmbH. Dir. Harry
Piel. Art Dir. W. A. Hermann. With Sybille
Schmitz, Siegfried Schürenberg.

MISS FANE'S BABY IS STOLEN. Paramount Pictures. Dir.
Alexander Hall. Art Dir. Hans Dreier. With
Dorothea Wieck, Alice Brady.

MOSCOW LAUGHS (VESYOLYE REBYATA). Mosfilm. Dir.
Grigori Alexandrov. Art Dir. Alexander Utkin.
With Leonid Utyosov, Lubov Orlova.

NINTH GUEST. Columbia Pictures. Dir. Roy William
Neill. Art Dir. uncredited. With Genevieve Tobin,
Donald Cook.

RIPTIDE. MGM. Dir. Edmund Goulding. Art Dir.
Cedric Gibbons. With Norma Shearer, Robert
Montgomery.

SADIE MCKEE. MGM. Dir. Clarence Brown. Art Dir.
Cedric Gibbons. With Joan Crawford, Gene
Raymond.

LA SIGNORA DI TUTTI. Novella–Film. Dir. Max Ophuls.
Art Dir. Giuseppe Capponi. With Isa Miranda,
Federico Benfer.

STAND UP AND CHEER. Fox Film Corp. Dir. Hamilton
MacFadden. Art Dir. uncredited. With Madge
Evans, Warner Baxter.

365 NIGHTS IN HOLLYWOOD. Fox Film Corp. Dir.
George Marshall. Art Dir. uncredited. With Alice
Faye, James Dunn.

WONDER BAR. First National Pictures. Dir. Lloyd
Bacon and Busby Berkeley. Art Dir. Jack Okey.
With Kay Francis, Dick Powell.

1935

AFTER OFFICE HOURS. MGM. Dir. Robert Z. Leonard.
Art Dir. Cedric Gibbons. With Constance Bennett,
Clark Gable.

ARTISTEN. Ariel–Film GmbH. Dir. Harry Piel. Art
Dir. Willi Hermann. With Susi Lanner, Harry Piel.

BIG BROADCAST OF 1936. Paramount Pictures. Dir.
Norman Taurog. Art Dir. Hans Dreier, Robert
Usher. With Jack Oakie, George Burns.

LE BONHEUR. Pathé–Cinéma. Dir. Marcel L'Herbier. Art Dir. Guy De Gastyne. With Gaby Morlay, Charles Boyer.

BROADWAY MELODY OF 1936. MGM. Dir. Roy Del Ruth. Art Dir. Cedric Gibbons. With Eleanor Powell, Jack Benny.

GOLD DIGGERS OF 1935. Warner Bros. Dir. Busby Berkeley. Art Dir. Anton Grot. With Gloria Stuart, Dick Powell.

LA KERMESSE HÉROÏQUE. Société des Films Sonores Tobis. Dir. Jacques Feyder. Art Dir. Lazare Meerson, Alexandre Trauner, Georges Wakhévitch. With Françoise Rosay, Jean Murat.

NO MORE LADIES. MGM. Dir. Edward H. Griffith. Art Dir. Cedric Gibbons. With Joan Crawford, Robert Montgomery.

PARIS IN SPRING. Paramount Pictures. Dir. Lewis Milestone. Art Dir. Hans Dreier. With Mary Ellis, Ida Lupino.

PRINCESS TAM-TAM. Productions Arys. Dir. Edmond T. Gréville. Art Dir. Lazare Meerson, Pierre Schild. With Josephine Baker, Albert Préjean.

RECKLESS. MGM. Dir. Victor Fleming. Art Dir. Cedric Gibbons. With Jean Harlow, William Powell.

ROBERTA. RKO. Dir. William A. Seiter. Art Dir. Van Nest Polglase, Carroll Clark. With Irene Dunne, Fred Astaire.

THE SCOUNDREL. Paramount Pictures. Dir. Ben Hecht and Charles MacArthur. Art Dir. Walter Keller, Albert Johnson. With Julie Haydon, Noel Coward.

SPLENDOR. Samuel Goldwyn Production. Dir. Elliott Nugent. Art Dir. Richard Day. With Miriam Hopkins, Joel McCrea.

STARS OVER BROADWAY. Warner Bros. Dir. William Keighley. Art Dir. Carl Jules Weyl. With Jane Froman, Pat O'Brien.

TOP HAT. RKO. Dir. Mark Sandrich. Art Dir. Van Nest Polglase, Carroll Clark. With Ginger Rogers, Fred Astaire.

THE TUNNEL. Gaumont. Dir. Maurice Elvey. Art Dir. Ernö Metzner. With Leslie Banks, Richard Dix.

WINTERNACHTSTRAUM. Boston–Film Co. Dir. Géza von Bolvary. Art Dir. Emil Hasler. With Magda Schneider, Wolf Albach-Retty.

1936

AFTER THE THIN MAN. MGM. Dir. W. S. Van Dyke. Art Dir. Cedric Gibbons. With Myrna Loy, William Powell.

ANYTHING GOES. Paramount Pictures. Dir. Lewis Milestone. Art Dir. Hans Dreier, Ernst Fegté. With Ethel Merman, Bing Crosby.

BIG BROADCAST OF 1937. Paramount Pictures. Dir.
Mitchell Leisen. Art Dir. Hans Dreier, Robert Usher. With Jack Benny, George Burns.

BORN TO DANCE. MGM. Dir. Roy Del Ruth. Art Dir. Cedric Gibbons. With Eleanor Powell, James Stewart.

CLUB DE FEMMES. S.E.L.F. Dir. Jacques Deval. Art Dir. Lucien Aguettand, Jean Bijon. With Danielle Darrieux, Betty Stockfeld.

DODSWORTH. Samuel Goldwyn Production. Dir. William Wyler. Art Dir. Richard Day. With Mary Astor, Walter Huston.

FOLLOW THE FLEET. RKO. Dir. Mark Sandrich. Art Dir. Van Nest Polglase, Carroll Clark. With Ginger Rogers, Fred Astaire.

GOLD DIGGERS OF 1937. Warner Bros. Dir. Lloyd Bacon. Art Dir. Max Parker. With Joan Blondell, Dick Powell.

THE GREAT ZIEGFELD. MGM. Dir. Robert Z. Leonard. Art Dir. Cedric Gibbons, Merrill Pye, John Harkrider. With Myrna Loy, William Powell.

LIBELED LADY. MGM. Dir. Jack Conway. Art Dir. Cedric Gibbons. With Jean Harlow, William Powell.

MODERN TIMES. Charles Chaplin/United Artists. Dir. Charles Chaplin. Art Dir. Charles D. Hall. With Charles Chaplin, Paulette Goddard.

MY MAN GODFREY. Universal Pictures. Dir. Gregory La Cava. Art Dir. Charles D. Hall. With Carole Lombard, William Powell.

NON-STOP NEW YORK. Gaumont. Dir. Robert Stevenson. Art Dir. Walter Murton. With Anna Lee, John Loder.

PICCADILLY JIM. MGM. Dir. Robert Z. Leonard. Art Dir. Cedric Gibbons, Joseph Wright, Edwin B. Willis. With Frank Morgan, Robert Montgomery.

SAMSON. Paris–Film–Production. Dir. Maurice Tourneur. Art Dir. Guy de Gastyne. With Gaby Morlay, Gabrielle Dorziat.

SMALL TOWN GIRL. MGM. Dir. William Wellman. Art Dir. Cedric Gibbons. With Janet Gaynor, Robert Taylor.

STAR FOR A NIGHT. Twentieth Century–Fox. Dir. Lewis Seiler. Art Dir. uncredited. With Claire Trevor, Jane Darwell.

SWING TIME. RKO. Dir. George Stevens. Art Dir. Van Nest Polglase, Carroll Clark, John Harkrider. With Ginger Rogers, Fred Astaire.

THEODORA GOES WILD. Columbia Pictures. Dir. Richard Boleslawski. Art Dir. Stephen Goosson, Lionel Banks. With Irene Dunne, Melvyn Douglas.

THINGS TO COME. London Films. Dir. William Cameron Menzies. Art Dir. Vincent Korda. With Raymond Massey, Cedric Hardwicke.

TOPAZE. Films Marcel Pagnol. Dir. Marcel Pagnol. Art Dir. Louis David. With Sylvia Bataille, Arnaudy.

WIFE VS. SECRETARY. MGM. Dir. Clarence Brown. Art Dir. Cedric Gibbons. With Jean Harlow, Clark Gable.

1937

ARTISTS AND MODELS. Paramount Pictures. Dir. Raoul Walsh. Art Dir. Hans Dreier, Robert Usher. With Ida Lupino, Jack Benny.

THE AWFUL TRUTH. Columbia Pictures. Dir. Leo McCarey. Art Dir. Stephen Goosson, Lionel Banks. With Irene Dunne, Cary Grant.

BROADWAY MELODY OF 1938. MGM. Dir. Roy Del Ruth. Art Dir. Cedric Gibbons, Merrill Pye. With Eleanor Powell, Robert Taylor.

DOUBLE WEDDING. MGM. Dir. Richard Thorpe. Art Dir. Cedric Gibbons. With Myrna Loy, William Powell.

★EASY LIVING. Paramount Pictures. Dir. Mitchell Leisen. Art Dir. Hans Dreier, Ernst Fegté. With Jean Harlow, Edward Arnold.

GANGWAY. Gaumont. Dir. Sonnie Hale. Art Dir. Alfred Junge. With Jessie Matthews, Barry MacKay.

HISTORY IS MADE AT NIGHT. Walter Wanger Production/ United Artists. Dir. Frank Borzage. Art Dir. Alexander Toluboff. With Jean Arthur, Charles Boyer.

HO PERDUTO MIO MARITO! ENIC/Astra Film Production. Dir. Enrico Guazzoni. Art Dir. Giorgio Pinzauti. With Paola Borboni, Nino Besozzi.

LIVE, LOVE AND LEARN. MGM. Dir. George Fitzmaurice. Art Dir. Cedric Gibbons. With Rosalind Russell, Robert Montgomery.

LOST HORIZON. Columbia Pictures. Dir. Frank Capra. Art Dir. Stephen Goosson. With Jane Wyatt, Ronald Colman.

NOTHING SACRED. Selznick International/United Artists. Dir. William Wellman. Art Dir. Lyle Wheeler. With Carole Lombard, Fredric March.

LES PERLES DE LA COURONNE. Impéria–Film, Cinéas. Dir. Sacha Guitry and Christian-Jaque. Art Dir. Jean Perrier. With Jacqueline Delubac, Sacha Guitry.

SAILING ALONG. Gaumont. Dir. Sonnie Hale. Art Dir. Alfred Junge. With Jessie Matthews, Roland Young.

SHALL WE DANCE. RKO. Dir. Mark Sandrich. Art Dir. Van Nest Polglase, Carroll Clark. With Ginger Rogers, Fred Astaire.

IL SIGNOR MAX. ENIC/Astra Film Production. Dir. Mario Camerini. Art Dir. Gastone Medin. With Assia Noris, Vittorio De Sica.

A STAR IS BORN. Selznick International/United Artists. Dir. William Wellman. Art Dir. Lyle Wheeler. With Janet Gaynor, Fredric March.

TOP OF THE TOWN. Universal Pictures. Dir. Ralph Murphy. Art Dir. John Harkrider. With Ella Logan, George Murphy.

TOPPER. Hal Roach Production/MGM. Dir. Norman Z. McLeod. Art Dir. Arthur I. Royce. With Constance Bennett, Cary Grant.

DER UNWIDERSTEHLICHE. Tobis–Magna–Filmprod. GmbH. Dir. Géza von Bolvary. Art Dir. Emil Hasler. With Anny Ondra, Hans Söhnker.

WOMAN CHASES MAN. Samuel Goldwyn Production/ United Artists. Dir. John G. Blystone. Art Dir. Richard Day. With Miriam Hopkins, Joel McCrea.

1938

BIG BROADCAST OF 1938. Paramount Pictures. Dir. Mitchell Leisen. Art Dir. Hans Dreier, Ernest Fegté. With Martha Raye, W. C. Fields.

BLUEBEARD'S EIGHTH WIFE. Paramount Pictures. Dir. Ernst Lubitsch. Art Dir. Hans Dreier, Robert Usher. With Claudette Colbert, Gary Cooper.

BRINGING UP BABY. RKO. Dir. Howard Hawks. Art Dir. Van Nest Polglase, Perry Ferguson. With Katharine Hepburn, Cary Grant.

CAREFREE. RKO. Dir. Mark Sandrich. Art Dir. Van Nest Polglase, Carroll Clark. With Ginger Rogers, Fred Astaire.

INVENTIAMO L'AMORE. Scalera. Dir. Camillo Mastrocinque. Art Dir. Carlo Enrico Rava. With Evi Maltagliati, Gino Cervi.

JUST AROUND THE CORNER. Twentieth Century–Fox. Dir. Irving Cummings. Art Dir. Boris Leven. With Shirley Temple, Bill Robinson.

MAD MISS MANTON. RKO. Dir. Leigh Jason. Art Dir. Van Nest Polglase, Carroll Clark. With Barbara Stanwyck, Henry Fonda.

MANPROOF. MGM. Dir. Richard Thorpe. Art Dir. Cedric Gibbons. With Myrna Loy, Franchot Tone.

THREE LOVES HAS NANCY. MGM. Dir. Richard Thorpe. Art Dir. Cedric Gibbons. With Janet Gaynor, Robert Montgomery.

DIE VIER GESELLEN. Tonfilmstudio Carl Froelich & Co./ UFA. Dir. Carl Froelich. Art Dir. Franz Schroedter. With Ingrid Bergman, Sabine Peters.

THE YOUNG IN HEART. Selznick International/United Artists. Dir. Richard Wallace. Art Dir. Lyle Wheeler. With Janet Gaynor, Douglas Fairbanks, Jr.

1939

AI VOSTRI ORDINI, SIGNORA. Aurora-Fono, Roma. Dir. Mario Mattoli. Art Dir. uncredited. With Elsa Merlini, Vittorio De Sica.

I GRANDI MAGAZZINI. Era-Amato Prod. Dir. Mario Camerini. Art Dir. Guido Fiorini. With Assia Noris, Vittorio De Sica.

LOVE AFFAIR. RKO. Dir. Leo McCarey. Art Dir. Van

Nest Polglase, Alfred Herman. With Irene Dunne, Charles Boyer.

THE PRIVATE LIVES OF ELIZABETH AND ESSEX. Warner Bros. Dir. Michael Curtiz. Art Dir. Anton Grot. With Bette Davis, Errol Flynn.

THE STORY OF VERNON AND IRENE CASTLE. RKO. Dir. H. C. Potter. Art Dir. Van Nest Polglase, Perry Ferguson. With Ginger Rogers, Fred Astaire.

THE WOMEN. MGM. Dir. George Cukor. Art Dir. Cedric Gibbons. With Norma Shearer, Joan Crawford.

1940

CHRISTMAS IN JULY. Paramount Pictures. Dir. Preston Sturges. Art Dir. Hans Dreier, Earl Hedrick. With Ellen Drew, Dick Powell.

DOWN ARGENTINE WAY. Twentieth Century–Fox. Dir. Irving Cummings. Art Dir. Richard Day, Joseph C. Wright. With Betty Grable, Don Ameche.

PARIS–NEW YORK. Regina Production. Dir. Yves Mirande. Art Dir. Andrei Andrejew. With Gaby Morlay, Gisèle Préville.

LA PECCATRICE. Manenti Prod. Dir. Amleto Palermi. Art Dir. Antonio Valente. With Paola Barbara, Gino Cervi.

1941

CITIZEN KANE. RKO. Dir. Orson Welles. Art Dir. Van Nest Polglase, Perry Ferguson. With Joseph Cotten, Orson Welles.

THE LADY EVE. Paramount Pictures. Dir. Preston Sturges. Art Dir. Hans Dreier, Ernst Fegté. With Barbara Stanwyck, Henry Fonda.

MOON OVER MIAMI. Twentieth Century–Fox. Dir. Walter Lang. Art Dir. Richard Day, Wiard Ihnen. With Betty Grable, Don Ameche.

SULLIVAN'S TRAVELS. Paramount Pictures. Dir. Preston Sturges. Art Dir. Hans Dreier, Earl Hedrick. With Veronica Lake, Joel McCrea.

1942

WOMAN OF THE YEAR. MGM. Dir. George Stevens. Art Dir. Cedric Gibbons, Randall Duell. With Katharine Hepburn, Spencer Tracy.

1945

THE LOST WEEKEND. Paramount Pictures. Dir. Billy Wilder. Art Dir. Hans Dreier, Earl Hedrick. With Ray Milland, Jane Wyman.

ROMA, CITTÁ APERTA. Excelsa–Film. Dir. Roberto Rossellini. Art Dir. R. Megna. With Anna Magnani, Aldo Fabrizi.

1946

THE BEST YEARS OF OUR LIVES. Samuel Goldwyn Production/RKO. Dir. William Wyler. Art Dir. George Jenkins, Perry Ferguson. With Myrna Loy, Fredric March.

1947

CROSSFIRE. Dore Schary Production/RKO. Dir. Edward Dmytryk. Art Dir. Albert S. D'Argostino, Alfred Herman. With Robert Mitchum, Robert Ryan.

1948

A FOREIGN AFFAIR. Paramount Pictures. Dir. Billy Wilder. Art Dir. Hans Dreier, Walter Tyler. With Jean Arthur, Marlene Dietrich.

1949

THE FOUNTAINHEAD. Warner Bros. Dir. King Vidor. Art Dir. Edward Carrere. With Patricia Neal, Gary Cooper.

1954

A STAR IS BORN. Warner Bros. Dir. George Cukor. Art Dir. Malcolm Bert. With Judy Garland, James Mason.

Bibliography

Adams, Thomas. *The Regional Plan of New York and Its Environs*. New York: Regional Plan of New York and Its Environs, 1931.

Aloi, Roberto. *L'Arredamento Moderno*. Milan: U. Hoepli, 1934.

Appelbaum, Stanley. *The New York World's Fair, 1939/1940*. New York: Dover Publications, 1977.

Applegate, Judith. "Paul Nelson: An Interview." *Perspecta: The Yale Architectural Journal* 13–14 (1971): 74–129.

"L'Arredamento Moderno nel Cinema." *La Casa Bella* 11 (November 1932): 32–41.

Bablet, Denis. *The Revolutions of Stage Design in the 20th Century*. Paris and New York: Léon Amiel, 1977.

Bandini, Baldo. "Lo Scenografo Lazare Meerson." *Cinema* (November 1941): 316–18.

Bandy, Mary Lea, ed. *Rediscovering French Film*. New York: Museum of Modern Art, 1983.

Banham, Reyner. *The Architecture of the Well-Tempered Environment*. London: Architectural Press; Chicago: University of Chicago Press, 1969.

Bardèche, Maurice, and Brasillach, Robert. *Histoire du cinéma*. Paris: André Martel, 1953.

Barr, Alfred H., Jr. "Notes on Russian Architecture." *The Arts* (February 1929): 103–6, 144, 146.

———; Hitchcock, Henry-Russell, Jr.; Johnson, Philip; and Mumford, Lewis. *Modern Architecture*. New York: Museum of Modern Art and W. W. Norton, 1932.

Barsacq, Léon. *Caligari's Cabinet and Other Grand Illusions: A History of Film Design*. Translated by Michael Bullock. Revised and edited by Elliott Stein. Boston: New York Graphic Society, 1976.

———. *Le Décor de Film*. Paris: Editions Seghers, 1970.

Battersby, Martin. *The Decorative Thirties*. London: Studio Vista, 1971.

———. *The Decorative Twenties*. London: Studio Vista, 1969.

Bel Geddes, Norman. *Horizons*. Boston: Little, Brown, 1932.

Benevolo, Leonardo. *History of Modern Architecture*. Cambridge: M.I.T. Press, 1971.

Bletter, Rosemarie Haag, and Robinson, Cervin. *Skyscraper Style—Art Deco New York*. New York: Oxford University Press, 1975.

Bogdanovich, Peter. "Edgar G. Ulmer." In Todd McCarthy and Charles Flynn, eds., *Kings of the Bs: Working Within the Hollywood System*. New York: E. P. Dutton, 1975.

Browne, K[enneth] R[obert] G[ordon], and Robinson, W[illiam] Heath. *How to Live in a Flat*. London: Hutchinson, 1936.

Brownlow, Kevin. *The Parade's Gone By*. New York: Alfred A. Knopf, 1968.

Brunhammer, Yvonne. *The Nineteen Twenties Style*. London: Paul Hamlyn, 1966.

Bucher, Felix. *Screen Series: Germany*. London: A. Zwemmer; New York: A. S. Barnes, 1970.

Buckberrough, Sherry A. *Sonia Delaunay: A Retrospective*. Buffalo, N.Y.: Albright-Knox Art Gallery, 1980.

Burch, Noël. *Marcel L'Herbier*. Paris: Editions Seghers, 1973.

Bush, Donald. *The Streamlined Decade*. New York: George Braziller, 1975.

Carrick, Edward. *Art and Design in the British Film*. London: Dobson, 1948.

————. "Moving Picture Sets: A Medium for the Architect." *Architectural Record* 67 (May 1930): 440–4.

"A Century of Progress Exposition . . . Chicago, 1933." *Architectural Record* (July 1933): 72.

Charensol, Georges. *Le Cinéma*. Paris: Librairie Larousse, 1966.

Chavance, René. "Chez un cinéaste (Marcel L'Herbier)." *Art et Décoration* 52 (1927): 43.

Cheney, Sheldon. *The New World Architecture*. New York: Longmans, Green, 1930.

————, and Cheney, Martha Candler. *Art and the Machine*. New York: Whittlesey House, 1936.

Chiericetti, David. *Hollywood Costume Design*. New York: Harmony Books, 1976.

Cincotti, Guido; Marchi, Virgilio; and Montesanti, Fausto. *La Scenografia Cinematografica in Italia*. Rome: Bianco e Nero, 1955.

Clarens, Carlos, and Corliss, Mary. "Designed for Film: The Hollywood Art Director." *Film Comment* 14 (May–June 1978): 25–60.

Clark, John R. "Expressionism in Film and Architecture." *Art Journal* 34 (Winter 1974–75): 115–22.

Croce, Arlene. *The Fred Astaire and Ginger Rogers Book*. New York: Galahad Books, 1972.

Curtis, William J. R. *Modern Architecture Since 1900*. Englewood Cliffs, N.J.: Prentice-Hall, 1983.

Cutts, Anson Bailey. "Homes of Tomorrow in the Movies of Today." *California Arts and Architecture* 54 (November 1938): 16–8.

De Mille, Cecil B. *The Autobiography of Cecil B. De Mille*. Englewood Cliffs, N.J.: Prentice-Hall, 1959.

De Mille, William C. *Hollywood Saga*. New York: E. P. Dutton, 1939.

Deshoulières, Dominique, and Jeanneau, Hubert, eds. *Rob Mallet-Stevens: Architecte*. Brussels: Archives d'Architecture Moderne, 1980.

Downing, Patrick, and Hambley, John. *The Art of Hollywood*. London: The Victoria and Albert Museum, 1979.

Dreier, Hans. "Designing the Sets." In Nancy Naumberg, ed., *We Make the Movies*. New York: W. W. Norton, 1937.

Eisner, Lotte H. *Fritz Lang*. New York: Oxford University Press, 1977.

————. *The Haunted Screen*. Berkeley: University of California Press, 1969.

Encyclopaedia Britannica, 14th ed. (1929–36), s.v. "Motion Picture Sets." By Cedric Gibbons.

Erengis, George P. "Cedric Gibbons." *Films in Review* (April 1965): 217–32.

Erté. *Things I Remember*. New York: Quadrangle, 1975.

Essoe, Gabe, and Lee, Raymond. *De Mille: The Man and His Pictures*. New York: A. S. Barnes, 1970.

Eustis, Morton. "Designing for the Movies: Gibbons of MGM." *Theatre Arts Monthly* 21 (October 1937): 783–98.

Ferriss, Hugh. *The Metropolis of Tomorrow*. New York: Ives Washburn, 1929.

Filmlexicon degli Autori e delle Opere. Rome: Bianco e Nero, 1958.

Fiorini, Guido. "Scenografia cinematografica." *Bianco e Nero* 7 (1941): 49–56.

Flint, Ralph. "Cedric Gibbons." *Creative Art* 11 (October 1932): 116–19.

Floherty, John J. *Moviemakers*. New York: Doubleday, Doran, 1935.

Forty, Adrian, and Newman, Geoffrey. *British Design*. Milton Keynes: The Open University Press, 1975.

"The Fountainhead." *Journal of the American Institute of Architects* 12 (July 1949): 27, 28, 31.

Frampton, Kenneth. *Modern Architecture: A Critical History*. New York: Oxford University Press, 1980.

Frankl, Paul T. *Form and Re-Form*. New York: Harper & Brothers, 1930.

French, Philip. *The Movie Moguls*. London: Weidenfeld and Nicholson, 1969.

Fülop-Müller, René, and Gregor, Joseph. *Das amerikanische Theater und Kino*. Zurich: Amalthea, 1931.

Gain, André. "Le Cinéma et les Arts décoratifs." *Amour de l'Art* (September 1928): 321–30.

Gebhard, David. *Shindler*. New York: Viking, 1972.

————, and von Breton, Harriette. *Los Angeles in the Thirties, 1931–1941*. Layton, Utah: Peregrine Smith, 1975.

————. *Lloyd Wright, Architect*. Santa Barbara: The Art Galleries, University of California, 1971.

————. *Kem Weber—The Moderne in Southern California, 1920 Through 1941*. Santa Barbara: The Art Galleries, University of California, 1969.

Genauer, Emily. *Modern Interiors Today and Tomorrow*. Illustrated Editions Co., 1939.

Gibbons, Cedric. "The Art Director." In Stephen Watts, ed., *Behind the Screen; How Films are Made.* London: Arthur Barker, Ltd., 1938.

———. "Every Home's a Stage." *Ladies' Home Journal,* July 1933.

Giedion, Sigfried. *Space, Time, and Architecture: The Growth of a New Tradition.* Cambridge: Harvard University Press, 1954.

Giovanetti, Eugenio. "Architettura Cinematografica di Giuseppe Capponi." *Architettura* (July 1933): 424–28.

Gropius, Walter, ed. *Internationale Architektur.* Munich: Langen, 1925.

Gruen, Victor. "Mountain Heads from Mole Hills." *Arts and Architecture* (May 1949): 32.

Gunn, James. *Alternate Worlds: The Illustrated History of Science Fiction.* Englewood Cliffs, N.J.: Prentice-Hall, 1975.

Haver, Ronald. *David O. Selznick's Hollywood.* New York: Alfred A. Knopf, 1980.

Higham, Charles. *Cecil B. De Mille.* New York: Charles Scribner's Sons, 1973.

Hillier, Bevis. *Art Deco.* London: Studio Vista, 1968.

Hines, Thomas S. *Richard Neutra and the Search for Modern Architecture.* New York and Oxford: Oxford University Press, 1982.

Hitchcock, Henry-Russell, Jr., and Johnson, Philip. *The International Style: Architecture Since 1922.* New York: W. W. Norton, 1932.

Hoffman, Herbert. *Die Neue Raumkunst in Europa und Amerika.* Stuttgart: Julius Hoffmann Verlag, 1930.

"Hollywood's *Fountainhead:* All dynamite will be charged to the clients." *Architectural Forum* 90 (June 1949): 13–14.

Huaco, George. *Sociology of Film Art.* New York and London: Basic Books, 1965.

"Introduction à l'Exposition." *Art et Décoration,* May 1925.

Jacobs, Lewis. *The Rise of the American Film: A Critical History.* New York: Teachers College Press, 1968.

Jarratt, Vernon. *The Italian Cinema.* London: The Falcon Press, 1951.

Joel, David. *Furniture Design Set Free: The British Revolution from 1851 to the Present Day.* London: J. M. Dent and Sons, 1969.

Johnson, Julian. "Marietta Serves Coffee." *Photoplay* (October 1920): 31–3, 132.

Johnson, Philip. *Mies van der Rohe.* New York: Museum of Modern Art, 1947.

Jourdan, Robert. "Le Style Clair-Meerson." *La Revue du cinéma* (1931): 32–3.

Kaul, Walter. *Schöpferische Filmarchitektur.* Berlin: Deutsche Kinemathek, 1971.

Khazanova, V. "A. Burov, 1900–1957." *Architectural Design* (1970): 101–4.

Koenig, John. *Scenery for Cinema.* Baltimore: Baltimore Museum of Art, 1942.

Koolhaas, Rem. *Delirious New York: A Retroactive Manifesto for Manhattan.* New York: Oxford University Press, 1978.

Korda, Michael. *Charmed Lives.* New York: Random House, 1979.

Kracauer, Siegfried. *From Caligari to Hitler.* Princeton, N.J.: Princeton University Press, 1947.

Kuter, Leo K. "Art Direction." *Films in Review* (June–July 1957): 248–58.

Lachenbruch, Jerome. "Interior Decoration for the 'Movies': Studies from the work of Cedric Gibbons and Gilbert White." *Arts and Decoration* 14 (January 1921): 204–5.

———. "Art and Architectural Artifice." *The American Architect* 118 (3 November 1920): 563–68.

Laing, A. B. "Designing Motion Picture Sets." *The Architectural Record* 74 (July 1933): 59–64.

Lasky, Jesse L. *I Blow My Own Horn.* Garden City, N.Y.: Doubleday and Co., 1957.

Lawder, Standish D. *The Cubist Cinema.* New York: New York University Press, 1975.

"Lazare Meerson." *Sight and Sound* 7, no. 26 (Summer 1938): 68–9.

[Leader]. "L'Arredamento di un Film." *La Casa Bella* 9 (October 1931): 22–36.

Le Corbusier. *Towards a New Architecture* (*Vers une Architecture,* originally published in London, 1927). New York: Praeger Publishers, 1970.

Le Style Moderne. Paris: A. Calavas, 1925.

Lesieutre, Alain. *The Spirit and Splendour of Art Deco.* New York: Paddington Press, 1974.

Leyda, Jay. *Kino.* New York: Macmillan, 1960.

L'Herbier, Marcel. *La Tête qui tourne.* Paris: Pierre Belfond, 1979.

Lindsay, Vachel. *The Art of the Moving Picture.* Macmillan, 1915, 1922.

Lubschez, Ben J. "*The Cabinet of Dr. Caligari.*" *Journal of the American Institute of Architects* 9 (January 1921): 213–16.

Lynd, Robert S., and Lynd, Helen Merrell. *Middletown in Transition: A Study in Cultural Conflicts.* New York: Harcourt, Brace, 1937.

MacFarland, James Hood. "Architectural Problems in Motion Picture Production." *The American Architect* 118 (21 July 1920): 65–70.

MacGowan, Kenneth. *Behind the Screen.* New York: Delacorte Press, 1965.

———. "Enter—The Artist." *Photoplay* (January 1921): 73–5.

————. *Theatre of Tomorrow*. New York: Boni and Liveright, 1921.

Machine Age Exposition Catalogue. New York: Little Review, 1927.

Mallet-Stevens, Robert. "Le Décor." In *L'Art cinématographique IV*. Paris: Felix Alcan, 1927.

————. *Le Décor moderne au cinema*. Paris: Charles Massin, 1928.

Maltin, Leonard. *The Art of the Cinematographer*. New York: Dover Publications, 1978.

Mancini, Elaine, "The Free Years of the Italian Film Industry, 1930–1935." Doctoral dissertation, School of Cinema Studies, New York University, 1981.

Mandelbaum, Howard, and Myers, Eric. *Screen Deco: A Celebration of High Style in Hollywood*. New York: St. Martin's Press, 1985.

Meikle, Jeffrey. *Twentieth Century Limited: Industrial Design in America, 1925–1939*. Philadelphia: Temple University Press, 1979.

Méliès, Georges. "Les Vues Cinématographique. " *La Revue du cinéma* (October 15, 1929).

Mock, Elizabeth, ed. *Built in U.S.A., 1932–1944*. New York: Museum of Modern Art, 1944.

Moholy-Nagy, László. *Vision in Motion*. Chicago: Paul Theobald, 1969.

Moholy-Nagy, Sibyl. *Experiment in Totality*. Cambridge, Mass.: M.I.T. Press, 1950, 1969.

Monaco, Paul. *Cinema and Society: France and Germany During the 1920s*. New York, Oxford, and Amsterdam: Elsevier, 1976.

Mordden, Ethan. *The Hollywood Musical*. New York: St. Martin's Press, 1981.

"Motion Pix Producers Recognize Efforts of Architects in the Productions." *The American Architect* (4 February 1920): 157.

Moussinac, Léon. "Le Décor et le costume au cinéma." *Art et Décoration* 50 (1926): 128.

Mujica, Francisco. *History of the Skyscraper*. Paris: Archaeology and Architecture Press, 1929.

Munden, Kenneth W. *The American Film Institute Catalog of Motion Pictures*. New York: Bowker, 1971.

Myerscough-Walker, R. *Stage and Film Decor*. London: Pitman, 1945.

Nelson, George. "Mr. Roark Goes to Hollywood." *Interiors* 108 (April 1939): 106–11.

Park, Edwin Avery. *New Background for a New Age*. New York: Harcourt, Brace, 1927.

Pehnt, Wolfgang. *Expressionist Architecture*. New York: Praeger, 1973.

Pells, Richard. *Radical Visions and American Dreams*. New York: Harper & Row, 1973.

Piacentini, Marcello. "Giuseppe Capponi, Architetto." *Architettura* 18 (1939): 267–82.

Plummer, Kathleen Church. "The Streamlined Moderne." *Art in America* (January–February 1974): 46–53.

Polglase, Van Nest. "The Studio Art Director." In Joe Bonica, comp., *How Talkies Are Made*. Hollywood: J. Bonica and Co., 1930.

Ponti, Gio. "Architettura 'nel' Cinema." *Lo Stile*, February 1942.

Porter, Allen W. "Hollywood Interiors." *Interiors* 100 (April 1941): 22–27, 57–60.

Powdermaker, Hortense. *Hollywood: The Dream Factory*. Little, Brown, 1950.

Prampolini, Enrico. "Evoluzione e Avvenire della Scenotecnica." *Lo Schermo* (June 1936): 28–9.

Pratt, George C. *Spellbound in Darkness: A History of the Silent Film*. Greenwich, Conn.: New York Graphic Society, 1973.

Ratzka, Helena, and Rosenthal, Rudolph. *The Story of Modern Applied Art*. New York: Harper & Brothers, 1948.

Rava, Carlo Enrico. "Stile negli Interni di Film." *Lo Stile* (April 1941): 54, 55, 79.

Rimberg, John David. *The Motion Picture in the Soviet Union, 1918–1952*. New York: Arno Press, 1973.

Robbins, George W., and Tilton, Deming L. *Los Angeles: Preface to a Master Plan*. Los Angeles: Pacific Southwest Academy, 1941.

Robertson, Howard, and Yerbury, F. R., eds. *Examples of Modern French Architecture*. New York: Charles Scribner's Sons, 1928.

Rotha, Paul. *The Film Till Now*. London: Vision Press, 1949.

Rye, Jane. *Futurism*. London and New York: Studio Vista and E. P. Dutton, 1972.

Sadoul, Georges. *French Film*. London: Falcon Press, 1953.

Savio, Francesco. *Ma l'amore no*. Milan: Casa Editrice Sonzogno, 1975.

Scagnetti, Jack. *The Intimate Life of Rudolph Valentino*. Middle Village, N.Y.: Jonathan David Publisher, 1975.

"Screen Glamour to Sell Fashions to Fans." *Design for Industry* 19 (July 1935): 19.

Sedeyn, Émile. "Le Décoration moderne au cinéma." *L'Art et les Artistes* 4 (1921–22): 153–60.

Shand, Philip M. *Modern Picture Houses and Theaters*. Philadelphia: J. B. Lippincott, 1930.

Sharp, Dennis, ed. *Glass Architecture/Alpine Architecture*. London: November Books Ltd., 1972.

Sklar, Robert. *Movie-Made America: A Cultural History of American Movies*. New York: Random House, 1975.

Spencer, Charles. *Erté*. New York: Clarkson N. Potter, 1970.

St. John Marner, Terrence. *Film Design*. London: Tantivy Press; New York: A. S. Barnes, 1974.

Swanson, Gloria. *Swanson on Swanson*. New York: Random House, 1980.

"The Architecture of Motion Picture Settings." *The American Architect* 118 (7 July 1920): 1–5.

"The 3 Most Popular Movie Sets of the Last 20 Years . . . and What They Mean." *House Beautiful,* December 1946.

Thorp, Margaret Farrand. *America at the Movies*. London: Faber and Faber, 1946.

"Three Sets from the Picture 'Shall We Dance?' " *California Arts and Architecture* 52 (October 1937): 30.

Urban, Joseph. "The Cinema Designer Confronts Sound." In Oliver M. Sayler, ed., *Revolt in the Arts*. Brentano's, 1930.

Vardac, Nicholas A. *Stage to Screen: Theatrical Method from Garrick to Griffith*. Cambridge, Mass.: Harvard University Press, 1949.

Verdone, Mario, ed. *La Scenografia nel Film*. Rome: Ateneo, 1956.

White, Palmer. *Poiret*. London: Studio Vista, 1973.

"Why the Movies Are Influencing American Taste." *House Beautiful,* July 1942.

Wolf, Peter M. "Eugène Hénard and the City Planning of Paris, 1910–1914." Doctoral dissertation, New York University, 1968.

Wollengerg, H. H. *Fifty Years of German Film*. London: Falcon Press, 1948.

Index

(Numbers in **boldface** refer to pages with illustrations.)

Grateful acknowledgment is made to the following for permission to reprint illustrative material (numbers refer to illustrations):

Academy of Motion Picture Arts and Sciences (78, 91, 127, 133); American Museum of the Moving Image, Stanley Cappiello Collection (120); Mrs. André Barsacq (139); Bibliothèque Nationale (39, 46, 51, 53); Cheseley Bonestell (158); The British Film Institute (38, 49, 50, 62, 65, 113, 154, 156, 157); Chicago Historical Society, ICH, #19855 (21); Chicago's Museum of Science and Industry (22); Cinémathèque Française (40, 41, 43–45, 47, 48, 54–56, 115, 130); Joseph Urban Collection, Rare Book and Manuscript Library, Columbia Library (37); Mrs. Anton Grot (102, 103); The Kobal Collection (99, 112, 126, 144, 153); John Mansbridge (109); Metro-Goldwyn-Mayer Corporation (76, 95, 97, 98, 105, 114, 117, 122, 123, 132, 136, 159–163); The Museum of Modern Art (10, 12–14, 16, 17, 19, 60, 64, 92, 93); The Museum of Modern Art Film Still Archive (27–30, 32, 36, 42, 57, 75, 84–86, 89, 90, 94, 96, 110, 111, 116, 125, 128, 131, 137, 141–143, 145 (courtesy RKO General), 146, 148–151); The Museum of The City of New York (23–25, 147); Mrs. Paul Nelson (1–6, 140); Billy Rose Theatre Collection, New York Public Library at Lincoln Center, Astor, Lenox, and Tilden Foundations (124); Paramount Pictures Corporation (118); The Rank Organisation (108); The Royal Film Archive of Belgium (34); Sevenarts Ltd., London (88); Elliot Stein Collection (118); Dr. Franz Stoetner (155); Ezra Stoller © ESTO (26); Architectural Drawing Collection, The University of California at Santa Barbara (79); University of Southern California, Archives of Performing Arts (121); David O. Selznick Collection, Harry Ransom Humanities Research Center, The University of Texas at Austin (101, 129); Wisconsin Center for Film and Theater Research, University of Wisconsin at Madison (134); Richard Wurts (18).

Source Notes

Architecture (35); *Architettura* (73, 74); *Art & Politics in the Weimar Period: The New Sobriety, 1917–1933,* by John Willett. London: Thames & Hudson, 1980 (106); *Bianco e Nero* (31, 104); *California Arts and Architecture* (87); *Casabella* (69–72); *Country Life* (119); *Creation Is a Patient Search,* by Le Corbusier. New York: Praeger Publishers, 1960 (7, 11, 15); *The Decorative Thirties,* by Martin Battersby. London: Studio Vista, 1971 (138); *The Decorative Twenties,* by Martin Battersby. London: Studio Vista, 1961 (8); *How to Live in a Flat,* by K. R. G. Browne and W. Heath Robinson. London: Hutchinson, 1936 (107); *Progressive Architecture* (20); *Realites* (9, 52); Staatliches Filmarchiv der DDR (33, 68, 135); Stiftung Deutsche Kinemathek (59, 61, 63, 66, 67); Charles L. Turner Collection (58).

Every reasonable effort has been made to trace the ownership of all copyrighted materials included in this volume. Any errors that may have occurred are inadvertent and will be corrected in subsequent editions provided notification is sent to the publisher.